100 Million
Unnecessary Returns

100 Million Unnecessary Returns

A Simple, Fair, and Competitive Tax Plan for the United States

MICHAEL J. GRAETZ

Yale University Press　New Haven and London

Set in Minion type by Integrated Publishing Solutions, Grand
Rapids, Michigan.
Printed in the United States of America.

Library of Congress Cataloging-in-Publication Data
Graetz, Michael J.
100 million unnecessary returns : a simple, fair, and competitive
tax plan for the United States / Michael J. Graetz.
    p.   cm.
Includes bibliographical references and index.
ISBN 978-0-300-12274-9 (cloth : alk. paper)   1. Income tax—Law
and legislation—United States.   2. Taxation—Law and
legislation—United States.   I. Title.   II. Title: One hundred
million unnecessary returns.
KF6369.G73   2008
343.7305′2—dc22   2007023130

A catalogue record for this book is available from the
British Library.

The paper in this book meets the guidelines for permanence and
durability of the Committee on Production Guidelines for Book
Longevity of the Council on Library Resources.

10 9 8 7 6 5 4 3 2 1

For Byron
whose unfailing optimism makes me believe that this
might actually happen

Contents

Prologue

The income tax system is a disgrace to the human race.

—*Jimmy Carter*

Inside the Washington beltway, politicians, pundits, and lobbyists all agree that sweeping tax reform is a long shot. Why, then, do I believe it to be inevitable? Because we have no alternative. Consider these facts.

First, our nation's basic tax structure came into place in the World War II era, when the United States essentially had all the money there was. Even a horrid tax system—with income tax rates up to 91 percent—could not then stall our economic progress. From 1946 through 1973, when OPEC quadrupled the price of oil, the economy grew by an average of 3.8 percent a year and unemployment averaged 4.5 percent.[1] Since 1973 our economy has grown more slowly, and so have the wages of middle-income Americans. Today the U.S. economy must compete for the investment capital essential for economic growth—capital necessary to produce a rising standard of living for the American people—with many countries throughout the world, including not only places like Europe and Japan but also China and India. Our tax system should advance the competitiveness of American workers and businesses, not stifle it.

Second, our tax revenues are not quite adequate to pay for our current spending, and, much more important, will fall far short of producing the revenues necessary to fund our government after the baby boom generation begins to retire and collect the benefits of Medicare and Social Security. An aging population and rising health care costs will make our current tax policy unsustainable. Today there are 3.3 workers for every recipient of Social Security benefits. By 2020 this number will fall only slightly, to 3.2 workers for every beneficiary. During the following twenty years, however, that number will drop to 2.2 contributors per beneficiary.[2]

While everyone agrees that, absent dramatic changes in our spending or tax policies, a large long-term gap between spending and revenues will emerge, the size of that gap will depend critically on future growth in health care costs and whether the tax cuts enacted in 2001 and 2003 actually expire as scheduled in 2010. The deficit projected by the Congressional Budget Office (CBO) for 2008 is $98 billion (0.7% of gross domestic product [GDP]).[3] By comparison, the *smallest* estimate by the Government Accountability Office (GAO) of the long-term fiscal gap from 2008 to 2050 is four times that large.[4] While in the short term relatively modest changes in spending or our tax system can balance the budget, in the long term—even assuming that Congress reduces the costs of the Medicare, Medicaid, and Social Security programs—only by restructuring our nation's tax system can we effectively finance our government.

Third, the scheduled expiration in 2010 of large tax cuts enacted in 2001 and 2003 builds a large tax increase into the current tax law. If Congress fails to act, income tax rates will rise, as will tax rates on capital gains and dividends, and people will lose many other current benefits, including credits for children and relief from marriage penalties. Moreover, the Alternative Minimum Tax (AMT) will be imposed on many more Americans. Under that scenario, the Congressional Budget Office estimates that federal revenues will exceed 20 percent of GDP, a level reached only once since World War II. In contrast, if the tax cuts are extended and the exemption from the AMT is indexed for inflation, tax revenues will be about 18 percent of GDP.[5] This is a large difference in revenues amounting to hundreds of billions of dollars each year. Congress therefore must reexamine our nation's tax laws by 2010. Doing nothing is not an option.

Fourth, our current income tax is a mess because politicians ask it to do too much. The result is a level of complexity that baffles experts, let alone ordinary Americans at tax time. Presidents and members of Congress from both political parties seem to believe that an income tax credit or deduction is the best prescription for every economic and social problem our nation faces. In the process, we have transformed the Internal Revenue Service from a tax collector into the administrator of many of the nation's most important spending programs. Here is one example: We know our nation's health care costs are growing too rapidly and that we have too many people—more than forty-five million—uninsured. To address this problem, Congress recently enacted tax-preferred "health savings accounts," and President Bush in his January 2007 State of the Union Address proposed a health insurance "standard deduction" for both income and payroll taxes. But even the president estimated that this would reduce the number of uninsured by only about five million. Our political leaders must be weaned from using tax deductions or credits as a cure-all for our nation's ills. The only path to success is to exempt most Americans from the income tax altogether.

Unfortunately, most of the tax reforms advanced by our political representatives in recent years are unrealistic bromides, ideas that won't work—plans designed to elicit political support rather than to finance our nation adequately in a manner that enhances American workers' and companies' ability to compete in the global economy. We need a competitive system that can produce the necessary tax revenues without unduly hindering our nation's economic progress. It must fit well in the global economy. And it must be fair and simple for the American people to comply with.

The plan I shall detail here would allow our government to raise the necessary revenues without limiting our nation's economic potential. It would substitute a tax on goods and services for much of the income tax, thus freeing the vast majority of Americans from having to deal with the IRS at all. Unlike many other tax reform plans that have been advanced, it would not shift the tax burden away from our wealthiest citizens to people with less income. It would be far simpler and less costly for the American people to comply with. It would be more favorable to savings, investment, and economic growth than our current tax system. And it would fit well with international arrangements and improve the competitiveness of American businesses and workers. Finally, it would stop the madness of relying on tax breaks as the solution to the nation's social and economic problems.

Our nation can no longer afford our broken tax system. It hampers our economy; it is uncompetitive; it distracts us from forging genuine solutions to our nation's most pressing problems; and it wastes enormous resources due to its over-whelming complexity. Three decades ago, when he was running for president, Jimmy Carter described our nation's tax system as a "disgrace to the human race." And it still is.

Part I
Why We Need Tax Reform

I

The Case for Fundamental Reform

The current tax system is an abomination not worthy
of an advanced society.
—*Paul H. O'Neill, former Treasury secretary*

Except in extraordinary circumstances, the minimal requirement for a tax system should be that it raises sufficient revenue to pay for government expenditures. A good tax system ought to do so fairly, keeping its costs of compliance and administration as low as feasible. It ought to be conducive to economic growth. Finally, it ought to promote freedom by interfering minimally with private decision making. Our nation's tax system fails on every count.

It is time we do something about it. At present, our country faces enormous challenges at home and abroad: military conflict in the Middle East, health care and education systems that are universally considered broken, and bitter partisan division in our national politics. In such a climate, comprehensive reform of our tax system may seem a dry and rather abstract issue, a problem to leave to experts and number crunchers who will, we hope, keep our country's finances afloat long enough for us to attend to all our other problems. But in fact, if we don't solve the problem of a grossly inefficient system of raising revenues, all the other challenges our government faces will eventually be overwhelmed by one overarching reality: we will have too little money and will lack the means to raise it without damaging our economy.

Tinkering around the edges, giving a tax break here and raising a rate there, as politicians have done for decades, was never sufficient to the task and certainly won't solve our problems now. The time for fundamental reform has come. In a world immeasurably more interdependent than the world of the mid-twentieth century, when our current system of taxation took shape, a vital question for any reform proposal is: Will it make American workers and businesses more competitive in the global economy, while maintaining the progressive structure consistent with our nation's historical insistence on fairness? The proposal I offer in this book—what I will call the Competitive Tax—does just that. Unlike many of the alternatives currently being discussed in the halls of Congress, this proposal will have major benefits for businesses of all sizes *and* for all Americans. Perhaps most important of all, at a time when the federal government has strayed far from any sort of discipline in taxation or spending, it will help ensure that we fulfill our basic obligation to our country and our children: to responsibly fund our democracy.

The Mess We're In

When George W. Bush first took office in January 2001, the Congressional Budget Office estimated that the federal government would enjoy budget surpluses totaling $5.1 trillion in the decade ahead. That month Federal Reserve Chairman Alan Greenspan famously told Congress that the looming surpluses were so large that the federal government would soon pay off all its debt and would then have to invest in private assets like corporate stock, a scenario Greenspan abhorred. That problem has been solved. Congress enacted significant tax cuts in 2001 and in every year since until 2007. The nation's economy in 2007 was much stronger than it was in 2001, but the government's financial situation much weaker. The United States government now borrows nearly $3 billion every day. In January 2006, when Alan Greenspan left the Fed for private life, the federal debt exceeded $8 trillion, more than $2 trillion greater than when George W. Bush took office, and Congress was about to raise the federal debt limit to $9 trillion so that the government could continue to pay its bills.

Thus when Congress tackles tax reform, as it will eventually be forced to, it will not have the luxury of federal budget surpluses that might be tapped to finance an overall tax cut to sweeten the bitterness from the inevitable reduction and elimination of many tax breaks. This option was available in 2001, but George Bush took a different path.

During the past decade or so, our politicians have become complacent. Congress has not increased taxes since 1993, when Bill Clinton raised the top income tax rate in an effort to eliminate deficits. He did so then without any Republican votes. Clinton's policy may have worked—when he left office the budget of the federal government was in surplus for the first time in thirty years, and economic growth was strong during his second term—but its politics failed. The 1994 election gave Republicans a majority in the House of Representatives for the first time in forty years. George H. W. Bush had learned a similar political lesson a few years earlier when he lost his 1992 reelection campaign after breaking his "no new taxes" pledge in an effort to control federal deficits.

It should be a simple truth that tax revenues ought to be adequate to finance the government's spending. Economic conditions, to be sure, may occasionally call for deficits to provide a short-term economic stimulus. And unforeseen circumstances—a terrorist attack or a devastating hurricane, to name two—may create a temporary shortfall in government collections that will take time to correct. But routinely financing government with borrowing simply shifts the taxes to our children and grandchildren, and running up interest on the federal debt will inevitably require higher taxes from someone down the road. But because "someone down the road" does not yet vote, deficit finance is catnip to politicians. As Herbert Hoover put it, "Blessed are the young for they shall inherit the national debt."

Deficit finance increases our economic vulnerability when it is coupled with a substantial imbalance in trade. Because we import far more than we export, other nations accumulate dollars, which they use to purchase U.S. assets, including government debt. In 2006, for example, China held more than $300 billion of U.S. government bonds and about $1 trillion in total dollar reserves. And with its enormous trade surplus with the United States, China is accumulating many more dollars every day. If it were to dump those bonds or dollars on the market, a precipitous decline in the value of the dollar would result, possibly destabilizing our economy. Allowing foreign governments such control over our economic well-being may someday prove harmful not only to our economic health but also to our national interest and security. As the Harvard economist Benjamin Friedman puts it: "Government deficits, sustained year after year even when the economy is operating at full employment, reduce net capital formation and induce foreign borrowing. Both effects accumulate over time. Both are harmful."[1]

But Congress has been unwilling either to pay for the government we have or to fashion a substantially smaller government. The time has come to put our fiscal house in order. We must stop pretending that we can continue to live with a tax system inadequate to finance what we are spending. Controlling that spending—and cutting it down wherever we can—should be a priority. Our federal government cannot continue to spend 20 or 21 percent of GDP while raising only 16 to 18 percent in taxes.

Unfortunately, as time passes, the pressures will be for more spending, not less. Over the decades ahead, demographic changes will put great additional pressures on the budgets of both federal and state governments. Our nation's population is aging. In 2011 the oldest of the baby boom generation turns sixty-five. Life spans have been increasing and will continue to increase. The fastest-growing segment of the population is the so-called old elderly—those over age eighty—for whom the costs of health care and of long-term care rise exponentially. People age eighty-five or older now constitute less than 2% of the population; they will account for 5% in 2040.

Today many people retire for about one-third of their lives. A man who retires at age sixty-two can now expect Social Security to provide income and Medicare to pay for health costs for seventeen years; the average woman, twenty years. These numbers have been rising over time. To limit our receipt of those benefits to the span of retirement of the average worker of the 1940s and 1950s today would require people to keep working until they are seventy-four.

In addition, fertility rates are much lower than in the 1950s and 1960s, leaving fewer children to help care for elderly parents. Immigration will account for most of our population growth in the years ahead, but immigration cannot solve our long-term fiscal problems, and, in any event, the public is ambivalent about increasing immigration.[2]

As the elderly constitute a significantly greater share of the nation's population, new pressures will emerge in improving our nation's well-being. The elderly tend to be spenders, not savers. Most personal savings occurs when middle-aged workers save for their children's education or their own retirement. But even now, before the baby boom generation has begun to retire, our nation's savings rate is inadequate. According to the Commerce Department, in 2006 the U.S. personal savings rate was negative 1 percent, the poorest rate since 1933, during the Great Depression. During only four years in U.S. history have the American people spent more than they earned: 1932, 1933, 2005, and 2006.

Why is this important? Because there are only two sources of funds for business investments: national savings and capital imported from abroad. Lower business investment will over time reduce our nation's productivity and our level of national income. Going forward, other nations, whose populations are also aging—many much faster than ours—will have less savings to lend us or to invest here. Our need for investment capital demands a competitive tax system—one that encourages investments here by both Americans and foreigners. We want Americans to save and invest more and multinational companies to invest here rather than abroad.

A competitive tax system is also necessary because the aging of our population will put enormous budgetary pressures on Social Security, Medicare, and Medicaid (the last of which is the major source of funding for long-term care today). One should always be skeptical of long-term projections, and I certainly am. Seventy-five years ago we were just coming out of the Depression. Imagine what the projections for today would have looked like from that perspective. But as Douglas Holtz-Eakin, former director of the Congressional Budget Office, told the Congress, "Doing nothing is not an option. The United States is highly unlikely to 'grow its way out' of the burden of the projected spending growth."[3] Yet nothing is precisely what we are doing. President Bush called for making the tax cuts of his first term permanent. In the meanwhile, Democrats accuse Republicans of favoring the rich and running large deficits, but have failed to offer any real alternative plans. It is as if Congress were paralyzed. Figure 1.1 illustrates the scope of the potential long-term fiscal problem.

Two things are clear: first, relying entirely on government borrowing to fund the fiscal gap is not sustainable—it will crowd out private investments, inhibit productivity, and increase interest rates, ultimately limiting Americans' standard of living. Second, government spending down the road is likely to be greater than it is today and higher than its historical levels. Social Security, Medicare, and Medicaid benefits will probably have to be reduced somewhat, and those programs may even be dramatically restructured, but it is foolhardy to assume that taxes will not also have to be raised. Although, as we shall see in Part II, not all tax reformers agree on how to proceed with fundamental reform, there is now broad consensus that our situa-

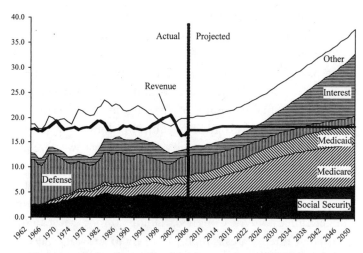

Figure 1.1. Federal spending by type, percent of GDP by year.
Note: Reflects CBO's intermediate-spending trajectory, which
assumes that spending per Medicare enrollee grows 1 percentage
point faster than per-capita GDP (compared with 2.9 percent
today); that defense spending gradually returns to its historical real
level; and that nondefense discretionary spending and other
mandatory spending remain at their historical levels as a share of
GDP. *Source:* Congressional Budget Office, *The Long-Term Budget
Outlook* (Washington, D.C.: Congressional Budget Office, 2005),
available at http://www.cbo.gov/ftpdoc.cfm?index=6982.&type=1.

tion is sufficiently grave that we must act. And, in today's global
economy, we should act in a way that enhances the competitiveness of workers and businesses in the United States.

Governance by Deduction

In our current system, presidents and other politicians use the
income tax the way my mother used chicken soup: as a magic
elixir to solve all difficulties. Special-interest lobbyists swarm

Congress to get their special breaks. This explains why there have been more than fifteen thousand changes to the tax law in the past two decades. Meanwhile, politicians use it to try to direct businesses' investments and people's spending and saving. If the nation has a problem in access to education, child care affordability, health insurance coverage, or the financing of long-term care, an income tax deduction or credit is the politicians' answer. When Newt Gingrich became speaker of the house in January 1995, one of his first acts was to urge the House Ways and Means Committee to enact a tax credit for laptop computers to help "poor children" become more effective in the new "third wave" information age. That idea was so bad that Gingrich himself soon called it "nutsy." But the tax code is laden with nutsy ideas.

Both political parties use the tax law this way. President George W. Bush and Congress, for example, in 2005 enacted a laundry list of income tax credits and deductions for energy production and conservation. In July 2006 Hillary Clinton unveiled her "American Dream Initiative" to the Democratic Leadership Council. It was larded with "targeted tax cuts," including a $5,000 refundable tax credit to help fund down payments for owner-occupied homes, an expanded tax credit for "savers," tax credits for employers enrolling employees in retirement accounts, a $3,000 college tuition tax credit, a new fringe benefit exclusion for housing, and a multipurpose tax-preferred "American Dream" account. All of these ideas have been poll-tested and no doubt are quite popular with the American public.

To keep track of all the ideas that actually become law, the federal budget each year is required to contain a list of "tax expenditures," defined as all tax credits, deductions, or exclusions that deviate from a "normal" income tax. The number of these tax expenditures has grown enormously in recent years. Forty-five percent—66 of 146—listed in the 2006 budget have been added since 1986. Their total cost in lost revenues is estimated at about $700 billion a year.[4] We are not talking here about narrow special-interest tax loopholes to benefit this company or that. These are tax breaks widely available to broad segments of the general public—tax cuts for the large middle class. The largest of these are very popular: tax advantages for employees' payments for health insurance and retirement savings, and deductions for home mortgage interest, state and local taxes, and charitable deductions. We have reached the point where Republicans in the Congress never see a tax cut they will not embrace, and Democrats view income tax benefits as practically the only way to achieve domestic policy goals without being labeled big spenders.

And yet we know that trying to solve the nation's problems through "targeted tax breaks" does not work. Take health insurance, for example. Our nation, contrary to others throughout the world, has long relied on a tax benefit for employers and employees as its main mechanism for covering Americans who are neither poor nor aged. What has been the result? Our health care costs are the highest in the world, and more than forty-five million Americans remain uninsured. Moreover, these costs are making American businesses and products less competitive in the world economy and are gobbling up wage increases of American workers. Nor has our tax-based energy policy produced better results. Nor do tax credits for working parents produce affordable child care. I could go on and on.

Historically, when competing policy ideas aimed at a common goal have emerged in Congress, the leaders of the tax-writing committees have fashioned a compromise provision with the advice of the Treasury Department and the chief of staff of the Joint Committee on Taxation. Now, given the dispersion of power within the Congress and the proliferation and expansion of tax staffs, Congress often compromises by enacting *all* of the ideas, leaving unsophisticated taxpayers bewildered about how to cope.

For a vivid illustration, consider the income tax incentives for paying for higher education. There are eight tax breaks for current-year education expenses: two tax credits, three deductions, and three exclusions from income. Five other provisions promote savings for college expenses. In 1987 only three provisions encouraged college expenditures or savings. The 1997 act alone added five provisions that were estimated to cost $41 billion over five years; together they represented the largest increase in federal funding for higher education since the GI Bill.[5]

Comprehending the tax savings provided by these provisions, their various eligibility requirements, how they interact, and their record-keeping and reporting requirements is mind-boggling.[6] Each of the provisions has its own eligibility criteria and definition of qualified expenses. For example, the various provisions do not provide consistent treatment of room and board, books, supplies and equipment, sports expenses, non-academic fees, or the class of relatives whose expenses may be taken into account. A student convicted of a felony for possession or distribution of a controlled substance is ineligible for one of the education credits, but such a conviction is no bar to another one. And this is just the tip of the iceberg.[7]

Relying, as we do, on income tax deductions and credits is about as successful a solution to our national needs as handing out more gunpowder at the Alamo. But lack of success does not curb our politicians' enthusiasm. Congress would rather whine about the current income tax and use the IRS as its whipping boy than embrace realistic tax reforms that would make it harder to use its favorite plaything—the income tax—as an instrument of public policy.

The truth is that our income tax is a mess. Today, no matter what their income, Americans confront extraordinary complexity in filing their taxes. In 1940 the instructions to Form 1040 were about four pages long. Today the instruction booklet spans more than one hundred pages, and the form itself has more than ten schedules and twenty worksheets. The tax code contains more than seven hundred provisions affecting individuals and more than fifteen hundred affecting businesses—a total of more than 1.4 million words—making the tax law four times as long as *War and Peace* and considerably harder to parse. The tax regulations contain another 8 million words, filling about twenty thousand pages (see Figure 1.2). And both the code and the regulations grow fatter every year.

No wonder more than 60 percent of income tax filers hire tax preparers (and many of the rest rely on computer programs) to tell them what to do. And tax return preparers have become notorious for peddling other products of dubious value to their customers, most notoriously so-called "refund anticipation loans," which often advance tax refunds by a few days at an exorbitant interest cost.

The income tax has become so complex and riddled with perverse incentives that Americans spend an estimated 3.5 billion hours each year preparing and filing their taxes. Families, businesses, and the federal government now spend a staggering $150 billion each year just to calculate and administer the system. It is $150 billion of wasted money. In fact, the income tax so confuses ordinary Americans that two million people pay more than $1 billion extra annually because they make the

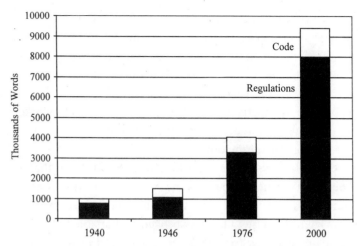

Figure 1.2. Tax code complexity: thousands of words in Internal
Revenue Code and Regulations. *Source:* Calculations based on
U.S.C. (1940, CCH 1952) and C.F.R. (1940, 1949) and Tax
Foundation calculations, based on Internal Revenue Code and
Federal Tax Regulations (1975); Joint Committee on Taxation, Study
of the Overall State of the Federal Tax System 4 (Washington, D.C.:
Joint Committee on Taxation, 2001), available at
http://www.house.gov/jct/pubs01.html.

wrong choice about whether to itemize or take the standard
deduction. And while these people overpay because of the
complexity, far more pay too little—many deliberately. The
IRS estimates that taxes are underpaid by about $300 billion
every year, which requires honest taxpayers to pay more than
$2,000 each to make up the loss.

In addition to these losses, the incentives in today's tax law
for unproductive expenditures, coupled with the efforts of individuals and businesses to structure their affairs in a tax-
favorable fashion, are estimated to cost our economy a further
$1 trillion a year. For a long time after the Second World War,

we could endure such waste and hardly notice. But today, when American businesses and workers are engaged in a highly competitive global economic environment, these are costs that we can no longer afford. We need a tax system that will encourage investment in the United States to create good jobs and will help make the goods and services our businesses and workers produce more affordable to consumers around the world.

Although the income tax now affects nearly everyone, that hasn't always been so. It wasn't until World War II that the federal government expanded the income tax beyond wealthy individuals to tax nearly all middle-income Americans. Sixty years later, this system is badly broken and unable to produce adequate revenues for the future without threatening economic growth. Relying as heavily as we do on income tax revenues to fund our government has become a liability in the current competitive international marketplace. As I shall detail in Part II, my Competitive Tax proposal would eliminate the income tax for most Americans, returning that tax to its original limited purpose, and my plan would make up for the lost revenue by introducing an administratively simpler tax on goods and services. To achieve fundamental reform we must recognize that the centerpiece of our overall tax system has grown too complex and has proven a failure as a mechanism for solving our nation's economic and social difficulties. The health of our nation's economy, the cohesion of our society, and the future of our nation's children all demand major changes. In our current political environment, this will not be an easy task.

II

The Broken Politics of Taxation

We can lecture our children about extravagance until we run out of voice and breath. Or we can cure their extravagance by simply reducing their allowance.

—*Ronald Reagan*

Despite powerful economic and structural forces pushing us toward tax reform, any responsible attempt to reform our tax system and create one more suitable to the global economy of the twenty-first century will face strong political headwinds. The public prefers tax reductions to tax reform, and politicians often pander to this preference. In addition, lobbyists and their clients will fight hard to retain the tax breaks that tax reformers seek to eliminate. To have any hope of actually implementing the proposal this book lays out, and to grasp why replacing most of the income tax with a tax on goods and services is the right way to go, it is vital to understand how we arrived at the mess we're in and why past reform efforts failed to solve the problem.

The first step in understanding the political landscape that has shaped the discussion of taxes in America for the past quarter-century is to recognize the profound impact of the modern conservative, antitax movement. What began in the 1960s and 1970s as a set of fringe ideas and jeremiads against big government became, with the 1994 Republican takeover of Congress and most clearly with George W. Bush's arrival in Washington, a forcefully implemented, governing ideology. Though not, as it turns out, one without serious contradictions.

The Beast That Will Not Starve

Modern conservatism, because it is ostensibly a movement to reduce the size of government (other than the military), has long been focused on the issue of cutting taxes. Given the popularity with the American people of the entitlement programs of Social Security and Medicare, it has proven difficult for conservatives to shrink the government by cutting spending. Thus, rather than attacking the size of government head-on, the idea emerged that conservatives should instead "starve the beast." That is, they should cut taxes as a way of denying government the revenues needed to pay for the spending programs. This, so the theory went, would eventually lead to a crisis in which raising taxes would prove even more unpopular than cutting entitlements, so the original goal would be achieved. To be sure, conservatives saw cutting taxes as a good unto itself, leaving more money in the hands of individuals and corporations, but the aggressive nature of the tax-cutting drive drew much of its force from this larger plan to deny the beast of federal expenditure the sustenance of tax revenues.

As the former Reagan economic adviser Bruce Bartlett has pointed out, it was the Nobel Prize–winning economist Milton Friedman who supplied the intellectual justification for this approach.[1] In a 1978 *Newsweek* column Friedman wrote, "I have concluded that the only effective way to restrain government spending is by limiting government's explicit tax revenue—just as a limited income is the only effective restraint on any individual's or family's spending."[2]

With the election of Ronald Reagan in 1980, this idea took hold for the first time as government policy. However, as observant conservatives quickly noticed, contrary to this dogma, in the absence of a balanced budget requirement, tax reductions do not necessarily mean spending reductions or a reduction of government size. That tax cuts are not necessarily accompanied by spending cuts was amply demonstrated during the Reagan presidency. Congress and the White House were quite ready to accept deficit spending instead. The presidency of George W. Bush has only reinforced the point. One of Reagan's own economists, William Niskanen, now at the libertarian CATO Institute, examined the relationship between deficits and federal spending from 1981 to 2005. He found that spending rises when deficits rise.[3] Deficits allow politicians to spend without the political discipline of having to ask anyone to pay through increased taxes. The federal debt, which had accumulated to nearly $1 trillion since George Washington's presidency, increased to $2.6 trillion during Reagan's time in office and is projected to increase from $5.6 trillion to nearly $10 trillion during the George W. Bush presidency. And since the government must pay interest on its borrowings, a dollar of federal debt ultimately requires more than a dollar of additional taxes. But these taxes are shunted off onto future generations who currently neither vote nor make political contributions. The fact that tax cuts have failed to curb government spending has not, however, dampened the enthusiasm of the "starve the beast" crowd for tax cuts.

Often those who would starve the federal government of tax revenues disguise their motives and confuse the public by relying on a handmaiden concept known as Rosie Scenario—the queen of what the comic Stephen Colbert famously calls "truthiness." David Stockman, Reagan's budget director, has told how Rosie came to the fore in the 1980s.[4] The idea then was to be relentlessly optimistic when forecasting key economic variables, routinely overestimating economic growth and other key economic predictions such as total wages or corporate profits that determine the size of total government spending and revenues. This provides an apparent rise in revenues without the need to raise taxes. These Rosie Scenarios then underestimated spending, both for unemployment and for interest on the federal debt. With rose-colored glasses firmly in place, every deficit could then seem a new surprise.

Politicians, of course, don't use the phrase Rosie Scenario. Instead they use a variety of techniques designed to make the federal budget picture appear much rosier than it really is. One example is the very aggressive use of what some call "dynamic scoring." As a method of budgetary accounting, dynamic scoring insists that optimistic projections of the positive impact of tax cuts on the economy should be used by Congress in estimating their revenue costs. This, of course, would allow Congress to fit even more tax cuts within a revenue target specified by the congressional budget process— something it seems quite willing and able to do without help. These new tax cuts themselves become eligible for dynamic scoring, perpetuating an illusory cycle. With scoring dynamic enough, our national debt could spiral out of control even faster. Disappointingly for some, when the Treasury issued its first dynamic scoring report in July 2006, it concluded that tax cuts *do not* pay for themselves. "A permanent reduction in taxes . . . would lead to an unsustainable accumulation of debt," the Treasury said.[5]

Another technique for understating the actual cost of tax cuts has come to the fore since 2001. This is the use of "sunsets," which terminate tax cuts unless Congress acts to extend them. In 2001, because of the Senate's procedures, it was necessary to sunset the entire legislation in 2010 in order to get it through the Senate with fewer than sixty votes—more votes than the bill's supporters could muster. The 2003 cuts in dividend and capital gains rates also expire in 2010 for a similar reason. The Congressional Budget Office (CBO), Congress's official scorekeeper, is required by law to provide estimates of the government's financial condition using current law—in other words, assuming that all the tax cuts do actually expire. To CBO's great credit, it now also provides estimates of deficits under alternative—less rosy—scenarios. The differences are sizable. For example, CBO projects that revenues will equal 20.1 percent of GDP in 2017—a level reached only once since World War II—if current law is unchanged, but 18 percent of GDP if the all the tax cuts scheduled to expire are extended. The difference in total deficits (or surpluses) under these two scenarios for the ten-year period 2008 through 2017 is $2.8 trillion.[6]

Both the president's budget and CBO's include in their projections of receipts amounts that would be collected if the Alternative Minimum Tax (AMT)—which now requires people to calculate income tax two ways and pay the higher amount—were actually extended to the thirty-five million to fifty million people who would be affected if current law remains unchanged. Again, the amounts at issue are large—$745 billion under current law (more than $1.3 trillion if the 2001 and 2003 tax cuts are extended) over the next ten years.[7] But this is counting a tax that Congress never intended to levy and money the federal government will undoubtedly never collect. Indeed most taxpayers who would become subject to the AMT have been protected by one-year "patches" enacted on a "temporary" basis by Congress. Just making these "patches" permanent will cost the government a lot of tax revenues: from $450 billion to $730 billion over ten years. But both the Congress's and the president's official projections of government revenues ignore these costs entirely.

Any lingering doubt that Rosie Scenario remains a potent force in American politics should have been erased by George Bush's statements about the federal deficit for 2006. In August of that year, the president's budget office predicted a deficit of $296 billion and one totaling $339 billion for 2007. What was George Bush's response? He held media events praising his tax cuts for "working" and attributing the "strong economy" to them. The fact that at the beginning of his administration he had estimated that 2006 would produce a $304 billion surplus was never mentioned. He apparently believes Dick Cheney's canard that Ronald Reagan proved that "deficits don't matter."

This idea is no doubt an attractive one, given the rank failure of either party to control spending. Whatever the target, neither the right nor the left has enjoyed much success in trimming its least-favored government expenditures. Ronald Reagan's defense buildup is widely credited with hastening the demise of the Soviet Union, and since September 11, 2001, attacking spending for defense or homeland security is political suicide. So our federal defense expenditures are now greater than the rest of the world's combined.

Nor has the right yet made any progress in curbing stubbornly popular entitlements. George W. Bush's effort to substitute personal savings accounts for a portion of Social Security was an abysmal failure, and ironically, by adding a prescription drug benefit, his administration enacted the largest increase in Medicare spending since it was originally passed as a key aspect of Lyndon Johnson's "Great Society" in 1965. (This was the first time a major new federal entitlement was created without any revenue source to pay for it.) Spending on defense and entitlements, along with interest on the federal debt, accounts for the bulk of federal spending—nearly 70 percent in 2007 (see Figure 2.1). And Congress has shown little ability to constrain the rest. An Alaskan "bridge to nowhere" in the 2005 highway legislation became a national symbol for how out of control government spending has gotten. Despite all the rhetoric to the contrary, and although the Bush administration has cut taxes substantially, the beast has continued to grow.

The Last Serious Attempt at Reform— And What Went Wrong

The Tax Reform Act of 1986 was widely heralded as the most significant change in our nation's tax law since the income tax was extended to the masses during World War II. It was the crowning domestic policy achievement of President Ronald Reagan, who proclaimed it "the best anti-poverty measure, the best pro-family measure and the best job-creation measure ever to come out of the Congress of the United States."[8] The law's rate reductions and reforms were mimicked throughout the Organisation for Economic Co-operation and Development (OECD).[9] Even

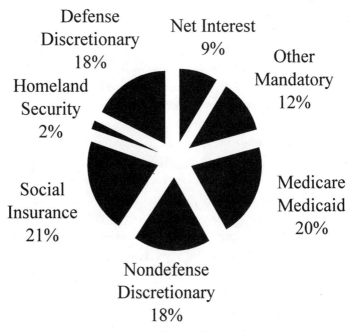

Figure 2.1. Federal government spending: an insurance company
and a borrower with an army. *Note:* "Other Mandatory" includes
various education and training programs, federal employee
retirement and disability, unemployment compensation, food and
nutrition assistance, supplemental security income, the earned-
income tax credit, payments to states for foster care and adoption
assistance, housing assistance, and other federal programs.
Medicare/Medicaid outlays include federal spending on the state
children's health insurance fund. *Source:* Office of Management and
Budget, budget for fiscal year 2007.

at the time, however, reading the paeans to this legislation was
like watching a Tennessee Williams play: something was terribly
wrong, but nobody was talking about it.

Two decades later, the changes wrought by the 1986 act
have proven neither revolutionary nor stable. The legislation

was a rearrangement of the income tax law in which marginal tax rates were reduced and the tax base was broadened by limiting or eliminating various loopholes, deductions, and exemptions. The act did enhance both the equity and efficiency of the income tax, but it was far from the purist cleansing of the tax code that some of its more ardent admirers implied.

The 1986 act substantially increased the permissible amount of tax-free income, removing about six million low-income people from the income tax rolls; lowered and flattened income tax rates; shut down mass-marketed tax shelters for high-income individuals; curtailed the ability to shift income to lower-income family members subject to lower tax rates; and taxed capital gains at the same rates as ordinary income.[10] An increase in corporate tax revenues was used to finance an overall reduction in individual income taxes, although by cutting back on deductions for plant and equipment, Congress found the money to reduce the corporate tax rate (from 46 to 34 percent).

The Tax Reform Act neither spurred American productivity, as some of its admirers hoped, nor destroyed it, as many of its detractors had warned. The University of Michigan economist Joel Slemrod estimated that the 1986 act may have spurred as much as a 1 percent increase in hours worked—a genuine benefit, but hardly a new American revolution.[11] In addition, the act ultimately fell short of creating a substantially fairer income tax because it left in place many avenues for tax-favored treatment. Tax-exempt fringe benefits like health insurance and pensions were hardly touched. Complex new rules limited personal-interest deductions to homeowners, disadvantaging renters, who lost their ability to deduct interest on their credit cards. Many provisions offering incentives for specific investments, such as tax-deferred annuities and tax-exempt state and local bonds, were continued, and new ones were added. Families were given a tax reduction when a child turned fourteen, no doubt to offset the additional burdens of having an adolescent in the household. Hundreds of scattershot "transition" rules were enacted to give special tax breaks to particular companies or individuals.

Compromise is often the handmaiden of tax complexity, and the 1986 legislation was forged out of hundreds of political compromises. Rather than eliminating provisions of dubious merit, Congress settled for reducing their benefits or restricting their use. Examples abound: the tax law now contains rules distinguishing at least seventeen categories of interest expenses; the 1986 rules for international investments were stupefying in their complexity; and the alternative minimum tax (AMT) provisions require two ways of calculating income, each with its own rate schedule.

The ink had hardly dried on the 1986 tax act before Democrats, most notably Speaker of the House Jim Wright of Texas, called for rate increases, and supply-side Republicans initiated tax incentives for savings and investments. In the two decades since 1986, Congress has amended the tax law annually, adding thousands of pages of new legislation.[12] The 1986 coalition of supply-side Republicans and tax-reforming Democrats has subsequently disintegrated. Republicans typically now favor low rates applied to a narrow income tax base, while Democrats prefer higher rates on a different but also narrow base.

In retrospect, the inherent weaknesses of the 1986 Tax Reform Act have become easy to identify. First, as I have said, the fragile political coalition that enacted the law left in place a variety of ongoing complexities, inequities, and inefficiencies. Second, the 1986 act had little public support even when it was passed. On June 25, 1986, the day after the Senate passed the bill by a 97–3 vote, the *New York Times* reported that fewer than one-third of Americans believed that it would produce a fairer tax system or reduce their own taxes.[13] Third, and most important, the 1986 tax act was based on retaining and strengthening the income tax itself, rather than heeding the calls of many economists and politicians to replace it with some form of tax on purchases of goods and services. Given the internationalization of economic activity during the past two decades, the 1986 act's reliance on increased taxation of income from capital and corporate income has made the United States economy less competitive with other national economies that tax corporate income at a relatively lower rate.[14] (This is a problem that my tax proposal, as laid out in Part II, would directly address.)

For all these reasons, tax experts now regard the 1986 act as a promise failed. There are, however, some experts who continue to think that the best path for tax reform is to reprise the 1986 act and simply improve the income tax. In fact, that is one of the proposals endorsed by the latest government panel to take a serious look at comprehensive reform.

The President's Panel

George Bush's second term began as if he intended to follow through on his campaign promise to "lead a bi-partisan effort to reform and simplify" the nation's tax law. Two weeks before his second inaugural, on January 7, 2005, he issued an executive order establishing the President's Advisory Panel on Federal Tax Reform. He charged it to submit to the Treasury secretary "revenue neutral options for reforming the Federal Internal Revenue Code." Bush picked two savvy former senators to head this group: Connie Mack (R-FL) and John Breaux (D-LA).

Bush's nine-person panel traveled the country, holding twelve public meetings in five states and in Washington, D.C. It took testimony from experts of all political persuasions, who offered devastating criticisms of the current income tax and many suggestions for how to fix or replace it. In November 2005, four months later than originally anticipated, the panel issued a 272-page report detailing two proposals that it supported unanimously and a third option, closely connected to the plan I recommend here, which it described as "worthy of further discussion." The panel also explained in detail why it had rejected complete replacement of the federal income tax with a "flat tax" or a national sales tax.[15]

The president thanked the members for their work, said the Treasury secretary would study the report, and kissed the panel good-bye. John Breaux was miffed. Five months later he said he thought the Treasury and the White House must have put the panel's report in "the library maybe and filed it, or it got put in a closet and they closed the door and they don't know where it is." When the press is not around, Breaux tells of walking around during a meeting in the White House Oval Office, peering into cupboards and corners. When the president asked, "What are you looking for, John?" Breaux responded, "My panel's report, Mr. President." Breaux insists that the country "universally agrees the federal tax law should be simplified" and says that President Bush missed a "golden opportunity" in his 2006 State of the Union Address to provide the presidential leadership essential to get tax reform moving.

Meanwhile, Bush was urging Congress simply to make permanent the tax cuts of his first term, which are scheduled to expire in 2010. Indeed, in May 2006, Ed Lazear, a member of the tax reform panel, who became the president's chief economic adviser, was asked why the president had not advanced any plan for tax reform. "I would argue that there actually has been tax reform," Lazear replied, "[although] not probably the broad tax reform you have in mind." Lazear then pointed to cuts in taxes on capital gains and dividends and the creation of tax-favored health savings accounts as examples of what *he* had in mind. To reassure his disappointed interrogator, Lazear added, "I wouldn't give up. The President has said that [tax reform] is something he will be thinking about over the next couple of years. I would expect something along those lines sometime in the future."[16]

What happened? Why did a president who had seemed determined to make reforming the nation's tax system a priority of his second term turn stony silent on the subject?

Because with its extensive study and thoughtful report, the president's handpicked panel injected an unwelcome dose of reality into the tax reform debate. Less truthiness, more truth. The panel's report carefully considered the two ideas that have garnered the most political support among congressional Republicans—a flat tax and a national sales tax—and rejected them both, thereby disappointing many of the president's most ardent supporters in Congress. Instead, the panel proposed two alternatives: an income tax restructuring that echoes the 1986 tax reform and the combination of a new consumption tax with a tax on some income from capital. Both of the panel's recommended plans would (1) reduce the top marginal tax rate—to 33 and 30 percent, respectively; (2) eliminate the alternative minimum tax (AMT); (3) replace the earned-income tax credit and refundable child credits with a refundable "work credit"; (4) replace personal exemptions, the standard deduction, and child tax credits with a "family credit"; (5) eliminate all deductions for state and local taxes; (6) extend tax breaks for interest on home mortgages and charities to non-itemizers, but reduce the amounts that can lower tax; (7) cap the fringe benefit for employer-provided health insurance; and (8) expand and simplify tax-favored savings opportunities. Both plans also would eliminate many other income tax deductions and credits.

Once the panel decided to eliminate the AMT, which would cost more than $1 trillion during the next ten years, it was not able to reduce tax rates substantially, and it had to struggle to find offsetting revenues. This required attacking political sacred cows, such as the mortgage interest deduction, the charitable deduction, and the deduction for state and local taxes. Predictably, this met with opposition from both sides of the congressional aisle. As John Breaux observed, "None of us [on the panel] is running for reelection."

For Politicians, Difficult Choices and Small Rewards

Since President Bush had instructed his tax reform panel to produce proposals that were revenue neutral—that is, proposals that would keep current revenues steady but with a different mix of taxes—it could not avoid taking on some politically unpopular proposals.[17] Unfortunately for the prospects of serious reform, politicians who lead a tax reform effort cannot expect a large political payoff.

Ronald Reagan put his political capital on the line to get the 1986 reform through Congress, making a crucial trip to the Capitol to save the bill from being buried by House Republicans. And he lauded the tax reform legislation he ultimately signed. But even though he ultimately achieved a top income tax rate of 28 percent—the lowest since Calvin Coolidge was president and Andrew Mellon Treasury secretary—Reagan is barely remembered for his tax reform efforts. His admirers far more frequently cite the tax cuts of his first term, his efforts to strengthen our national defense, and his confrontations of the Soviet Union. And although the congressional leaders most crucial to the bill's enactment, Robert Packwood of Oregon, the Republican Senate Finance Committee chairman, and Dan Rostenkowski, the Democratic chairman of the House Ways and Means Committee, shared the cover of *Time* magazine for their efforts, their fame was short-lived. Both soon left Congress in disgrace for other misadventures. Some other congressional tax reform leaders fared a bit better: Democrat Dick Gephardt became House majority leader; his Senate counterpart Bill Bradley mounted an unsuccessful campaign for president; and Jack Kemp, the former Buffalo Bills quarterback and New York congressman and an outspoken advocate for low tax rates, secured the Republican nomination for vice president in Bob Dole's unsuccessful 1996 campaign. But the kudos these politicians garnered hardly suggest that leading a tax reform effort is the path to national prominence. There are far less risky issues to tackle for those with that ambition.

Even so, it is surprising that Democrats have, with few exceptions, let Republicans lead the charge for tax reform. For the past three decades, Republicans have attempted to persuade the public that only their party can be trusted on the tax issue. They frequently claim that low taxes are needed to keep an avaricious government at bay. Bill Schneider, a former Harvard political scientist and now CNN's political analyst, says that "tax hatred is what holds the Republican Party together."[18] But the Republicans' antitax message has gained less traction with the public than is generally believed. A March 2007 *New York Times*/CBS poll, for example, found 60 percent of Americans ready to pay more taxes for universal health insurance. And even in the face of the Republican anti-IRS, antitax onslaught, the Democrats have held their own with the public on the tax issue. Americans are suspicious about the Republicans' true goal; they think Republicans are far more likely than Democrats to reward the rich.

When people are asked which political party will do a better job of holding taxes down or keeping taxes low, the Republicans have the advantage, although not by much.[19] Over time, answers to these questions have tended to vary with general economic conditions. So when the economy was strong during Bill Clinton's presidency, the edge went to the Democrats. And Democrats often enjoy an advantage over Republicans when the question is phrased in terms of "handling taxes" or "managing tax policy." In March 2006, for example, both the *Time*/SRBI and NBC/*Wall Street Journal* polls gave the Democrats a 7- to 9-percentage point advantage over Republicans on "dealing with" the federal tax system. So why have the Democrats been silent about tax reform?

Democrats cede the tax reform issue to the Republicans at their peril. They put at risk the very principles of tax justice they seek to protect. As former senator Bill Bradley has said, "Tax reform is ultimately a discussion about values." And when the income tax is the issue, the stakes are high.

To achieve the kind of comprehensive reform our tax system clearly needs will require politicians from both parties to put the national interest ahead of the short-run advantage of any particular segment of their supporters. Yet as we shall see in the chapter that follows, the prospect for such statesmanship is dimmed by the ever-burgeoning ranks of special interest groups and their highly organized and well-financed lobbying campaigns that often promise one thing to the public in order to achieve another for their backers. If fundamental reform is to succeed in simplifying Americans' lives, creating a competitive tax system for America and retaining basic fairness—as my proposal would—its proponents must first understand the ways in which public opinion and popular resentment are being channeled in today's political environment. A movement for change that does not craft its arguments in such a way as to respond convincingly to these forces will soon find itself swept aside.

III

Of Pleaders, Zealots, and the Rest of Us

One night at Boston Harbor, the tea flew overboard.
They said, "We don't owe King George a thing, we answer to
our Lord."
They built this land of freedom but things have changed since then.
Perhaps we need a Tea Party again.
—Banks Burgess and Paul Shane, "Perhaps We Need a Tea
Party Again" (The Fair Tax Song)

One of the most important underlying dynamics of tax politics, and a key to understanding the obstacles to fundamental reform, is the variety in levels of intensity that different groups bring to the issue. When the topic is taxes, it is fair to say there are two kinds of people: the high-intensity folks and the rest of us. Of course, this could be said of many political issues, from abortion to immigration to the environment. The difference is that the tax code directly—and as we all know, annually—regulates the financial life of every American individual and corporation, and it does so in ways that distinctly advantage some and disadvantage others. The income tax in particular has become the conduit through which nearly all federal social and economic policy is attempted, be it by libertarian Republicans or by liberal Democrats. Tax policy, then, has become the ground on which nearly all other major policy battles are eventually fought.

In addition, unlike the more symbolically loaded and often religiously infused debates that dominate our national attention on issues of domestic policy, the effects of the tax law on each American can be measured precisely, in dollars and cents. Most of us accept, however dolefully, the reality that taxes are a necessary aspect of funding a working government, and we try to minimize the amount of time we spend thinking about them. But the high-intensity folks are different. They come in two varieties: the special pleaders and the would-be populists. The special pleaders are mostly corporations and industry groups, while the would-be populists, more central to the debates of fundamental reform, have grown adept at channeling the low-intensity resentment of the public at having to pay taxes into high-intensity legislative campaigns that seek to reshape not only the tax code but the place of government in American life.

For those interested in serious, responsible reform of how we fund our democracy, it is important to understand both groups in order to see clearly the challenges we face.

The Would-Be Populists

In May 2006, on a sultry Wednesday night north of Atlanta, forty-five hundred people jammed into the Gwinnet Convention Center had come to rail against the income tax. Another hundred or so hung around the parking lot to listen to the rally on their car radios. A couple thousand more were turned away. Some drove hundreds of miles. Bob Ivey and his wife, Kitty, from Live Oak, Florida, said that they spent $120 on gas for their recreational vehicle and many hours driving just to be there. Local Republican Congressman John Linder, formerly a dental surgeon, now the field general in a campaign to replace the income tax with a national sales tax, or what its proponents have somehow labeled the FairTax, led the charge. The former Senate candidate Herman Cain, a powerful orator, who turned the Kentucky Pizza chain from a failing business into a highly profitable company, brought the crowd to its feet complaining about the income tax and the IRS. The *Atlanta Journal-Constitution* likened the event to the Boston Tea Party but said that this "modern mob" must have made a lot more noise.

Naysayers may claim that the crowd came just to gawk at celebrities, most notably Fox's Sean Hannity, ABC's John Stossel, and the local radio talk show host Neal Boortz, but they would be badly mistaken. Republican candidates and elected officials have been nurturing anti–income tax sentiment for decades. They now have many thousands of avid supporters.

Nearly a decade before this Georgia rally, Congressmen Dick Armey (R-TX) and Billy Tauzin (R-LA), now both retired from Congress, held a "Scrap the Code" road show, traveling the country to debate whether the income tax should be replaced with a national sales tax or a flat tax. In October 1997, side by side with Georgia's Speaker of the House Newt Gingrich, Armey and Tauzin drew nearly two thousand people to the Cobb County Galleria Ballroom. They attracted similar crowds to many forums throughout the country, and the crowds always cheered loudly whenever Tauzin echoed Ways and Means Committee Chairman Bill Archer's refrain: "We need to pull the income tax out by its roots."

Armey and Tauzin announced their Scrap the Code tour the same week that Senator William Roth (R-DE), chairman of the Senate Finance Committee, held dramatic hearings on alleged IRS abuses. Several citizens, including a retired Catholic priest, related their personal horror stories of IRS misfeasance and malfeasance. One of the complainants, Katherine Lund Hicks, a California bank employee, described a ten-year saga of IRS computer screwups, liens, levies, audits, and compounding interest and penalties that she claimed led to her divorce and bankruptcy. "Our lives are now forever altered," she said. "We will pay additional taxes every year as a result. Our confidence in the integrity of the IRS has been completely shattered. . . . My credit is completely destroyed, and my husband's credit is seriously damaged. We will suffer the effects of this IRS collection for the rest of our lives." Roth's constituent Tom Savage, owner of a construction management firm in Lewes, Delaware, claimed that the IRS had cost him $250,000 he did not owe by insisting he pay taxes due from an unrelated business. The most dramatic moments of the Roth hearings came, like a scene from a bad movie about the mob, when six IRS agents, testifying from behind screens through voice-altering microphones, detailed the agency's misconduct. The star witness, who testified openly, was Jennifer Long, a career IRS agent in Houston. She said the IRS was targeting poor taxpayers and people who had suffered personal tragedies or financial crises. The IRS, she said, wants to "stick it" to people who "can't fight back."

Faced with this apparently populist outrage, the IRS uncharacteristically did not fight back. Instead, the acting commissioner apologized to the American people. The hearings made great television and generated front-page headlines throughout the country. Only later did investigations show that many of that day's allegations were false. But for many Americans the hearings served only to confirm what they already feared: that the IRS is an out-of-control agency routinely willing to trample on the rights of ordinary law-abiding folks.

Later that year, Congress passed legislation revising the governance and many operations of the IRS and enhancing legal protections for taxpayers. Even though the legislation was mostly the product of a bipartisan effort led by Representative Rob Portman (R-OH), who later became George W. Bush's budget director, and Senator Bob Kerrey (D-NE), William Roth took the lion's share of credit in his 1999 book *The Power to Destroy*. Senator Roth had grabbed the headlines and the public's attention.

The IRS itself did some serious backpedaling. In addition to its public apologies for "abuses," it spent years trying to convert from an "enforcement" to a "service" agency and to treat taxpayers as "customers" of the agency. Bill Clinton's Treasury Department required the IRS to provide "customer surveys" to people whose tax returns were audited. Nearly a decade passed before the agency once again emphasized its "enforcement" function. But to little avail. The IRS remains the villain. Americans, by a 51 to 34 percent majority, would rather have a root canal than an IRS audit.

Over the past fifteen to twenty years, conservative Republicans and allied industry groups have proven remarkably effective at organizing this resentment and linking it to their tax reform agendas. Republicans commonly and quite deliberately mislabel the nation's tax law the "IRS Code," as if the

Congress is no more than a bystander in producing it—rather than its author. During Roth's hearings, Senator Don Nickles (R-OK) ostentatiously placed a copy of the tax code and the Bible side by side on the dais, and in case anyone had missed his emphasis on the code's larger size and its lesser worth, said: "[The tax law] is about ten times the size of the Bible, and unlike the Bible contains no good news."

Representative Steve Largent (R-OK), who enjoyed far greater success as a wide receiver at the University of Tulsa and for the Seattle Seahawks than as a legislator, introduced the Tax Code Termination Act, which would have ended the income tax on December 31, 2001. Largent's bill had one small shortcoming: it failed to specify what kind of tax law would replace the current one. Nevertheless, in June 1998 the House passed the bill 219–209, with almost all Republicans voting in favor and almost all Democrats against. The Senate, no doubt regarding the House action as a bit irresponsible, failed to follow suit. This legislation is routinely updated. No "Save the Code" countermovement has emerged.

Even now, long after the Roth hearings, attacking the IRS always arouses the crowd's passions and brings people to their feet applauding and screaming. Rarely have politicians had such a ready target. Who wants to stand up for the tax collector? No one. So promises to abolish the IRS are commonplace. Boortz and Linder's best-selling *FairTax Book* shouts the end of the IRS from its cover. "Scrap the Code" T-shirts were festooned with the same "No IRS" logo. John Linder advised George W. Bush that he should run for reelection in 2004 by railing against the IRS. "Take the focus off Iraq and attack the Internal Revenue Service," advised Linder. Steve Forbes had tried this, in 1992 running for president principally on his flat-tax plan (which received more support from the electorate than he did), claiming that the "IRS [would] be RIP" if only he were elected.

It is stunning that so many Americans seem to believe that the federal government can collect taxes—no matter on what or whom—without a tax collection agency, but many apparently do. To be sure, a responsible tax reform could be fashioned to free most Americans from having any contact with the IRS by shifting tax collections away from individuals and onto businesses. (This is one of the major advantages of a tax on goods and services over an income tax, as I shall explore in detail subsequently.) But the IRS will not just vanish. The rallying cry of many sales tax advocates—that they will eliminate the IRS altogether and have federal taxes collected by the states—is rubbish. But what should a thoughtful and honest politician do? Stand up and defend the IRS? Not if he values his political life. So silence on the other side is palpable.

As we have seen, claims that the IRS will disappear are just one instance in the tax reform debate of Colbert's truthiness. Colbert himself seems only slightly out of the mainstream when he adds, "I'm not a fan of facts; you see, facts can change, but my opinion will never change no matter what the facts are."[1] Unfortunately, tax reform provides a perfect occasion for a pandemic of truthiness. As we saw with Rosie Scenario, predictions of glorious economic benefits from one's favorite reform can readily be generated by complex econometric models whose results turn on assumptions buried so deep in the mathematical interstices that not even a CIA agent could find them.[2]

Despite all this apparently populist fuss, taxes tend to be a rather low-intensity issue with the public—trailing not only terrorism and the spread of nuclear weapons but also often education, job security, health insurance, and even gas prices in Americans' lists of their greatest concerns. But tax reform is always on the list. In a November 2002 PSRA/ *Newsweek* poll, "major reform of the federal income tax system" ranked second out of eleven categories. In an ABC/ *Washington Post* poll a month later, nearly one-fifth of the respondents said that tax reform should be the highest priority. A similar poll in January 2005 produced exactly the same result, and when ranked according to "highest priority," tax reform tied for ninth out of twelve categories. In Harris polls conducted in 2005 and 2006, 77 to 80 percent of the public said that the federal tax system needs major change or should be completely overhauled.[3] About half urged a complete overhaul. Nearly 80 percent of respondents in the December 2002 ABC/ *Washington Post* poll ranked tax reform at least a "high priority." A *Los Angeles Times* poll the same month found that the public, by a 59–24 margin, thought that tax reform should be one of President's Bush's top priorities in his second term. So polling data reveal that a large majority of Americans wants major tax reform.

Despite the centrality of antitax sentiment in holding the Republican coalition together, however, neither political party enjoys a clear edge on the tax issue. And because the tax issue is one of relatively low intensity to the general public, there is great leeway for polling data to be manipulated by the phrasing of questions and by the structure of the poll. People's responses are remarkably sensitive to the way questions are phrased. A surprising example can be found in polling about the public's support for reducing income inequality. While a plurality favor such reductions, polls conducted simultaneously by the same organization show a significantly greater degree of support when the question refers to "high-income people and low-income people" than when the poll asks about "people with high incomes and people with low incomes." Go figure.

Ian Shapiro and I detailed in our book *Death by a Thousand Cuts* the brilliant use of polling in 2001 by those who wanted to repeal the estate tax.[4] By separating repeal from the broader context of the federal budget and from other tax and spending issues and isolating the "death tax" as a stand-alone issue, repeal advocates were able to transform a low level of interest by the general public into a clear perception by both politicians and the press of overwhelming public support for repeal. When the polling was conducted differently, much of the apparent support evaporated. The activities of the repeal advocates in structuring, disseminating, and promoting their polls offers a virtual playbook on how to transform low-intensity public preferences into a powerful political sword that may be wielded in Congress by those with a lot of money at stake and a high-intensity desire for a particular outcome. Effective political leadership can transform the "running room" of such public opinion into a major legislative victory. This is what happened with the estate tax.

And it may be happening again now with the so-called FairTax or proposed national sales tax. While FairTax is not yet a household name, its backers are organizing in much the same way the estate-tax repeal advocates did. For this reason alone, it is worth understanding just why this proposal doesn't come close to making sense.

FairTax Follies

In their *FairTax Book,* Neal Boortz and John Linder advocate a national sales tax to replace both income and payroll taxes, claiming that under their plan workers would receive 100 per-

cent of their paychecks with no taxes withheld; they also claim
that the sales tax would not increase prices.[5] Thus, they would
have it, the sales tax will be completely pain free; wages will not
fall and prices will not go up. Now while either of these things
could be true, they cannot both be true simultaneously. The
sales tax must be paid either out of people's wages, like the income tax, or at the store when people buy goods and services.
While preparing for a New York City debate with Boortz, I
wrote to the Harvard economist Dale Jorgenson, whom Linder
and Boortz cite for their claim that prices won't rise:

> Dale, I'm confused about some of the claims made
> by the "FairTax" national sales tax advocates. They
> cite you for the proposition that prices won't go up.
> At the same time, they claim people will take home
> pay equal to their before-tax wages, so wages won't
> go down. I don't see how both of these things can be
> true. Either prices will rise or wages will go down.
> Both ends of a seesaw cannot be up at the same
> time. Can you help me?

Professor Jorgenson replied: "Dear Michael, I agree with you. I
am responsible only for the part about prices." The economist
responsible for Boortz and Linder's claim that wages will not go
down, Laurence Kotlikoff of Boston University, assumes that
prices will rise. Boortz and Linder selected the most favorable
assumptions from each and claimed the best of both worlds—
a hefty dose of truthiness. The difficulty is that most Americans
cannot sort through the competing claims. Even experts often
have trouble reaching agreement about the facts.

Taking a step back, what we need to understand about
this proposal is that it is designed to further the ultimately

untenable starve-the-beast agenda discussed in the previous chapter. The technique is simple: advance a flat tax or national sales tax proposal with a rate significantly lower than what would be necessary to replace the revenues forgone from the taxes it replaces. Thus Linder and Boortz claim that they could replace the federal corporate and individual income taxes, payroll taxes, and the estate tax with a national sales tax of 30 percent (which they call 23 percent).[6] The president's panel, using Treasury Department estimates, reported that even assuming low rates of sales tax evasion, it would take a 34 percent rate to replace only the individual and corporate income taxes. Replacing payroll taxes as well would require a rate roughly double that. Even Kotlikoff, perhaps the most respected economist supporting the national sales tax, has confessed that a 30 percent rate would require federal spending to decline by $280 billion each year to be revenue neutral.[7] The goals of the FairTax crowd are clear: they not only want to change the nation's tax system, but they also want to use tax reform to reduce government spending. We may agree that these goals are laudable, but, as we saw in the previous chapter, given our experience for more than two decades, using tax reform as the way to make spending cuts happen is foolhardy.

Assuming large increases in economic growth or major spending cuts in fashioning tax reform proposals carries obvious political advantages. It allows lower tax rates, thereby increasing the number of winners and reducing, or—with a scenario rosy enough—eliminating, the losers. This, of course, enhances the political appeal of any proposal. At the same time, it makes other more realistic proposals, with their higher tax rates, considerably less appealing.

President Bush's tax reform panel unanimously rejected the idea of completely replacing the income tax with a retail sales tax for several reasons. In addition to the panel's conclusion that a "rate of 34 percent and likely higher" would be required to eliminate the income tax alone, it viewed the idea as not "appropriately progressive," declared that a cash grant proposal associated with the idea "would inappropriately increase the size and scope of government," and foresaw that a retail sales tax so high would probably be difficult to collect.

Nevertheless, the FairTax movement is well financed and extremely well organized. Neal Boortz relentlessly trumpets the idea on his nationally syndicated radio show and his Web site. Leo E. Linbeck, Jr., a Houston construction magnate with connections to Republican leaders, among others, has supplied the financial wherewithal. FairTax backers have spent millions to fund sympathetic economic research, to conduct focus groups and polling, and to advertise on radio, television, and the Internet. Their umbrella organization, Americans for Fair Taxation, has chapters in all fifty states holding meetings, hosting speakers, sponsoring dinners and other social events, distributing information advocating their plan, and coordinating letter-writing and e-mail campaigns to Congress. It is, by far, the best-organized and best-financed national effort to change our tax laws. And this plan has more congressional cosponsors than any other tax reform idea.

A proposal such as this, coupled with its inevitable call to abolish the IRS, seems designed more to rally antitax Republicans than to make a serious attempt at restructuring our tax system. The political goals are clear. The Republican political consultant and language guru Frank Luntz, who insisted that Republicans always call the estate tax the "death tax," claims that "nothing guarantees more applause and more support than the call to abolish the IRS."

Grover Norquist, the peripatetic leader of Americans for Tax Reform and a close adviser to the Bush White House, uses the same playbook. As he puts it: "All tax cuts are good tax cuts." Newt Gingrich has described him as "the person who I regard as the most innovative, creative, courageous, and entrepreneurial leader of the antitax efforts and of conservative grassroots activism in America." Norquist has spent more than twenty years getting politicians (now numbering more than two hundred in the House and nearly forty in the Senate) to sign his so-called Taxpayer Protection Pledge stating that they will oppose "any and all" tax increases. He is clear about his ultimate policy goal. "I don't want to kill the government," he says. "I just want to get it down to a size where I can drown it in a bathtub." Norquist considers his antitax crusade as the linchpin to a long-term Republican majority. Insisting that taxation is the "central vote-driving issue," he adds: "You win this issue, you win—over time—all issues."

That a significant segment of the Republican Party views tax reform as the best way to attack government spending and as a political move to outflank Democrats limits the prospect of a bipartisan coalition in Congress, an essential element in enacting a new tax system that has any realistic chance at long-term stability and success. Using tax reform to serve the political ambitions of one political party substantially reduces the chances that reform will actually happen. Asking tax reform to carry the burden of reining in federal spending is demanding something of it that it cannot do. In crafting a responsible reform of our tax system, we cannot allow the faux populism of certain high-intensity advocates to drown out the larger public interest in appropriately funding our government.

Special Pleading

Since responsible tax reform in the current context cannot cut taxes overall, it inevitably will produce both winners and losers. Simplifying the tax code requires cutting back on someone's deductions or credits, eliminating someone's special tax breaks, and closing someone's loopholes. In exchange, everyone can have lower tax rates. So there should be more winners than losers. But the losers may lose a lot, while the more numerous winners will each gain only a little. If so, the losers will scream loudly enough to drown out the winners' quiet applause.

Politicians also fear the reactions of the large numbers of Americans who could lose all or part of their treasured deductions and tax credits, and politicians are, of course, afraid of powerful special-interest groups. When the president's panel issued its report, Congress heard immediate complaints, for example, from the Council on Foundations about the reductions in the tax deduction for charitable giving. The life insurance industry instantly claimed that panel proposals to eliminate income tax breaks for its products "represent a retreat from America's historic commitment to helping Americans achieve financial and retirement security . . . by setting arbitrary limits on the ability of Americans to protect their families through life insurance and annuities." The National Retail Federation described one of the panel's proposals as "a huge new tax increase for American consumers that would dramatically drive up the price of everyday necessities" and urged President Bush and Treasury Secretary John Snow to reject the proposal. The American Society of Pension Professionals and Actuaries described the panel's recommendations as "devastating to the retirement security of millions of American workers." And this is just a small sample of complaints lodged on the day the panel's report was released. Needless to add, members of each of these groups are important contributors to congressional and presidential campaigns.

Several years ago, I experienced firsthand the intensity of special pleaders' reactions even to mild threats. In a few pages of a book on the shortcomings of the income tax, I suggested a possible tax reform—the reform I detail here in Part II— that would free 150 million Americans from filing tax returns and paying income tax. My book had hardly hit the bookstores before I received a call from Robert A. Weinberger, vice president and Washington representative for H&R Block, the nation's largest tax return preparation firm. He wanted to buy me lunch and explain to me how bad it would be for the country if all those people did not have to file tax returns. Bad for H&R Block, to be sure. Not bad for the country.

My experience was trifling compared to what happened to the Stanford law professor Joe Bankman when he spearheaded California's Ready Return program, under which the state provided filled-out tax returns to thousands of low-income and elderly Californians. The eleven thousand beneficiaries of this pilot program loved it. They said it saved time and alleviated their anxieties about doing their taxes. They said that it was something government should do routinely. The California legislature was poised to extend this experiment to a million people and make it permanent, until Intuit, the producer of the tax preparation software program Turbo-Tax, spent hundreds of thousands of dollars to kill it and another $1 million unsuccessfully trying to defeat a Ready Return supporter running for state controller. Tom Campbell, a former California budget director and a member of the state tax board that had initiated the Ready Return program, who had also been a state senator and congressman, said he had "never seen the public interest being overborne by private interests as clearly as it has been in this case. The argument was never presented in terms of the public interest." Joe Bankman was determined to fight back, so he spent $30,000 hiring his own business lobbyist (instead of remodeling his kitchen). Nevertheless, he faced an uphill fight.

The California legislature initially yielded to opponents of the Ready Return program and let it die. In December 2006, however, California's Franchise Tax Board decided to revive Ready Return for the 2007 tax year and expand it to cover one million taxpayers. California's legislative leaders said that they would not try to block the board from going ahead with the program.[8] It is unlikely, however, that a similar service could be implemented on a federal level, in no small part due to Intuit's entrenched position under agreements with twenty-one states whereby low-income taxpayers may obtain TurboTax free through an IRS-backed effort known as Free File.

Attempting a major overhaul of any system of government in this day and age means confronting the highly organized and well-funded opposition that is bound to come from those special interests who have something to lose.

This is why any successful effort to implement the Competitive Tax proposal I am putting forward in this book must include as part of its effort an education of Congress and the business community to the *overall* advantages of eliminating the income tax for most Americans, lowering both individual and corporate tax rates, and instituting a tax on goods and services. Flying blind into the thicket of special pleaders will assure any serious tax proposal's quick demise.

The Road Ahead

The American people are notoriously optimistic. Usually this is a wonderful attribute. In the context of tax reform, however, it makes the public very susceptible to manipulation and misinformation. There are many billions of dollars at stake. Shifting taxes to someone else is what legislative contests over tax policy are typically about. For the would-be populists this means organizing the resentment of average Americans, often through of use of faulty arguments, in order to further their own ideological goals. For the special pleaders this means hiring lobbyists to try to shift the tax burden elsewhere. Meanwhile, the rest of us have to work to know what's at stake, and ultimately have to rely on the president and our representatives in the Congress to protect us. This has proved a risky proposition.

And yet history demonstrates that the only political leader who can get tax reform through Congress is the president of the United States. Tax reform requires both a president genuinely committed to a major restructuring of the nation's tax system and House and Senate leaders with the knowledge and the power to get the legislation through Congress. Such politicians, unfortunately, are in short supply. Once they learn that tax reform has serious political downside risks, as President Bush did when his tax reform panel issued its report, politicians are far more likely to turn away from tax reform than to embrace it—unless and until either the American public and its business leaders insist reform is essential or a financial crisis emerges. It is far easier to rail against what is wrong with the income tax—or to score political points by attacking the IRS—than to fashion a reasonable and realistic solution.

Nonetheless, ready or not, Congress will soon face a major dilemma. By 2010 it will have to choose which of President Bush's tax cuts to make permanent and also avoid the AMT train wreck heading down the tracks. Moreover, if we don't get our government's finances in order, a major fiscal catastrophe may be looming in the more distant future when we face an aging population along with massive holdings of our debt abroad. The president and the Congress will be forced to act.

The question is: what is the honest and responsible form of action if what we want is a truly fair, simple, and competitive tax system?

IV

Until the Second Child Speaks: First Principles of Responsible Reform

People want just taxes more than they want lower taxes.

—Will Rogers

T he Competitive Tax proposal I put forward here takes as its first principles the traditional goals of tax reform: produce adequate revenue; promote economic growth; increase international competitiveness of U.S. products, workers, and businesses; minimize interference with private decision making; streamline compliance and administration; and, finally, distribute the burden of taxation fairly in accordance with people's ability to pay.

Before turning to the details of the proposal itself and demonstrating how it fulfills these principles, I want to take a moment to underline that final principle: the fair distribution of taxation's burdens.

In our country today, the gap between the wealthy and the poor is wider than it has been since the roaring twenties. One has to go back eighty years to find a chasm so big between the ultrawealthy and the least well off in our society. Much of the success of the far-right, tax-cutting fundamentalists comes from their rhetorical insistence that even to notice this fact, much less do something about it, amounts to an endorsement of some utterly leveling socialism or even communism. This is nonsense. And dangerous nonsense at that. As Andrew Jackson, Teddy Roosevelt, and the Progressives understood, the establishment of a permanent economic aristocracy is inimical to the American ideal of fairness for all its citizens. George W. Bush in February 2007 recognized the issue: "The fact is that income inequality is real; it's been rising for more than twenty-five years." And Henry Paulson, in his first speech as Bush's Treasury secretary identified "wage growth and income distribution" among the major economic challenges facing our nation. Any serious reform of our tax system must retain as one of its first principles the progressive structure we have used for nearly a century.

James Q. Riordan, a staffer for the conservative Tax Foundation, said that "the need for a progressive tax system is imprinted on the American DNA." This sentiment has been echoed by the liberal congressman Richard Neal (D-MA), who said, "From the Boston Tea Party to now, tax fairness is firmly parked in the American psyche." And even schoolchildren know it to be true: one need go no further than your local elementary school to realize how basic this American instinct for tax justice really is.

The Progressive Intuition

Forty years ago, Dan Throop Smith, a Harvard economist who served as the Treasury Department's top tax adviser during the Eisenhower administration, accepted the invitation of his daughter, a teacher, to visit her one-room school in Montana. To get a better handle on tax equity, Smith asked three children what would be a fair tax on a family with an income of $5,000, if a family with an income of $2,000 paid a tax of $200.

The first child said, "five hundred dollars," thereby showing a predisposition for proportional burdens and perhaps a desire to make use of a newly acquired familiarity with percentages. A second child immediately disagreed, adding the comment that the payment should be more than $500 because "each dollar isn't so important" to the family with the larger income. A third child agreed with the second, but with the reservation that the additional tax over $500 shouldn't be "too much more or they won't work so hard." Smith subsequently relayed this story in a scholarly article, adding: "Elaborate theoretical structures concerning diminishing utility and incentives and disincentives are all really refinements of the quasi-intuitive opinions of those children and may not lead to any greater certainty."[1]

Shortly after publication of my book *The Decline (and Fall?) of the Income Tax,* which retells Smith's story, my daughter's fifth-grade teacher asked me to visit her classroom to talk about it. While there, I repeated Dan Throop Smith's experiment. I asked the identical question, and, remarkably, the first three students to speak gave the identical answers in exactly the same order. Children's intuitions about progressive taxation in the 1990s in New Haven, Connecticut, mirrored precisely those of the Montana children of the 1960s. After I told them that they had given exactly the same answers in exactly the same order as did children more than three decades earlier in a one-room Montana schoolhouse, a number of the students wrote to me remarking how "cool," "neat," "amazing," and "weird" that was. One concluded, "I guess that must be fair, if both of the schools got the same answers."

These two experiments should serve as a caution to those who believe that the American public will view as fair the complete replacement of a progressive tax on income with a flat-rate tax on goods and services. That sentiment will last only until the second child speaks.

And yet both the flat tax and FairTax proposals would reduce taxes on those at the top and make up the lost taxes from people with less income or wealth. This seems particularly untimely when between 1979 and 2006 the income of the richest 1 percent of Americans nearly doubled, while the income of middle-class Americans increased by only about 11.5 percent, according to the most reliable numbers.[2] Over the same period, the wage at the 10th percentile, near the bottom of the wage distribution, rose just 4 percent, while the wage at the 90th percentile, near the top of the distribution, rose 34 percent. The share of after-tax income garnered by the top 1 percent of households increased from 8 percent in 1979 to 14 percent in 2004.[3] Even within the top 1 percent the distribution of income has recently widened. And although the nation's economy grew by 11.7 percent in the period 2001–5, the income of the median household fell by 0.5 percent in that period.

Wealth is even more unevenly distributed than income, with the wealthiest 1 percent owning about one-third of all wealth in the United States. The bottom 50 percent hold just 2.25 percent of all wealth. As the University of Chicago economist Austan Goolsbee has pointed out, "The average net worth of the top 10 percent of American families is almost 30 times greater than the average net worth of families in the middle 50 percent of the spectrum—and these disparities in net worth have been growing even faster than the disparities in income."[4]

To be sure, people move in and out of these wealth and income classes; some of the rich lose money and some poor people become rich over time.[5] But while Americans can debate forever what constitutes a fair distribution of taxes, surely it is not appropriate to shift the tax burden downward now, when those at the very top are doing so very much better than everyone else. This, however, is exactly what proposals like the flat tax and the FairTax would do.

Those who advocate such a shift claim it to be essential for economic growth, but they offer little credible evidence for that proposition. They also cite polls showing that many people regard a single tax rate as "fair." Their opponents shout: "Tax cuts for the rich, tax cuts for the rich." And they reply, "class warfare, class warfare." This shouting match is a prescription for stalemate—or, if something does pass Congress, for future instability and uncertainty.

I have long thought we could not do much better than the former *New York Times* columnist William Safire's maxim of tax fairness: "Most of us accept as fair this principle: the poor should pay nothing, the middlers something, the rich the highest percentage."[6] Today's tax reform debate has reopened the contest between, on the one hand, what Stephen Weisman in his book *The Great Tax Wars* labeled "virtue," which views "wealth as a product of hard work, thrift, ingenuity and risk taking"—something the state should encourage and protect—and, on the other, "justice," which, according to Weisman, is taxation based on ability to pay, with progressive taxes on income or wealth. Weisman, like most

Americans, views progressive taxation as necessary to "soften the edges of the distribution of wealth in the interest of justice and fairness."[7]

Drawing appropriate lines in the battle between virtue and justice has always haunted tax lawmaking. But today's tax reform debate raises fundamental questions that many thought were settled by the enactment of the income tax nearly a century ago—questions that have not been at issue since the income tax was extended to the masses to finance World War II. Advocates for replacing the income tax with a flat tax or the FairTax are willing to sacrifice tax justice to promote economic virtue and reward success. One need not view the current tax distribution as ideal to be convinced that tax reform should not be used to shift the tax burden away from those at the top down the income scale.

In addition to producing a simple tax system that will raise adequate revenue without inhibiting economic growth, the critical challenge for tax reformers today is to fashion a tax reform that will better reward virtue and promote economic growth *without* sacrificing tax justice, *without* shifting the tax burden downward. Last century's solution—the progressive rate income tax—has fallen into disrepair and disrepute. Relying—as we now do and have since World War II—exclusively on the income tax as the solution to this dilemma no longer seems viable.

The current income tax is a horrible mess. But it is quite progressive today. More than two-thirds of the total income tax is paid by the highest 10 percent of earners, more than one-third by the top 1 percent.[8] It is impossible to duplicate this distribution by completely replacing the income tax with a flat rate tax on consumption. In restructuring our tax system, we need not, and should not, enact a massive tax reduction for the country's wealthiest people—those who least need such relief—while increasing taxes for those with less income or wealth. Many Democrats would go even further and increase taxes at the top.

In 1986 Congress was able to achieve a bipartisan tax reform only by agreeing to leave the distribution of the tax burden as it was. Maintaining the existing distribution of the tax burden may somewhat complicate the task of tax reform and limit the options available, but, at a minimum, it is essential if reform is to be fair. Despite several tax reform plans currently before Congress that throw into question the century-old American principle that taxes should be distributed in accordance with people's ability to pay, replacing much of our income tax with a tax on goods and services need not strip away the progressivity we have in our system. As the Competitive Tax Plan, which we now turn to in detail, demonstrates, this distribution can be maintained with a new mix of taxes in a far simpler system that can produce adequate revenue as our population ages—and in a manner much more conducive to economic growth.

Part II
Funding a
Competitive America

V

Tax Spending

If you don't drink, smoke, or drive a car, you're a tax evader.
—*Thomas S. Foley, Former Speaker of the House*

When it comes to meeting its funding requirements, a government has four basic choices as to what it can tax: income, wages, consumption, or wealth. These are the four tax bases robust enough to produce the revenues a modern government requires that are also connected in some way to people's ability to pay. Most governments around the world use all four rather than picking among them. But from these four basic categories of revenue, we in the United States have, since World War II, chosen two—income and wages—as our primary forms of funding our federal government. Together, our individual and corporate income taxes, along with our payroll tax on wages, account for about 92 percent of federal revenues annually. State and local governments rely on their own versions of income taxes in addition to taxes on sales and property. And while the federal government imposes a handful of excise taxes—taxes on purchases of specific goods, such as alcohol, tobacco, and gasoline—unlike the rest of the world, we do not have a national tax on the third category, consumption. That is a tax on people's spending, their purchases of goods and services.

It is the central contention of this book, and the centerpiece of my Competitive Tax Plan, that the fundamental reform required to create an internationally competitive, administratively efficient, and viable long-term solution to our funding requirements is to make a different choice: we should impose tax on purchases of goods and services. I am not the first to propose the adoption of a consumption tax. Indeed, except for a handful of holdouts, who believe that our dysfunctional tax system can be fixed simply by patching up our income tax, virtually every serious proponent of tax reform has suggested the need for a federal tax on consumption. Some, who are principally concerned with the funding of Social Security and health insurance for our aging population, would simply add to our existing system a relatively low-rate tax—say 3 to 5 percent—on goods and services. Others want to substitute a consumption tax for all or part of the payroll tax that now funds Social Security and Medicare (an idea I take up in Chapter 8). The most radical propose eliminating the income tax altogether and substituting a consumption tax for it. Instead, I believe we should free the overwhelming majority of Americans from the income tax and replace the revenues lost with a broad-based tax on consumption.

My plan, unlike some national sales tax proposals such as the FairTax currently making the rounds in our capital, offers a nonideological, reasoned, fiscally sound, and feasible way to modernize our tax system. It would avoid shifting the tax burden away from those most able to pay to families with less income or wealth, while allowing us to fund our government in a manner more conducive to economic growth and increasing standards of living for all Americans.

The first, overarching point that must be addressed is how a consumption tax would work in practice. Unfortunately, this is not a straightforward inquiry. Consumption taxes can take many forms. Academicians have designed taxes on consumption that may be collected from individuals or partially from individuals and partially from businesses, and some of these ideas have been embraced by politicians. The flat tax, supported by former presidential candidate Steve Forbes and former Congressman Dick Armey, is an example. These kinds of consumption taxes can look so much like taxes on income that the nonexpert may not even know what is being taxed. However, the consumption taxes used widely throughout the world—value-added taxes and retail sales taxes—are collected only from businesses. Let's begin with these.

The Value-Added Tax

The United States is a relatively low-tax country. Looking at total taxes, including federal, state, and local taxes, as a percentage of total economic output (GDP), the United States at about 25 percent has considerably lower taxes than the European Union (EU), which averaged about 40 percent of GDP before the recent addition of ten new lower-tax members, mostly from eastern Europe. Our taxes are also lower than the average of approximately 36 percent of GDP of the thirty countries of the Organization for Economic Cooperation and Development (OECD). Our income tax level is comparable, however. We collect about 12 percent of our GDP in corporate and individual income taxes, while the OECD nations average about 13 percent and Europe around 14 percent. Our corporate income tax rate is actually higher than virtually all of the OECD countries. The biggest difference in our tax structure is that most other nations rely much more heavily on consumption taxes than we do. Indeed, we are the only OECD nation that does not impose a national-level tax on sales of goods and services.

This was not always true. For this nation's first century, taxes on consumption in the form of excise taxes on specific commodities and tariffs on imported goods were virtually the only taxes imposed by the federal government. During World War I, however, tariff revenue became uncertain and unstable as the war disrupted international commerce. Since then, tariffs have fallen into disrepute because of the economic distortions they entail for both international trade and domestic production.

The most common types of modern consumption taxes are retail sales taxes and value-added taxes (VATs). Retail sales taxes in the United States are commonly imposed by state and local governments. As most Americans know, retail sales taxes are paid by consumers to retail businesses, who then pay the tax to the government. Often retail sales taxes exempt such items as food or clothing, requiring someone to decide whether a chocolate Easter bunny is food or a toy and whether a Halloween mask or costume qualifies as exempt clothing. States vary in their sales tax coverage and exemptions, and many local governments also impose sales taxes. In 2006 there were 7,579 retail sales tax jurisdictions in the United States.[1] Large multistate corporations commonly file more than two hundred state and local sales tax forms *monthly*.

Elsewhere in the world, the most common form of consumption tax is the VAT, a tax on the value added to goods and services. (These taxes are sometimes called goods and services taxes, or GSTs, but I will use the more common VAT label here.) The difference between the value of a business's purchases and its sales is the value it has added to its products or services, and it is this increase in value that is taxed. A VAT is much like a retail sales tax, except in a value-added tax system it is not only retailers who collect the tax and pay it to the government. Wholesalers and manufacturers also withhold tax as products move through the chain of production, distribution, and sale. In other words, a retail sales tax taxes only sales directly to consumers, while a VAT collects a portion of the tax at each level of production. The cumulative value added at all stages of production and distribution of a good or service necessarily equals the total value of the retail sale, with the result that a retail sales tax and a VAT of the same rate are economically equivalent, even though they are collected differently. It is these collection advantages that have made the VAT the consumption tax of choice throughout the world.

The previous paragraph may give the impression that the real difference between a retail sales tax and a VAT is that the VAT taxes more levels of production. Indeed, many people who oppose such taxes characterize them as if they actually taxed the same retail sale many times. This, however, is simply incorrect. In a value-added tax, businesses receive a tax credit for the amount of VAT they have paid on their own purchases of goods and services from other businesses.

To illustrate how this works, consider a farmer who sells barley and other supplies to a brewer for $20. The brewer brews the beer and sells it to a retailer for $60. The retailer, in turn, sells the beer to customers for $100. The tax liability of the farmer under a 20 percent VAT is $4 (20 percent of his sales price to the brewer, assuming he hasn't made any purchases that have been subject to a VAT). The brewer's tax liability is $12 (20 percent of $60), less the credit he receives for the tax paid by the farmer ($4), for a net tax liability of $8. Similarly, the retailer's tax liability is $20, less the taxes previously paid on his purchases ($4 by the farmer, and $8 by the brewer), for a net tax liability of $8. Across the three levels of production, there has been a total tax liability (net of credits) of $20, or 20 percent of the final retail sales price, exactly what a retail sales tax at the same rate would collect entirely from the retailer.

This widely used "credit-method," which requires invoices for sales and purchases, decreases the opportunities for noncompliance under a VAT since the records from one firm can be used to check other firms' sales and purchases. A VAT therefore works essentially like a system of withholding for sales taxes. A VAT does not eliminate compliance issues altogether—a Belgian study estimated that the United Kingdom lost nearly $18 billion to VAT fraud between June of 2005 and June of 2006.[2] Nonetheless, a U.S. VAT could help reduce the "tax gap"—the difference between what taxpayers should pay and what they actually pay on a timely basis—estimated by the IRS to be more than $300 billion annually.

Value-added taxes are now imposed by all of the other OECD countries and by nearly 150 countries worldwide. In the OECD the VAT rates range from a low of 5 percent in Japan to a high of 25 percent in Sweden, Hungary, Norway, and Denmark. The lowest European VAT rate is 16 percent. Ireland—which because of its low 12.5 percent corporate tax rate has been called by the *Wall Street Journal* the "Hong Kong of the west with the fastest pace of economic growth and jobs in the Eurozone"—imposes a VAT of 21 percent. VATs generate the revenues in Ireland and elsewhere that make low income tax rates possible (see Figure 5.1).

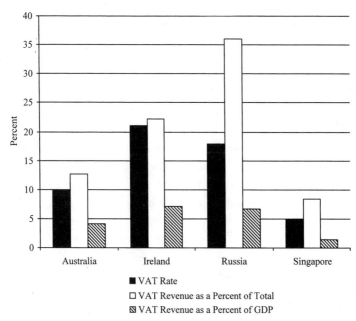

Figure 5.1. VATs in countries with low income taxes.
Source: OECD data (2005).

In the United States, a VAT at a rate of 10 to 14 percent could fund an income tax reform that would exempt families with income of $100,000 or less from the income tax and allow substantially lower income tax rates for both individuals and corporations. (These reforms will be described in subsequent chapters.) Like retail sales taxes, the amount of VAT should be separately stated so that consumers know how much tax is imposed each time they purchase goods or services. As with retail sales taxes, the ultimate consumers—nonbusiness purchasers—receive no credits with respect to their purchases.

In order to keep a VAT tax rate as low as possible, I propose that the base for this tax—that is, the total universe on which the tax will be charged—should be broad, covering nearly all goods and services. A broad VAT base with a single tax rate would minimize its economic distortions. However, as with any tax, there is the question of what will be exempt.

Both value-added and retail sales taxes are typically imposed on less than a full consumption base. Certain services are typically excluded from the tax base. Common examples include such things as medical and hospital care, services provided by state and local governments, education, religion, foreign travel, and sometimes public transportation and legal and accounting services. Appropriately taxing financial services provided by banks and other financial institutions under a VAT has proved difficult, although this may be changing.[3]

Typically, nations that impose value-added taxes exempt exports but tax imports so that the tax is imposed only by the country where the goods and services are actually consumed. To the extent that VAT revenues are used to replace corporate income taxes, this may help make American products become more competitive in the global economy.[4]

Some countries also exempt certain products, like food or clothing, in an effort to alleviate the VAT burdens of low- and moderate-income families, and some impose higher rates on luxuries. In general, however, having a single tax rate and limiting exemptions would further simplify compliance and administration.[5] As I shall discuss in Chapter 10, there are better ways to relieve the regressive impact of such consumption taxes on lower-income families than by exempting food, clothing, and housing.

My Competitive Tax Plan, however, makes one simple exemption from the outset: all businesses with gross receipts of less than $100,000 annually (which account for nearly 65 percent of the country's twenty-five million businesses) would be freed from collecting VAT or filing returns. Such an exemption would reduce the number of VAT returns to about nine million. An exemption for small businesses would also relieve them from the costs of compliance and relieve the tax collector from having to chase after small amounts of tax.[6] Large businesses are used to collecting VAT; they do so throughout the world. Collecting taxes from businesses, rather than from families, is a great advantage of the VAT, since most Americans would have nothing to do with the collection or enforcement of the tax, even though they would pay the tax when they purchase goods or services.

The Congressional Budget Office, using favorable assumptions, estimated that the costs of complying with a VAT could be as low as 10 percent of the compliance costs under the current corporate and individual income tax system. (European countries spend anywhere from two-thirds to four-fifths less on compliance than we do in trying to maintain our mess of an income tax.)[7]

Another key feature common to consumption taxes, regardless of how they are structured, is that the total tax base is generally sales, so the tax imposes no burden on savings or investments. Under an income tax, unless the particular form of savings gets special treatment, such as an exemption from tax, as is the case with most savings for retirement, the pretax return on savings is reduced by the tax rate. In other words, an income tax of 20 percent generally reduces a 10 percent pretax return on savings to 8 percent after tax. In contrast, the distinguishing characteristic of a consumption tax is that the pretax and after-tax rates of return on savings are identical; savers typically get the full 10 percent pretax return. If a person spends less than her current income, the difference—her savings—is exempt from taxation. If a person spends more than her current income, either by withdrawing prior savings or by borrowing, a consumption tax should be imposed on such spending.

Young people and the elderly often spend more than their current incomes, while people in middle age tend to save part of their current incomes for retirement, their children's education, or the down payment on a house. Thus, in comparison with a tax on wages or income, a consumption tax tends to impose relatively greater burdens on the young and the old. Wage and income taxes typically impose their greatest burdens in the higher-earning years of middle age. Many middle-income people, however, consume essentially whatever they earn, so for them there may be little difference in the timing of the burdens imposed by these kinds of taxes. Likewise, for very wealthy people, age may make little difference; their income will almost always be greater than their consumption in any particular year. Since many retirees tend to spend more than they earn, however, taxing consumption will require them to contribute to funding our government. Retirees who rely on Social Security will not be affected, since their Social Security benefits will automatically be increased to reflect any increases in prices resulting from the new consumption tax.

Avoiding the Mistakes of the Past

The federal government has frequently considered imposing a national consumption tax. For example, in 1921, when the income tax was only eight years old and a fraction of its current size, Chester Jordan, a public accountant from Portland, Maine, told the Senate Finance Committee that he could reduce the size of his accounting firm from eight to three members if Congress would substitute for the income tax a tax on "spendings."[8] That idea was strongly seconded by Ogden Mills, then a congressman from New York, who later served as Herbert Hoover's secretary of the Treasury.[9] After Congress refused to go along, Chester Jordan changed his name to Price Waterhouse and the rest is history. (I made that last part up, of course, but you get my point: income tax compliance has become an industry unto itself—and an unnecessary and wasteful one at that.)

Chester Jordan's proposal for taxing consumption rather than income was not a new idea, even in the 1920s. John Stuart Mill had been a fan of taxing consumption, and Alexander Hamilton had only praise for consumption taxes. Hamilton claimed that with consumption taxes people could choose how much to pay; as he put it, "The rich may be extravagant, the poor may be frugal."

In 1942 Franklin Roosevelt's Treasury secretary Henry Morgenthau advanced a progressive, graduated rate tax on spendings to finance the Second World War, but Congress again rejected it.[10] Instead, the Revenue Act of 1942 began the conversion of the income tax, which had applied only to high-income people, into a tax on the masses. Had this episode turned out differently, the income tax might have remained narrowly targeted to high-income people, and a consumption tax, rather than the income tax, might have become the federal government's mainstay revenue raiser.

In the early 1970s President Richard Nixon came close to proposing substituting a value-added tax for all or part of our corporate income and payroll taxes.[11] Several years later, in 1979, Ways and Means Chairman Al Ulman did recommend a 10 percent value-added tax. Although the best evidence supports other reasons—he did not even have a home in his congressional district, for example—some people claim that Ulman's stance cost him reelection in 1980, and his experience has made American politicians leery of suggesting a VAT.

Many observers thought that the political movement to replace the income tax with a consumption tax died when Ronald Reagan and the Congress retained and strengthened the income tax in the 1986 tax reform. The success of Democrats' political efforts in the 1990 and 1992 campaigns to portray the tax changes of the 1980s as excessively favorable to the rich, coupled with accumulating evidence that most of the gains in real wages during the period since 1973 have been garnered by high-income families, also made any serious effort to repeal the income tax seem far-fetched.

But the Republicans' sweep of the congressional elections of 1994 dramatically changed the political landscape. Proposals for substituting a consumption tax for the income tax vaulted back into the forefront of the nation's political dialogue. Republican Senate Budget Committee Chairman Pete Domenici of New Mexico and Democratic Senator Sam Nunn of Georgia in 1995 introduced legislation to replace the individual income tax and a portion of the Social Security payroll tax with a progressive rate tax on consumption and to substitute a value-added tax for the corporate income tax. The new Ways and Means Committee chairman, Bill Archer of Texas, and 1996 Republican presidential candidate Senator Richard Lugar of Indiana said that they too wanted to replace the income tax with a consumption tax. Archer never said what kind of consumption tax he favored. Lugar proposed a retail sales tax to be collected by the states, which he claimed would put the IRS out of business. As we have seen, this torch is now being carried by John Linder and the FairTax movement. In 1995 Dick Armey of Texas, the new Republican majority leader, and Republican presidential candidate Steve Forbes urged replacing the corporate and individual income taxes and the federal estate tax with a flat-rate tax on consumption, which they called a flat tax.[12] The Princeton economist David Bradford added a second rate to the flat tax to make it more progressive and named this the "X-tax."[13] In 2005 President Bush's tax reform panel added a third rate and a supplemental income tax on dividends, interest, and capital gains and called it the "Growth and Investment Tax Plan." All the rejiggering and relabeling makes it impossible for the public to know exactly what is being proposed. But we can be sure that the president's panel did not mean to impose a tax on growth and investment.

In addition to the president's panel, which considered consumption taxes to be an important piece in restructuring our tax system, many others, including the conservative economist Bruce Bartlett, who served in both the Reagan and George H. W. Bush administrations, and the Committee for Economic Development, a research and policy organization of more than two hundred business leaders and educators, urge a VAT for the United States. These proponents view a VAT as the best source for future federal revenues.

Notwithstanding all the support, a VAT has long been a difficult political sell in the United States. Republicans have worried that a VAT will be a money machine for the federal government and inevitably will lead to greater spending. Democrats have been concerned that a VAT is regressive, placing a higher burden on the less well-off. Larry Summers, a former

Treasury secretary and Harvard president, has quipped that a VAT will be enacted as soon as the Democrats recognize its potential as a money machine and Republicans realize that it is regressive.

The recent ascendancy of consumption tax proposals raises three fundamental questions. First, should the United States adopt a national tax on sales of goods and services? Second, if so, in what form? How should such a tax be structured? And third, how should the revenues from such a tax be used? In particular, what other tax reforms should accompany introduction of a national consumption tax? The answers to these questions will determine whether and how much tax reform will improve the simplicity, fairness, and economic wisdom of our tax system.

The United States has had an extremely low—and sometimes negative—rate of savings for many years. Similarly, the U.S. rate of private investment has been lower than that of other countries. Moreover, compared with other OECD nations, a far greater proportion of this nation's private savings goes into housing than into the corporate sector. Investments by the corporate sector are better at generating jobs. There is now a consensus among economists that, relative to an income tax, a consumption tax will increase national savings and economic output—so long as it does not result in greater deficits. There is disagreement, however, about the size of these benefits.

The simplification advantages of a consumption tax depend on how it is implemented. As noted earlier, retail sales taxes and VATs are collected from businesses rather than from families, greatly easing the compliance burdens of households and freeing them from having to deal with the tax collector. Other forms of consumption taxes, such as the flat tax, tax individuals on the wage element of value added and thus require households to file tax returns. Since under the flat tax only individuals' wages would be taxed, and all deductions, exclusions, and credits would be eliminated, its proponents claim that the annual tax return will shrink to a postcard that everyone would be able to fill in quickly and easily. Adding more than one tax rate—as, for example, the president's panel recommended—does not substantially complicate matters.

Two problems remain, however. First, the flat tax (as well as its variations) is a consumption tax, invented by academics, which is untried and untested anywhere in the world. All experience warns us that even if such a tax could be enacted in its pure form with all deductions, exclusions, and credits eliminated—a real long shot—the tax would stay neither pure nor flat for very long. Tax breaks for home ownership, charitable gifts, and education expenses, to name only a few, would soon make their way back into the tax law. The income tax Form 1040 itself could have once fit on a postcard. As it grew, so would the flat tax form.

Second, as the president's panel discovered, taxing only individuals' wages and not their income from investments offends our notions of tax justice. This is why the panel—hardly a bunch of liberals and none of them, as John Breaux is fond of reminding us, standing for reelection—coupled their consumption tax proposal with a tax on interest, dividends, and capital gains, albeit at a lower 15 percent rate. The panel concluded, correctly in my view, that the American public will not accept taxing families only on their wages and not on the income they receive from their investments or savings.

In the 1990s Senators Sam Nunn and Pete Domenici proposed coupling a VAT with a progressive rate tax on consumption—a so-called expenditure tax. The senators designed their proposal this way to avoid the substantial tax cut for high-income families that would occur under a retail sales or value-added tax or any other flat-rate consumption tax that completely replaces the income tax. Again, unlike the VAT or retail sales tax, a progressive consumption tax is essentially untested, although it has long been discussed and often applauded in academic circles. Only India and Sri Lanka have ever enacted an expenditure tax, and both repealed the tax shortly after it was enacted.

Senators Nunn and Domenici modified the standard form of expenditure tax in an effort to make their proposal more appealing politically. Their proposals would exempt, for example, much consumption financed out of sales of people's existing assets and would defer the tax on spending from borrowed funds. These modifications required complex rules to track both borrowing-financed consumption and consumption from dispositions of preenactment assets. Indeed, the Nunn-Domenici plan foundered because of its inability to solve problems of transition from an income tax to this type of consumption tax and its failure to tax consumption financed with borrowing. In combination, these two problems would have allowed people with assets or the ability to borrow to avoid the tax.[14] The personal tax was essentially a tax on wages, but by borrowing for consumption and reinvesting the proceeds of asset sales, people could have avoided even the wage tax. Senators Nunn and Domenici also concluded that it was necessary politically to retain a number of existing income tax preferences, including, for example, exempting interest on state and local bonds. This created other opportunities to consume tax free. The Senators called their tax a Uniform Savings Allowance, or "USA" tax. Maybe the *U* really stood for *unusual*.

Senator Nunn has since left the Senate, and Senator Domenici has not recently reintroduced this proposal. The Nunn-Domenici experiment suggests that enacting a coherent, progressive, and personalized tax on consumption is probably not politically viable. This is hardly surprising since no other nation relies on such a tax.

What all this history of attempts to enact a consumption tax teaches us is that in order for such a tax to become a politically viable alternative to our current income tax system, it will have to produce an outcome that is better for businesses, better for savings and investment, feasible, and fair to middle-income Americans. I believe the proposal that is laid out in the chapters that follow meets these criteria. Other plans currently popular in Washington do not.

Beware of Imitators

To date, the looks and labels of both the flat tax and the Bush panel's Growth and Investment Tax (GIT) have deflected the public from learning that both these proposals are unusual and untested kinds of value-added taxes. The critical details have remained buried with experts.

The fact is, both the flat tax and the GIT are variations on a type of value-added tax that in form resembles an income tax. They are what is called "subtraction-method value-added taxes." This kind of VAT taxes the difference between the total receipts from a business's sales of goods or services and the total amount of the business's purchases of goods or services from other businesses. The difference between sales and purchases is the business's value added, and the tax rate is applied to that amount. A subtraction-method VAT has been used in New Hampshire (and used and then repealed in Michigan) and currently enjoys great favor among some consumption tax advocates.

At the same tax rate, a retail sales tax, a subtraction-method VAT, and the much more common credit-method VAT should, in theory at least, produce identical results. Take, for example, a retailer who purchases a product from a manufacturer for $2,000 and sells it to consumers for $3,000. With a 10 percent retail sales tax, the retailer is required to pay $300 in taxes. The value added by the retailer is $1,000. Under a 10 percent credit-method VAT, the retailer must pay tax of $100 ($300—10 percent of sales—less the $200 credit for the taxes previously paid by the manufacturer). The retailer's tax of $100 plus the manufacturer's tax of $200 equal $300 (10 percent of the retail sales price). With a 10 percent subtraction-method value-added tax the retailer would subtract $2,000 of purchases from $3,000 of sales and pay 10 percent of the $1,000 difference—or $100, exactly the same amount. Applying the same tax rate to sales minus purchases should give identical results to taxing sales and offsetting the tax on sales by that paid on purchases, as under the more common credit-method VAT.[15] A subtraction-method VAT, however, has the political virtue of looking more like a corporate income tax, and it does not show up as a separate charge to consumers. It is a consumption tax disguised to look like an income tax.

The flat tax and the panel's GIT proposals essentially split the collection of a single-rate subtraction-method VAT between businesses and individuals. Rather than denying businesses any deduction for wages, as is usual under a value-added tax, the flat tax allows businesses to deduct wages in addition to purchases from other businesses. This type of consumption tax is collected at each stage of production, as under a typical value-added tax, except that the tax on wages is directly remitted by individual workers. In combination, the total of the business and individual tax bases should equal total sales, putting aside any exemptions.

The principal advantage of dividing a value-added tax between businesses and individuals is that it enables the exemption of a certain amount of wages from tax and is a way to eliminate, for wage earners, the regressivity of a standard flat-rate tax on consumption. The amount of the exemption will, of course, vary depending on the flat tax rate and the other exclusions, deductions, or tax credits allowed. (As I will illustrate in Chapter 10, there are other methods of addressing this issue under a VAT or retail sales tax.) This division of the consumption tax-base tax also allows the imposition of progressive rates on wages, as the panel's GIT demonstrates, though it is a bit mysterious why only wages and not investment income should be subjected to progressive tax rates.[16]

A Major Problem with the Alternatives: They Do Not Work Well Internationally

We live in a more globally competitive economic environment than we did in the years of the post–World War II economic boom. American businesses and workers are now competing with a vastly increased array of foreign companies and economies. In the 1960s the total value of all our imports made up just 3.2 percent of our GDP. By 2005 that number had risen to 13.6 percent.[17] Amid all the talk of how to make our economy more competitive, one issue that is rarely brought to the public's attention is the possibility that our tax system might itself be a drag on our economy in the realm of international trade and investment.

While my proposal would harmonize our tax system with international standards and thus open up the possibility of real cost savings for companies doing business in more than one nation, the unusual nature of the methods used to collect the flat tax and the GIT create large difficulties under our international tax and trade treaties. The value-added taxes of the standard credit-invoice sort that I am proposing fit well with these agreements. They can be—and usually are—imposed only by the country where the consumption takes place. They therefore tax imports and exempt exports, so that the location where a good is produced is irrelevant. In contrast, income taxes are typically imposed on all domestic production, and the tax on production abroad is generally ceded to the country where the production occurs.

Mostly for compliance reasons, the president's panel decided—rightly in my view—that any U.S. consumption tax should be imposed in the standard manner: in the country where the consumption occurs. Otherwise, imports would not be taxed but exports would. The latter kind of tax is said to be imposed on an "origin" basis. This occurs under the flat tax. Thus, for example, if Ford sells cars manufactured in the United States to be used in the United States, their full retail sales value would be subject to the flat tax. Likewise, if Ford or any other U.S. automobile manufacturer sells automobiles in the United States to a foreign dealer for use abroad, the manufacturer's sales price would be subject to the U.S. flat tax. But a U.S. dealer of cars made in Japan, Germany, or another foreign country would be taxed only on the excess of the dealer's total receipts from its sales over the costs of the cars from the foreign manufacturer. As a result, the costs of manufacturing cars abroad would not be included in the U.S. consumption tax base; only the foreign car dealer's markup would be subject to U.S. taxation.

Economists, including the inventors of the flat tax, claim that we should be indifferent to this distinction because currency exchange rates—the value of the dollar relative to other currencies—will adjust to compensate for these tax differences. But U.S. automobile manufacturers and other U.S. companies that compete with products from abroad will not readily accept the economists' assurances that exchange rates will adjust so perfectly—especially when the country with whom we have the largest trade deficit, China, has yet to allow its currency to float freely against the dollar. U.S. businesses undoubtedly will resist rules that impose a U.S. tax on the full retail price of products manufactured in the United States but tax only the dealer markup of products manufactured abroad. They will view such a tax as fundamentally unfair to American businesses and perhaps as seriously disadvantaging U.S. manufacturers competitively.

In any event, the president's panel determined that imposing a consumption tax on an origin basis would raise major enforcement difficulties.[18] This will be an important, perhaps even decisive, issue.

The president's panel forthrightly acknowledged that its recommended consumption tax, the GIT, along with other consumption taxes such as the flat tax, which allow businesses to deduct wages and which tax individuals on those wages, cannot be imposed where the consumption occurs (taxing imports and exempting exports) without violating our major trade treaty—the GATT—and all eighty-six of our existing bilateral income tax treaties. Tax reform proposals so out of sync with international trade and tax arrangements as to require renegotiation of all our trade and tax treaties are essentially unrealistic.

It is puzzling that U.S. economists and policymakers have struggled to fashion novel consumption tax alternatives, like the flat tax or the Growth and Investment Tax, when there is a well-functioning consumption tax—the value-added tax— being used throughout the OECD and in nearly 150 countries worldwide. Given the interconnectedness of the world economy, tax reform does not seem the right occasion to insist on American exceptionalism. While, as we have seen, there are a variety of methods for imposing and collecting a consumption tax, the best alternative is the credit-invoice VAT of the sort used throughout the world. Experience demonstrates that such a tax works well. Since sellers of goods and services collect taxes and receive credits for VATs paid on their purchases, tax revenues are collected regularly throughout the year from companies at all levels of production, rather than just from retailers, thereby easing enforcement. A credit-method VAT also facilitates exemptions for small businesses (and for specific goods or services if such exemptions become necessary politically). The key point is this: the consumption tax should be collected only from businesses, and the tax should be imposed at a rate and on a broad enough base to raise sufficient revenues to free the vast majority of Americans from any income tax liability and any requirement to file tax returns.

Consumption taxes are used in our states and throughout the industrial world as a key part of tax systems that typically also contain progressive income taxes. Clearly consumption taxes have a role to play as a part of a modern tax system. As we shall see in the chapters that follow, enacting a VAT—in effect, a national sales tax with withholding by busi-

nesses other than retailers—would permit a major restructuring of our tax system into one that is vastly simpler and
far more conducive to savings, investment, and economic
growth. And this can be accomplished in a way that is fair: a
way that neither substantially increases the tax burden of low-
and moderate-income taxpayers nor shifts taxes away from
those at the top of the income scale. There is a limit, however,
to how much we can rely on consumption taxes to finance our
government. Today we rely too little on such taxes, but those
who would rely solely on such taxes to finance the federal government are playing Pollyanna. A national sales tax at a rate of
30 percent or higher, for example, as the FairTax plan requires,
is much higher than elsewhere and is simply not a practical
alternative.

My Competitive Tax Plan makes a different choice:
bring our tax structure closer into line with the rest of the
world by imposing a VAT at a 10 to 14 percent rate and at the
same time eliminate the income tax for at least 150 million
Americans. It is to the issue of how to shrink the income tax
that we turn next.

> *Competitive Tax Plan, Point 1:* Introduce a 10–14
> percent value-added tax on a broad base of goods
> and services, exempting all businesses with reve-
> nues of less than $100,000 a year from collecting
> the tax.

VI

Shrink the Income Tax

It's income tax time again, Americans: Time to gather
up those receipts, get out those tax forms, sharpen up that
pencil, and stab yourself in the aorta.

—*Dave Barry*

In the modernized tax system that would be ushered in under the Competitive Tax Plan, no family earning less than $100,000 would pay any tax on its income. In one fell swoop we would eliminate more than 100 million tax returns, freeing more than 150 million Americans from the income tax. This would allow the Internal Revenue Service to focus on enforcement where it really makes a difference and remove its much-maligned presence from the life of most Americans. Overall, we would save billions of dollars in compliance costs; reduce the possibility of cheating, thereby making the entire system fairer for those who do obey the law; and end the broken politics of taxation by curbing the congressional motivation to legislate special income tax breaks.

This all sounds good, but not infrequently when you mention reducing the size of the income tax so drastically and replacing it with a VAT, many people say: What? Use a system the Europeans use? A system the French use? That's not the American way. In truth, as far as the reach of the income tax goes, the drastic shrinking that I'm proposing is hardly radical. It's a return to its American origins.

Back to the Future

Although an income tax was used to help finance the Civil War, it did not become a permanent part of our nation's financial picture until World War I. The corporate income tax dates from 1909, but it was not until after the Sixteenth Amendment was ratified in 1913 that a tax on individual incomes was enacted. From the end of the Civil War until 1913, the federal government raised its revenue almost exclusively from tariffs on imported goods and excise taxes on this or that. By the beginning of the twentieth century, however, there was great dissatisfaction with this system. Tariffs and excise taxes raised the costs of goods for everyone, while large fortunes accumulating in real estate, corporate stock, and other investments were left untaxed. In 1893, for example, an Atlanta newspaper complained that "most of our tariff taxes . . . fall heavier on the poor."[1] The income tax was adopted—with the extraordinary public support necessary to amend our constitution—to fund a reduction in tariffs and to counterbalance the effect of those taxes on consumption with a tax more closely linked to people's ability to pay. When first enacted, the income tax was expected to contribute only a small portion of ordinary government revenues and to supplement other revenue sources in times of emergency.[2]

So the income tax was not originally supposed to play the central role in financing the federal government that it now does. Until World War II our income tax had exemptions that shielded most Americans from having to pay it. During World War I, these exemptions were lowered and rates increased so that the income tax played a crucial role in financing the war, but after that war ended, the tax was rolled back to a tax of limited scope. From 1918 to 1932 only 5.6 percent of the population filed taxable income tax returns, and from 1933 to 1939 that number dropped so that on average only 3.7 percent of the total population filed taxable returns. Public opinion polls in 1938 and 1939 showed that large majorities of Americans favored an exemption level that would exclude at least 75 percent of the population from income taxes.[3] Thus, through the economic shocks of the Great Depression and the creation and expansion of the New Deal, the reach of the income tax remained quite limited: a low-rate tax on a relatively small group of higher-income Americans. But World War II changed everything.

Legislation in 1940 and 1941 almost quadrupled the number of Americans subject to the income tax, from 7.4 million to 27.6 million. After the United States entered the war, the number of income taxpayers expanded dramatically. By 1943, taking into account both the regular income tax and a so-called Victory Tax of 5 percent on incomes higher than $624, fifty million Americans—nearly 70 percent of the population—were required to file income tax returns.

As we have seen in earlier chapters, this imposition of the income tax on nearly the entire population has led to perverse results in terms of complexity and congressional policymaking. And as our history shows us, it needn't be so.

What we should do now is return the income tax to its original, manageable purpose: to collect income tax only from high-income earners, who tend to have multiple income sources.

Among the many benefits of this change would be to address the growing problem of collecting what taxpayers owe.

The Crisis of Compliance

My father, who was too young to serve in World War I and too old for World War II, like Donald Duck (in Disney's World War II propaganda movie "Taxes to Beat the Axis"), never used aspirin when he filled out his tax return.[4] My mother took the aspirin. I remember well how, to my mother's great dismay, Dad took over the dining room table, sitting there struggling off and on from about mid-February until April 15 every year to fill out his tax return. My father was no Oliver Wendell Holmes, but he viewed taxes the same way Justice Holmes did: as the price we pay for a civilized society. However, this now seems a decidedly minority view.

In today's America, very few people share my dad's attitude toward taxes. Many people feel like "chumps" if they pay the taxes they legally owe. Young people, especially, admit that they feel no compunction when they don't fill out their tax forms honestly. And the Internet has facilitated growth of the "tax deniers" movement—people who preach rejection of the legitimacy of any income tax requirements, including the requirement for employers to withhold taxes on their employees' wages. Like Mickey Mouse battling the brooms in *Fantasia,* the IRS shuts down one Internet site only to have others replace it.

We are moving inexorably toward a crisis of compliance with our income tax. The Treasury and Congress are searching frantically for ways to close the estimated $300 billion annual tax gap. Filing a tax return no longer serves to connect the American people to their government. Instead it is just one more commercial operation. H&R Block, Jackson-Hewitt, and a legion of accountants sit between Americans and their government.

Moreover, the Internal Revenue Service is now incapable of administering and enforcing the income tax law. The fundamental problem is that the IRS is being asked to do too much. That agency may know precious little about alternative energy sources, for example, but when Congress decides to stimulate their use through income tax breaks, the IRS becomes the ultimate arbiter of what qualifies. Likewise, having to administer the earned-income tax credit (EITC)—the nation's wage subsidy for low-income workers—diverts IRS audit resources from corporate and high-income individual returns, leading to headlines that the IRS is targeting the poor. The IRS processes more than 130 million individual and corporate income tax returns and nearly 1.5 billion information documents each year. It is also supposed to issue regulations promptly implementing frequent and massive legislative changes, to ferret out and deter income tax protestors and those who create and market tax shelters, halt tax evasion, and bring the underground economy to the surface. The IRS cannot do all of these things well. Many it cannot do at all.

In addition to the problem of compliance, the current income tax has become convoluted by a series of changes in the twenty years since the last tax reform that in many ways underline how inefficient the tax is as our main instrument for generating federal revenues.

Complexity, Part I: Turning the
Tax Collector into a Benefit Agency

In the Tax Reform Act of 1986, Congress removed about six million low-income people from the income tax rolls and re-affirmed the principle that people at the poverty level should not be subject to income tax. At the bottom of the income scale, the most important changes since then have involved the earned-income tax credit (EITC) and child credits. The EITC was originally adopted in 1975. It provides a tax credit for low-income working parents. In 2006, for example, for a family with two children, the tax credit was worth 40 percent of income up to approximately the first $11,000 earned, so that the maximum credit was about $4,400. The amount of the tax credit remains flat as the family's income rises to approximately $15,000, and then the credit phases out, disappearing entirely when the family's income rises to about $38,000.[5] The tax credit is "refundable," which means that if the credit is more than the income taxes that would have been owed—a common occurrence for a low-income family with children—then the government pays the amount of the credit to the tax-payer. The rate of the credit and the income levels to which it applies and phases out vary according to the parents' marital status and the number of children. Taxpayers with investment income greater than a specified amount are not eligible to receive the credit.

The EITC was transformed in the 1990s from a relatively small adjustment in the progressivity of the tax system, intended mainly to offset Social Security taxes on low-income workers, into a partial replacement for welfare as a wage subsidy for low-income workers. In 1978, the year Congress made the EITC permanent, about $1 billion was refunded to working families, far less than the more than $6 billion in cash grants paid by Aid for Families with Dependent Children (AFDC), the main welfare program at that time. In 2005 nearly $40 billion in earned-income tax credits were claimed by more than twenty-two million taxpayers. Of that amount only roughly $5 billion was used to offset taxes; about $35 billion was paid out directly as refunds. The total amount of EITC was about twice the approximately $20 billion spent that year on AFDC's successor, Temporary Assistance for Needy Families (TANF). Welfare payments under TANF generally cannot be received for more than five years, but the EITC can be claimed annually by low-income workers without any time limit.

A second partially refundable credit, the child tax credit, was enacted in 1997, providing a $400 credit per child (rising to $500 in 1999). The 2001 act increased the credit to $1,000. (Like all of the 2001 tax act, this increase in the child credit is scheduled to terminate after 2010, when the law will revert to its pre-2001 status in the unlikely event that there is no further congressional action.) In 2005 child tax credits totaled more than $30 billion, with more than $10 billion of that amount refunded to taxpayers who otherwise owed no income tax.

The EITC and child tax credits have dramatically changed the income tax. Most low-income workers and many moderate-income families now file income tax returns only to claim refunds. In 2005, for example, a married couple with two children owed no income tax until their income reached $41,000. Then, the poverty threshold for a family of four was about $20,000, half the level at which income tax now applies.[6] To illustrate the same point another way, in 1987, 18.5 percent of the 103 million returns filed were nontaxable; by 2003 nearly one-fourth of the 130.4 million returns filed were nontaxable.[7]

The transformation of the Internal Revenue Service from solely a tax collector to also a check writer has produced difficulties. Now more than two-thirds of returns claiming the earned-income tax credit are prepared by paid preparers. The National Taxpayer Advocate Nina Olson has singled out the EITC as the most troublesome complex provision of the tax code. Her call for major simplification was seconded by the president's tax reform panel. In an effort to combat erroneous EITC claims, the IRS shifted audit resources away from high-income taxpayers to low-income families, provoking much criticism.[8]

By eliminating the income tax for families earning less than $100,000 a year, the Competitive Tax Plan would get the IRS out of the business of running what amounts to a social welfare program enmeshed in a tax code. It need not, however, lower the benefits received or raise the taxes paid by those already at the bottom of the economic ladder. As I will discuss later, there are better ways of maintaining progressivity than continually tinkering with marginal rates and credits as we have done for the past two decades.

Complexity, Part II: "Targeted Tax Cuts" and the Alternative Minimum Tax

Needless complexity doesn't afflict just the lower end of the income scale when it comes to administering our income tax system. So called "targeted tax cuts"—that is, income tax reductions for one expenditure or another generally made available only to taxpayers with a specified maximum income—have reduced tax burdens while greatly increasing complexity. When competing policy ideas aimed at a common goal emerge in Congress, Congress often enacts all of the ideas, leaving unsophisticated taxpayers bewildered about how to cope. The incentives for paying for higher education mentioned earlier—two tax credits, three deductions, three exclusions from income, and five provisions to promote savings for education—offer one vivid illustration. The multiple vehicles for tax-favored savings provide another.

Many people believe that tax incentives are enacted to reward campaign contributors or to satisfy lobbyists, and sometimes they are, but the most important complex provisions that now fill the tax code reflect congressional efforts to cater to the general public. This practice will not stop until most Americans are freed from income taxation.

After the tax rate reductions of the 2001 act, problems due to the alternative minimum tax (AMT) have taken center stage. Since 1969 the tax law has contained provisions intended to ensure that all high-income taxpayers would pay at least some income tax. Since 1982 the minimum tax has taken the form of an alternative tax schedule with a different calculation of taxable income and different rates than the regular tax: taxpayers are required to pay the taxes they owe either under the regular tax code or under the AMT, whichever is higher. But over the past two decades, the regular and alternative tax codes have evolved so that a greater share of taxpayers find themselves needing to pay the alternative minimum tax.

Under current law, a larger share of taxpayers will become subject to the alternative minimum tax in the years ahead. In 2002, 1.4 percent of tax returns were subject to the alternative minimum tax; by 2010, 20 percent of all returns will be subject to the alternative minimum tax, and revenues collected through the alternative minimum tax will exceed those collected through the regular tax.[9] More than thirty million

Americans will have to calculate their income tax two ways, surely a cruel waste of time and money. Members of Congress, the staff of the Joint Committee on Taxation, and President Bush's tax reform panel have all called for repeal of the alternative minimum tax. Repeal, however, is expensive. Only a systematic restructuring of our tax system can cure this problem without inflicting a hit on federal revenues in the range of $1 trillion over the next decade—a hit we cannot afford.

Rate Cuts at the Top

At the top end of the income distribution, the most significant legislative changes have involved revisions to the structure of tax rates and to the taxation of capital gains and dividends. Recent decades have also seen a significant shift in the distribution of income toward the very top, which has affected the share of taxes paid by this group.

When Ronald Reagan took office in 1981, the top marginal income tax rate was 70 percent, with a 50 percent maximum rate on "earned income," which is how the tax law generally refers to wage and salary income. His 1981 legislation dropped the top rate to 50 percent and the 1986 act further reduced it to 28 percent.[10] The first President Bush in 1990 agreed to raise the top rate to 31 percent, breaking his "no new taxes" pledge and alienating his conservative base in the process. In 1993 President Clinton raised the top rate to 39.6 percent in an effort to eliminate federal deficits. The 2001 act reversed field, phasing in a reduction in the top rate to 35 percent and eliminating two provisions enacted in 1990 (a phase-out at higher income levels of personal exemptions and a reduction of itemized deductions) that had surreptitiously increased the top rate a few percentage points above the statutory maxi-

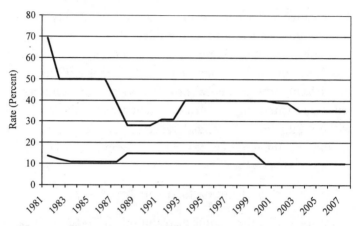

Figure 6.1. Highest and lowest marginal income tax rates by year.
Source: Joseph A. Pechman, *Federal Tax Policy,* 5th ed. (Washington,
D.C.: Brookings, 1987); updated with current IRS publications.

mum. The highest and lowest statutory income tax rates over
time are shown in Figure 6.1.

This reduction in top marginal tax rates has been accompanied by a greater share of income being concentrated at
the top of the income distribution. In the period between 1979
and 2002, the share of income reported by the highest quintile
rose substantially, while the shares of income of the four lowest quintiles declined. Most of the increase for the top quintile
occurred at the very top of the income distribution. For example, the income share of the top 1 percent of the income distribution rose steadily from a low of 9.6 percent in 1979 to a
high of 21.6 percent in 2000 before falling back to 16.9 percent
in 2002. At the same time, the income share of the top 0.1 percent grew from 3.3 percent to 10.5 percent. The amount of income needed to join this group more than quintupled in nominal dollars, from $234,000 in 1979 to $1,278,000 in 2002, and

more than doubled in real dollars from $321,679 to $710,661 (in constant 1982–84 dollars).[11]

As a result of this shift in income, we are now collecting a higher share of income taxes from upper-income people even with the lower tax rates. For example, the top 10 percent income group paid 55 percent of the total individual income tax in 1987 and 45.6 percent in 1988, while earning between 35 and 39 percent of all adjusted gross income (AGI) in those years. In 2002 the top 10 percent (with AGI of at least $92,663) earned 41.8 percent of adjusted gross income and paid 65.7 percent of the total individual income tax.

Capital gains tax rates have also come down. Capital gains, which are gains on assets held over a period of time, have always presented a difficult question for the tax code. One theoretical answer is to tax capital gains as they accrue, even if the asset has not been sold, but this approach has long been a political dead letter. Thus taxpayers have considerable discretion about when to sell assets and when to pay taxes. Advocates of lowering the capital gains rate claim that it will stimulate new investments, advance technology, trigger economic growth, and enhance democracy and freedom. With similar hyperbole, opponents of lower capital gains rates claim that taxing capital gains the same as ordinary income would eliminate tax shelters, dramatically simplify the law, and promote tax justice. Both sides' claims are overstated. Given the great discretion about when to realize capital gains, opportunities for taxpayers to postpone and avoid capital-gains taxes make high rates of capital gains tax unproductive; people will just hold on to their assets and borrow against them if they need cash. On the other hand, it is not at all clear that any revenue lost by taxing capital gains at 15 percent, as we now do, rather than say, 20 or 25 percent, is compensated for by increased savings, investment, or economic growth. While I generally will assume here that the 15 percent rate on capital gains would be retained, a reformed income tax might reasonably tax capital gains at any rate from 15 to 25 percent.

In 2003 the tax rate on dividends was also reduced to 15 percent to reduce the "double" tax on income earned by corporations. (The next chapter discusses this issue.) All of the rate reductions enacted since 2001 are currently scheduled to expire in 2010.

The Big Picture: Where the Changes Have Left Us

Tax changes and changes in the distribution of income since 1986 have dramatically altered the structure of the income tax and its distribution of burdens. Figure 6.2 shows the share of income tax liability by quintile from 1986 to 2002. Figure 6.3 shows the distribution of the federal income tax burden in 2006. In the bottom 40 percent of the income distribution, the overall income tax is negative, because of the refundable earned-income tax credit and child credits. For low- and moderate-income taxpayers—indeed, for the bottom 80 percent—the payroll taxes that support Social Security and Medicare, but are not shown in the tables, are more burdensome than the income tax.

The income tax remains quite progressive. However, it is difficult to determine in an airtight way whether the progressivity of the tax code has risen or fallen over time. To be sure, the share of taxes paid by the highest-income group has risen. But the share of income received by that group has also risen substantially, which would raise its share of taxes even with no change in the tax code at all. Taxes paid by high-income tax-

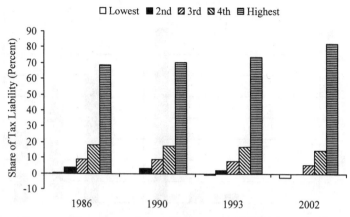

Figure 6.2. Percentage share of income tax liability by quintile.
Source: Computed using Internal Revenue Service statistics,
available at http://www.irs.gov/taxstats/indtaxstats/
article/0,,id=98123,00.html.

payers also often vary considerably because there are better
and worse times to realize capital gains, depending on changes
in asset values and the timing of changes in the tax code. In addition, the tax cuts since 2001 have helped to generate large
budget deficits that will ultimately have to be paid by taxes on
someone. A full model for determining the progressivity of the
tax code would need to take into account the distributional effects of how those budget deficits (and the interest on federal
borrowing) will be repaid over time. Nevertheless, the income
tax remains quite progressive, with about two-thirds of its revenue coming from the highest 10 percent of earners.

   The big difference between the Competitive Tax Plan and
most of the alternatives currently being discussed is that my
proposal would eliminate nearly all the complexity I have been
discussing, *while at the same time* maintaining the progressiv-

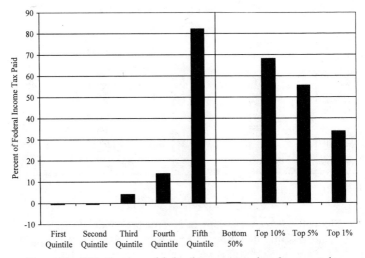

Figure 6.3. Distribution of federal income tax burden, 2006, by income percentile. *Source: Simple, Fair, and Pro-Growth: Proposals to Fix America's Tax System, Report of the President's Advisory Panel on Tax Reform* (Washington, D.C.: Government Printing Office, 2005), Figure A.1, available at http://www.taxreformpanel.gov/final-report.

ity that the current income tax system supplies and the public generally endorses.

Radical Surgery

In earlier chapters I have described how most of the prominent Republican tax reform proposals would completely replace the income tax with some form of tax on consumption. Those who reject that approach have focused instead on reforming the income tax. There are two recent proposals for income tax reform, each echoing the 1986 reform, that merit our attention. The first is the "simplified income tax" (SIT) proposal offered by President Bush's tax reform panel; the second is the "Fair Flat" tax proposal introduced in Congress in 2005 by Senate Finance Committee member Ron Wyden (D-OR) and House Ways and Means Committee member Rahm Emmanuel (D-IL). Both would eliminate the AMT and cut down on deductions and other tax breaks to pay for it.

Interestingly, Wyden and Emmanuel decided that the flat tax label had enough cachet to be worth imitating. But their proposal is hardly flat; it has three tax rates—15, 25, and 35 percent—not one, and it is an income, not a consumption, tax. Like the Armey-Forbes "flat tax," it does eliminate many deductions, exclusions, and credits and promises a shorter tax form. However, neither Wyden nor Emmanuel has yet given up his electoral ambitions, so they would retain many of the most popular provisions, including deductions for home mortgage interest and charitable gifts, the EITC and child credits, savings incentives for health care, retirement, and education, and various benefits for the elderly, disabled, soldiers, and veterans. They also would add a new refundable credit for 10 percent of state and local taxes. And they would tax dividends and capital gains at the regular tax rates.

As we have seen, President Bush's panel would convert some of the most popular deductions, including those for personal exemptions and home mortgage interest, into tax credits and would lower the top rate to 33 percent. The panel also would maintain, but revise, the tax benefits for charitable giving, dividends, and capital gains. For those interested in more detail, Table 6.1 contains a side-by-side comparison of the main features of the two plans. As Senator Wyden has put it, both would give the tax code "a good cleansing." He adds that this is what the "tax code desperately needs."

Table 6.1
A Side-by-Side Comparison of the Main Features
of the Two Income Tax Reform Plans

Provisions	Tax Reform Panel Income Tax	Wyden-Emanuel Fair "Flat Tax"
	Households and Families	
Tax rates	Four brackets: 15%, 25%, 30%, 33%	Three brackets: 15%, 25%, 35%
AMT	Repealed	Repealed
Personal exemption	Replaced with family credit available to all taxpayers: $3,300 for married couple, $2,800 for unmarried with child, $1,650 for singles, $1,150 for dependent taxpayer; additional $1,500 credit for each child and $500 for each other dependent	Unchanged
Standard deduction	*See* Personal exemption	$30,000 for joint filers, $15,000 for singles, $26,500 for head of household
Child tax credit	*See* Personal exemption	Unchanged
Marriage penalty	Reduced. All tax brackets, family credits, and taxation of Social Security for couples are double those of individuals	Persists
	Other Major Credits and Deductions	
Home mortgage interest	15% home credit, limited to average regional price of housing	Unchanged, except that interest paid on second home not deductible
Charitable giving	Deduction available to all taxpayers	Unchanged
Health insurance	Taxpayers may purchase health insurance with pretax dollars, up to the amount of average premium	Unchanged; requests report from Treasury on how to eliminate $10 billion in tax subsidies that create inefficiency in health insurance markets

Provisions	Tax Reform Panel Income Tax	Wyden-Emanuel Fair "Flat Tax"
	Other Major Credits and Deductions—*Continued*	
Education	Taxpayers can claim family credit for some full-time students	Unchanged
State and local taxes	Not deductible	New, refundable credit for 10% of state and local taxes available to all tax-payers
Itemized deductions	None	Eliminates deductions for wagering losses, elementary teachers' expenses, and moving expense. 2%-of-AGI floor eliminated
Exclusions from income	Eliminates exclusions for employer-provided group-term life insurance and most fringe benefits except meals furnished for the conven-ience of the employer	Eliminates exclusions for employer-provided group-term life insurance, work-er's compensation, rental value of personage, in-come earned abroad, most fringe benefits, and meals furnished for the conven-ience of the employer
	Individual Savings and Retirement	
Defined con-tribution plans	Consolidated into save-at-work plans that have simple rules	Unchanged
Defined ben-efit plans	Unchanged	Unchanged
Retirement savings plans	Replaced with save-for-retirement accounts ($10,000 annual limit)	Unchanged
Education savings plans	Replaced with save-for-family accounts ($10,000 annual limit) covering education, medical, new home costs, and retirement saving needs	Unchanged

(Continued)

Table 6.1—*Continued*

Provisions	Tax Reform Panel Income Tax	Wyden-Emanuel Fair "Flat Tax"
Individual Savings and Retirement—Continued		
Health savings plans	*See* Education savings plan	Cafeteria plans and FSAs eliminated
Dividends received	Exclude 100% of dividends of U.S. companies paid out of domestic earnings	Taxed at regular income tax rates
Capital gains received	Exclude 75% of corporate capital gains from U.S. companies	Taxed at regular income tax rates
Interest received	Taxed at regular income tax rates	Taxed at regular income tax rates
Social Security benefits	Married taxpayers with less than $44,000 in income pay no tax on Social Security benefits	Unchanged
Small Business		
Rates	Taxed at individual rates	Taxed at individual rates
Record-keeping	Simplified cash-basis accounting	Unchanged
Investment	Immediate expensing (except for land and buildings)	Straight-line depreciation over longer periods
Large Business		
Rates	31.50%	35% (on all corporate income)
Investment	Simplified accelerated depreciation	Straight-line depreciation over longer periods
International tax system	Territorial tax system	Deferral eliminated

While either of these proposals could improve current law, they do not, in my view, go far enough. As we all know, it doesn't take very long after a "good cleansing" for things to get very dirty again. Even those who applauded the 1986 act as a wildly successful tax reform must concede now that this legislation was not a stable solution. Over time, many of its reforms have been reversed. Its broad income tax base and low rates have been transformed into a narrower base with higher rates. How can anyone remain optimistic about fixing the income tax without radical surgery? What the nation needs is a new and better tax system, one that is far simpler, less intrusive for the American people, fair, and more conducive to savings, investment, and economic growth.

By enacting the Competitive Tax Plan, starting with a value-added tax, as described in the previous chapter, we could return the income tax to its pre–World War II status: a low-rate tax on a relatively thin slice of higher-income Americans. A VAT imposed at a rate of 10 to 14 percent could finance an exemption from income tax for families with $100,000 of income or less ($50,000 for singles) and would allow a vastly simpler income tax at a 20 to 25 percent rate to be applied to incomes over $100,000. In combination, these two taxes would produce revenues roughly equivalent to the current income tax. (For details on the revenue effects, see Appendix 1.)[12] And this proposal, unlike the flat tax, the FairTax, and other such proposals, would not dramatically shift the tax burden away from high-income families to middle- and lower-income families. Also, rather than relying on tax structures like the flat tax and progressive consumption taxes, which were invented in ivory towers and are untested in today's economy, this plan combines two of the world's most common tax mechanisms, while exploiting our nation's substantial economic advantages as a low-tax country.

As I have said, a $100,000 exemption would eliminate more than 100 million of the 140 million income tax returns that are now filed and would free about 150 million Americans from filing income tax returns (see Figure 6.4). These people would have no dealings at all with the IRS. For them, April 15 would be just another day.

The income tax law that would remain would be shrunken and simplified substantially, and would have a low rate of tax. The marriage penalties of the existing income tax would be eliminated. An exemption of $100,000 would automatically replace the standard deduction, personal exemptions, and nonrefundable child credits and would eliminate many of the special income tax credits and allowances that now crowd the tax code and complicate tax forms, since they are now targeted at people with incomes lower than that threshold. It also would permit reconsideration of the need for other deductions and credits.

One important question, for example, is what to do about state and local taxes. Currently, these taxes are deductible under the regular tax computation but not under the AMT. The president's panel recommended eliminating the AMT but also would eliminate the deduction for state and local taxes on the ground that payments for state and local government services "should be borne by those who want them, not by every taxpayer in the country." The Wyden-Emmanuel plan would substitute a limited tax credit for the deduction. Others would limit the amounts that could be deducted. While I tend to side with the president's panel on this particular issue (which is why for ease of exposition and revenue estimation I describe my plan as repealing the regular income tax rather than the AMT), any of these alternatives might emerge from the political process. Obviously, represen-

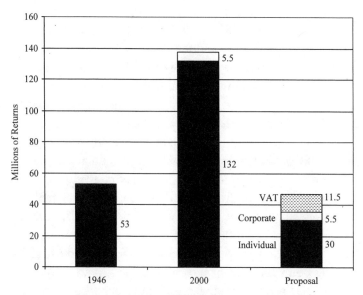

Figure 6.4. Number of income tax returns under current law and the proposed Competitive Tax Plan. *Note:* GAO has estimated that an exemption for small businesses with gross receipts of $100,000 or less would reduce the required number of VAT returns from 25 million to 9 million. We assume here that such a small-business exemption would be included in a VAT and show 11.5 million VAT returns filed, since some small businesses will opt into the VAT to obtain refunds and to account for growth since the GAO report was published. VAT Administrative Costs, GAO/GGD-93-78 (1993), 62. *Sources:* 1946: Statistical Abstract of the United States (1956); 2004: Internal Revenue Service Statistics of Income Bulletin (2004); Proposal: Treasury estimates (individual), author estimate (corporate), and updated GAO estimate (VAT).

tatives and senators from high-tax states will be most concerned with this question.

Likewise, an exemption of $100,000 could trigger a reconsideration of the deductions for charitable contributions and home mortgage interest. The former, for example, might be limited to contributions above some floor—the panel suggested 1 percent of income. And the latter might be limited to mortgages on one house and for less than $1 million. Until we get national health insurance, the deduction for large medical expenses should certainly be retained. In addition, employers should continue to have payroll and income tax incentives to provide their employees retirement savings plans and health insurance—at least until an adequate individual or family-based replacement is enacted.[13] Although reducing or eliminating deductions would permit lower tax rates, cutting back or eliminating any of the current deductions will inevitably be controversial politically. And the critical element in my plan is its major shrinking of the role and scope of the income tax. In adopting my Competitive Tax Plan, Congress could use as its starting point the current income tax, the AMT, the Wyden-Emmanuel income tax, the presidential panel's income tax proposal, or any other simplified income tax.[14]

The key point is this: families with incomes of $100,000 or less would owe no income tax. And because those higher-income families subject to the income tax would also be paying VAT on their purchases of goods and services, the income tax rate should be reduced. For families with incomes above $100,000, tax would be computed by applying the new rate (or rates) to income after subtracting the $100,000 exemption (which would be indexed for inflation) and other allowable deductions. For example, a family with $150,000 of income and $14,000 of allowable deductions (say, from charitable contributions and home mortgage interest) would have $36,000 of taxable income and owe $9,000 of income tax, if the rate were 25 percent, or $7,200 if the rate were 20 percent.

This plan is fair and balanced. It is fiscally sound, designed to maintain current federal government revenues and to provide room for future increases in revenues should they become necessary. Unlike proposals to replace the income tax completely with either a flat tax or a national sales tax and some other proposals, this plan does not entail a substantial tax cut for high-income individuals offset by a tax increase for those below the top tier. This tax system would make the United States similar to the average of OECD countries in taxing consumption relative to GDP and in terms of tax rates on consumption. Our income tax, however, would be much smaller—and could be much simpler—than what people generally face abroad. And our tax system would be far more favorable for savings and economic growth.

Such a fundamental reform as replacing the income tax on most Americans with a tax on consumption cannot responsibly be done, however, without a comprehensive plan for how such a change would affect other elements of our current law. Thus I must now address further elements of the overall picture: changes in the taxation of businesses and alternative ways to protect low- and moderate-income families from a tax increase due to the enactment of a value-added tax.

> *Competitive Tax Plan, Point 2:* Eliminate the income tax for all American families earning less than $100,000 a year ($50,000 for singles, with both indexed for inflation), thereby relieving 150 million people from having any dealings at all with the IRS. Maintain a low-rate income tax for all earners above $100,000. Retain some incentives for home ownership, charitable contributions, large medical expenses, and employer-sponsored health and retirement plans. Eliminate most other deductions and credits.

VII

Reduce the Corporate Income Tax Rate

Don't tax you; don't tax me;
Tax the corporations across the sea
—Dan Rostenkowski, former chairman, House Ways and
Means Committee

I f the Competitive Tax Plan is going to live up to its name, it has to make good on the promise of creating better conditions for American workers and businesses, domestically and internationally. The United States needs to be an attractive place for both domestic and foreign investments, and U.S. companies need to be positioned to take full advantage of the new global marketplace.

In order for this to happen, as part of the overall reform of our tax system, we need to lower corporate tax rates considerably. My plan calls for reducing the corporate income tax rate to at most 20 percent and perhaps as low as 15 percent, which would match the current capital gains and dividend rates. This would dramatically improve the competitive position of the American economy and reduce tax-sheltering behavior, and, if done right, it need not worsen our fiscal position.

The Shape of the Problem

The tax that the federal government imposes on large businesses, or the corporate income tax, as it is known, is an odd phenomenon, even by the mysterious lights of the tax law. Corporate taxes are popular with the public. People think that taxes remitted by corporations, especially large multinational companies, are paid by someone other than themselves. Indeed, the ditty that appears as the epigraph to this chapter was advanced by Congressman Rostenkowsi as a fitting second verse to the tax reform classic coined by Senate Finance Committee Chairman Russell Long (D-LA): "Don't tax you; don't tax me; / Tax the fellow behind the tree." But as Paul H. O'Neill, George W. Bush's first Treasury secretary, observed, "Corporations don't pay taxes, they collect them."

The question of who actually bears the economic burden of corporate income taxes—who ultimately pays them—has tormented public-finance economists since the tax first came into existence. Three candidates come instantly to the fore: people who own the companies, people who work for the companies, or people who buy the companies' products. Since the tax may affect wages, prices, and/or returns to capital, economists believe that workers, consumers, or owners of capital generally may bear the economic costs of the tax. For many years, the conventional wisdom among economists was that the tax principally reduced returns to capital, at least in the short run, and thus the tax was considered to be progressive, even if economically distortional. Ultimately, however, the reduced capital due to the tax might result in lower wages, so in the long run, workers might pay. As the economy has become more open internationally, recent economic studies have concluded that the tax is less likely borne by capital generally, but rather—at least in some substantial part—by workers or consumers in the form of lower wages or higher prices.[1] Owners of capital today have the ability to move their money anywhere in the world, but workers and consumers are considerably less mobile. All the uncertainty in the economics profession contributes to the public view that the tax is probably paid by someone else.

Economists are unanimous, however, that the corporate income tax is a bad one. It creates incentives for investing in noncorporate businesses and housing instead of corporations, and it induces many distortions in corporate finance. For example, since interest payments but not dividends are deductible and thereby not subject to the corporate tax, the tax creates a bias in favor of debt over equity finance. The combination of individual and corporate income taxes also has created an advantage for corporations to repurchase shares rather than paying dividends. The invention and deployment of innovative financial products has added new distortions as companies structure their financial transactions to achieve income tax advantages. And the internationalization of businesses, along with the greater mobility of capital, has made collecting corporate income taxes much more difficult. For example, companies now routinely adjust their corporate structures, finances, and intercompany prices to take advantage of lower corporate tax rates in other countries. These are just some of the reasons that economists hate a tax the public seems to love.

There are four fundamental issues that bedevil the corporate income tax today: (1) the relationship of corporate and individual income taxes; (2) the relationship of the corporate income tax to the taxation of noncorporate businesses; (3) the problem of corporate tax shelters; and, most important, (4) the future of the corporate tax in light of the internationalization of economic activity and the competition among countries for business capital. I will consider each of these issues in turn.

The Relationship of Corporate and Individual Income Taxes

The U.S. corporate income tax was originally enacted as a result of both fiscal and constitutional necessities. In 1909, four years before the Sixteenth Amendment created a constitutional basis for an income tax on individuals, Congress imposed a tax on corporate income. The government needed money, and the Supreme Court had in 1895 ruled an income tax on individuals to be an unconstitutional "direct" tax.[2] Employing some legal gymnastics, the Court subsequently upheld the corporate income tax as an "indirect" excise tax on the privilege of doing business in corporate form. Nevertheless, the primary justification for a separate tax on corporate incomes is as a complement to the individual income tax—it is impractical to tax income earned and retained by large corporations directly to their owners.

While many tax policy aficionados have advanced other arguments for taxing corporate income, they are generally unpersuasive. To my mind, the best argument for taxing corporate income is that, without such a tax, individuals could create and use companies to shelter their individual incomes from tax. With no corporate income tax at all, it would be child's play, for example, simply to move income-producing assets into a corporation and postpone tax until the income is needed by the owner and is paid out to him by the corporation. So the corporate income tax essentially serves as a backup tax to protect against erosion of the individual tax and to reach income not taxed directly to individuals. If we had no individual income tax, I would see no reason to tax corporate income.

Certain policy prescriptions flow naturally from this view. It makes no sense, for example, to impose a double tax on corporate income, taxing it once when earned by the corporation and again when paid out as dividends to shareholders. The corporate income tax, however, has long been a double tax in the United States, taxing corporate income first when earned and again when realized by equity holders in the form of dividends or capital gains.

Eliminating this double tax—or "integrating" corporate and individual income taxes, as it is known in tax policy circles—so that corporate income would be taxed only once at either the corporate or shareholder level, has recently attracted significant attention.[3] One option is to treat the corporate tax essentially as a withholding tax on shareholders' income and allow shareholders to credit any corporate taxes paid on dividends they receive. With this approach, corporate income would be taxed only once at the shareholder tax rates. The other major policy option for integrating corporate and shareholder taxes is to exclude from shareholders' income some or all corporate dividends—that is, profits paid out as dividends would be taxed at the corporate level but excluded from taxation at the shareholder level.[4] Until quite recently, many European countries limited double taxation of corporate income by providing full or partial shareholder credits for corporate taxes paid with respect to income distributed as a dividend. But after a series of decisions by the European Court of Justice holding that certain shareholder credit systems violated the free movement of capital guaranteed by the European Treaties, many European nations have replaced their shareholder credit systems with partial shareholder exclusions of dividends.[5]

In 2003 President Bush urged Congress to exclude from shareholders' taxable income dividends paid out of corporate income that already had been subject to U.S. corporate-level tax. Congress instead lowered the tax rate on dividends to 15 percent without requiring that the income had been previously taxed at the corporate level. The best evidence is that this change stimulated corporations to pay more dividends. At the same time, Congress reduced the capital gains rate to 15 percent, also in the name of reducing the double taxation of corporate income, but, again, without regard to whether the gains are attributable to earnings previously taxed at the corporate level. The current state of affairs does not seem stable. Many Democrats have since urged a return to higher rates on both dividends and capital gains, arguing that they should be taxed no more favorably than wages—in effect, ignoring the fact that they may also be taxed at the corporate level. Others, including the president's tax reform panel, have urged complete elimination of double taxes, at least for dividends paid by U.S. companies.

Noncorporate Business Entities and Tax Variations Across Industries

The president's panel was also concerned with the economic distortions resulting from differences in taxation among dif-

ferent types of business entities and differences in the effective
tax rates of different industries due to special tax benefits. It
therefore advanced proposals to make the corporate tax more
neutral among different business investments and to reduce
the distinctions in taxation between corporate and noncorporate businesses. Given the flexibility in choosing whether
and where to incorporate a business and the growing role of
private equity in the world economy, creating greater parity
between corporate and noncorporate businesses is a valuable
endeavor.

In the Competitive Tax Plan I am advocating here, one
important step would be to tax the income of small corporations on a flow-through basis, thereby eliminating the separate
corporate tax for small businesses and taxing their income directly to their owners. This would allow small-business income to qualify for the $100,000 income tax exemption. The
taxation of small businesses should also be simplified substantially. The corporate income tax would then apply only to
large, mostly publicly traded companies.[6]

Corporate Tax Shelters

In recent years, the corporate income tax has been haunted by
the proliferation of corporate tax shelters. They have reduced
federal revenues by many billions of dollars and undermined
the public's sense of tax fairness. The 1986 Tax Reform Act
halted the marketing of individual tax shelters by prohibiting
individuals from using "tax shelter losses"—investments in
which they had no active managerial involvement but that
were structured to create substantial losses on paper—to offset their income from earnings or investments. Although the
government has in recent years enjoyed considerable success

both in uncovering and challenging corporate tax shelters, no similarly effective solution has emerged to eliminate them.

The corporate tax shelter phenomenon dates from at least the early 1980s, when Congress rewarded corporate tax planning by enacting "safe-harbor leasing," a scheme that allowed corporations to sell tax savings that they couldn't use because the firm's tax bill had already been reduced to zero (by business losses, depreciation of plant or equipment, or foreign tax credits, for example). The straightforward way to allow companies to capture the value of tax breaks they could not use would have been to refund taxes, but this would have smacked of politically unpalatable "corporate welfare." Congress preferred instead to permit companies to sell tax benefits among themselves. This "lease-a-deduction" scheme became an object of popular satire; for example, Dianne Bennett, a tax lawyer from Buffalo, New York, suggested that low- and moderate-income families should be able to "lease" a welfare family to obtain their children's tax allowances. The political cartoonists had a field day. Only failure of imagination limits the possibilities for "leasing" tax breaks.

By 1986, when Congress eliminated safe-harbor leasing, corporate attitudes toward the income tax had changed. Many managers had come to regard their tax departments as potential profit centers. Corporations could increase shareholders' returns by producing better products, selling more goods or services, cutting costs, or reducing taxes. Tax savings were often the easiest.

A decade later, the character of corporate tax shelters had also changed. Corporate tax shelters now often have no nontax economic substance at all. One common technique is to create a financial transaction with offsetting gains and losses and have the losses allocated to a U.S. corporation while the gains are allocated to a taxpayer not subject to U.S. income taxation. Often, these "tax indifferent" parties are foreign financial institutions; sometimes they are tax-exempt charities or Native American tribes.

Most efforts to address the corporate tax shelter problem have employed greater disclosures of tax shelter transactions and greater penalties on those who enter into them. It is easy to define a tax shelter in general terms: a tax shelter is a deal done by very smart people that, absent tax considerations, would be very stupid. But translating this definition into legislative language to attack tax shelters or to justify enhanced penalties is difficult. To be effective, any attack on corporate tax shelters must change the incentives for corporate management to enter into such transactions. Many companies are willing to take the chance either that tax shelter transactions will not be discovered by the IRS or that, if the transactions are discovered, a court will uphold the company's view of the facts and the law. There is no natural counterforce to offset the potential benefits for a company playing what is, in effect, a tax audit lottery.

In fact, companies keep two different sets of books, one for tax purposes and one for reporting to shareholders. Corporate tax shelter deductions, credits, and losses reduce tax liability without reducing the income reported on the company's financial statements to shareholders. Thus tax shelters give a company the best of both worlds: lower taxes are paid to the government while higher profits are reported to shareholders. In the 1986 act, Congress linked the different corporate income statements, one for shareholders and one for taxes, in a corporate alternative minimum tax, but this linkage expired after three years. The IRS recently expanded its required disclosures of book-tax disparities, but a stable solution to the corporate tax shelter problem will probably require greater conformity between book and tax accounting for pub-licly traded companies.[7] Where Congress wants to maintain book-tax differences—such as for depreciation, research and development expenses, and foreign taxes, for example—these differences should be made explicit. Given companies' desire to report high earnings to shareholders, a stronger link be-tween book and tax accounting would discourage tax shelters for publicly held companies, which pay the lion's share of cor-porate taxes. This linkage would generally increase the amount of corporate income subject to tax, helping to finance the re-duction in the corporate tax rate I am urging here. The lower corporate tax rate, which is an important part of the Compet-itive Tax Plan, will also itself decrease the incentive for shelter-ing corporate income.

The Future of the Corporate Income Tax

The most dramatic and important changes in corporate taxa-tion since the last tax reform are due to the international-ization of the world economy. Cross-border activity of large corporations has greatly expanded. Corporations and other investors now move money quickly and easily around the world, making it much more difficult for any nation to tax their income. U.S.-headquartered companies no longer domi-nate the world economy as they once did. But they play an im-portant role in the U.S. economy. In 2004, for example, they accounted for nearly one-quarter of U.S. GDP, nearly half of U.S. exports, almost two-thirds of U.S. research and develop-ment, and 19 percent of domestic employment. In 1960, eigh-teen of the world's twenty largest corporations were head-quartered in the United States; by 1985 that number was twelve, and in 2005 it was nine. In addition, U.S. companies are

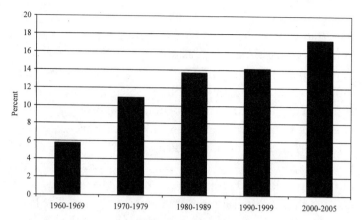

Figure 7.1. Share of U.S. corporate profits from foreign sources.
Source: PricewaterhouseCoopers, "United States in the World
Economy: 1960–2005."

now getting a larger share of their profits from foreign sources
(see Figure 7.1).

Flows of direct and portfolio investments into and out
of the United States have increased dramatically since the 1986
tax reform. In 1986 foreign-owned assets in the U.S. economy
totaled $1.5 trillion (measured at market value), while U.S.-
owned assets abroad were $1.6 trillion. By 2004 foreign-
owned assets in the U.S. economy climbed to $12.5 trillion,
while U.S.-owned assets abroad had reached $10.0 trillion
(see Figure 7.2).[8]

U.S. affiliates of foreign-headquartered multinationals
today perform many activities important for our economic
growth and a rising standard of living for Americans. In 2004
they contributed 5.7 percent to U.S. GDP and accounted for
18.8 percent of U.S. exports, 13.6 percent of U.S. research and
development, and 4.5 percent of domestic employment.

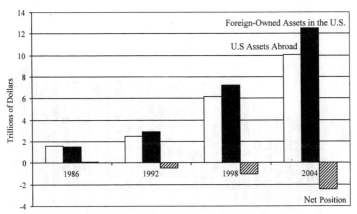

Figure 7.2. U.S. international investment position.
Source: U.S. Bureau of Economic Analysis.

Foreign financial and global trading centers offering favorable tax treatment are now commonplace. Often they are located on pleasant islands that impose no corporate income tax. These developments, along with new financial instruments and technologies, pose striking challenges for corporate income taxation. The United States, like other countries, has long wanted to avoid double taxing of corporate income earned abroad, but the United States also doesn't want American firms to shift income to related foreign companies to reduce taxes on their income earned domestically.

One vehicle by which companies have moved income abroad has been overpayment by U.S. subsidiaries of foreign companies to their foreign parents for intangible assets, such as patents or trademarks. Similarly, U.S. parent companies have shifted income to low-taxed foreign subsidiaries. During the 1990s the U.S. Treasury substantially revised its transfer-pricing regulations, and the IRS began entering into agreements with

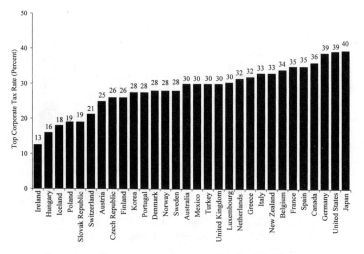

Figure 7.3. Top corporate tax rates in the OECD, 2005.
Source: OECD Tax Database, available at http://www.oecd.org/
document/60/0,2340,en_2649_34533_1942460_1_1_1_1,00.html.

companies and with other nations in an effort to curtail such practices. While these developments have helped, they have not solved the problem. Both U.S. and foreign companies are also able to strip earnings out of the United States by paying deductible interest to foreign affiliates in low-tax countries.

Many OECD nations have responded to the increasing internationalization of business by reducing their corporate tax rates, broadening their corporate tax bases, and reducing or eliminating various deductions for specified investments.[9] After the 1986 Tax Reform Act, the U.S. corporate tax rate was one of the lowest in the OECD. Now, as shown in Figure 7.3, it is one of the highest.

The internationalization of business has effectively capped the role of corporate income taxes as a source of federal revenue. Little U.S. tax revenue is now being collected from foreign-source business income.[10] In 1986 Congress attempted to limit tax benefits for income earned abroad. That legislation classified foreign income into nine separate categories for determining foreign tax credits in order to restrict the ability of companies to offset U.S. taxes with foreign taxes on unrelated income. The 1986 act also limited interest deductions for companies that invest abroad. The thrust of the 1986 legislation—tightening income tax rules for foreign investments by U.S. companies—has been reversed. Nations today want low corporate income taxes, both to attract domestic investments and to reduce the temptation of domestic companies to shift income abroad through intercompany pricing or other techniques. The 2004 act substantially liberalized a number of the limitations enacted in 1986 and also established a special, lower corporate tax rate for income from domestic manufacturing activities. This lower rate created an administrative nightmare—due to questions such as whether Starbucks is "manufacturing" coffee—though it did reduce the potential tax savings from taking manufacturing abroad.

Increasing taxes on corporations may be as popular with the public now as in 1986, but is far less feasible economically. Absent a fundamental reexamination of U.S. international income tax policies, the combination of sophisticated corporate tax planning and tax competition among nations may cause the taxation of international corporate income to unravel completely. Although President Clinton in 1993 got a 1 percentage point increase in the corporate tax rate (from 34 percent to 35 percent) through Congress and some politicians still look to the corporate income tax as a potential source of additional revenue, it now seems far more likely that, as I advocate here, U.S. corporate rates will decrease in the years ahead.

The 1986 Tax Reform Act managed to achieve a 28 percent top marginal rate for individuals and meet its goal of revenue neutrality by increasing the tax burden on corporations by $120 billion in the years 1987 through 1991.[11] This increase in corporate tax revenues was used to finance an overall reduction in individual tax revenues, although the corporate tax changes mainly reduced deductions so that the corporate tax rate was also reduced (from 46 to 34 percent). The increase in corporate tax revenues came largely from the repeal of tax benefits for new investments in real estate and equipment. In combination, these changes reduced the tax burden on service companies while increasing it for capital-intensive industries, including manufacturing firms and real estate—a change which made the income tax burden considerably more neutral across industries. This outcome became politically possible because corporate interests split between capital-intensive companies, which wanted favorable depreciation allowances that would allow them to write off their large capital expenses quickly, and service companies more interested in lower corporate tax rates.

The 1986 act reversed the trend, spurred by the 1981 tax cuts, of declining corporate taxes as a share both of federal revenues and of GDP. However, corporate income taxes, which are now just over 2 percent of GDP, are unlikely ever again to reach the levels of 4 to 5 percent of GDP that prevailed in the 1950s and into the 1960s.

It is no longer possible—given the integration of the world economy—to regard domestic tax reform and international tax reform as if they are different subjects. When Congress last enacted fundamental tax reform—in 1986—the stock of cross-border investment was less than 10 percent of the world's output. Today it equals about one-quarter of the world's output. The U.S. corporate tax affects both U.S.-based and foreign-based companies that do business in the United States, as well as U.S.-based businesses that do business abroad. It therefore affects the competitiveness of U.S. companies and the attractiveness of the United States as a place for investment of both domestic and foreign capital.

In my view, the most important corporate tax change Congress could enact—both to stimulate our domestic economy and to increase the competitiveness of U.S. companies throughout the world—would be to lower our corporate tax rate substantially. Although a 25 percent rate would put us in line with most OECD nations, it is worth trying to get that rate down to 15 percent—the rate now applicable to dividends and capital gains—or to no more than 20 percent.[12] A low corporate income tax rate would be good for the U.S. economy: it would make the United States a much more favorable location for business investments by both domestic and foreign corporations. There are many features of the U.S. economy critical to the competitiveness of U.S. businesses and workers—flexible labor markets and a highly skilled workforce, to name but two. Making the United States a more attractive place for businesses to invest is an important piece of this puzzle. Once large business investments in plant and equipment are made, they are often difficult to move. The evidence is clear that corporations will respond to tax incentives for locating investments and for shifting profits.

A lower corporate tax rate would also allow much simplification of our rules for taxing international business income. For example, a 15 percent rate would diminish the payoff from corporate tax shelters—which frequently have international aspects—and from intercompany transfer pricing that shifts U.S. income abroad while consuming great resources of the IRS and taxpayers alike.

But given the current financial condition of the federal government—with deficits and looming demands for spending on retirement income, health care, and long-term care for an aging population—it is not possible to achieve this kind of corporate rate reduction without a major restructuring of our domestic tax system. Corporate tax receipts were $279 billion in FY 2005 and $303 billion in FY 2006, about 2.3 percent of our GDP. While some corporate base broadening is surely feasible by eliminating or reducing tax loopholes and incentives for certain investments or industries and by forging a closer link between financial and tax measures of income, base broadening alone will not produce enough revenue to pay for the kind of rate reduction I am urging here. Lowering the corporate tax rate significantly—a priority for international competitiveness of the U.S. economy and for international tax reform—cannot happen without domestic tax reform.

As I have said, one goal of tax reform should be to enhance U.S. savings and investment by reducing our nation's reliance on income taxes and increasing our reliance on consumption taxation. Enacting a value-added tax on goods and services at a 10 to 14 percent rate, as I have suggested, would not only allow us to eliminate 150 million Americans from the income tax, but it would also permit the kind of corporate rate reduction I am advocating here.

It is crucial now that any major domestic tax reform fit well with international tax practices. For example, while I found much to admire in the 2005 Report of the President's Panel on Tax Reform, a critical weakness of its proposal for a consumption tax alternative to the income tax—its so-called

Growth and Investment Tax—is that it does not mesh well with long-standing international practices. Indeed, adopting that proposal would not only require the votes of the Congress and the signature of the president, but also would require the United States to renegotiate all eighty-six of our bilateral income tax treaties as well as the General Agreement on Trade and Tariffs (GATT). If the proposal had no other major shortcomings (which it does), it is so out of sync with our international tax and trade arrangements that it is unrealistic as a practical matter. The panel, in my view, also failed to take into account the potential responses of other nations to the kind of major tax reform it was suggesting.

Incremental improvements in our system for taxing international income can occur in the absence of fundamental tax reform. Some international tax reforms can even be done independently of domestic tax reform on a revenue neutral basis. But the benefits for the American people of such changes will be small relative to the potential benefits achievable through a fundamental restructuring of our nation's domestic and international tax system.

Competitive Tax Plan, Point 3: Reduce the federal corporate tax rate to 15–20 percent, making the United States a more attractive economy for both domestic and foreign investment, with the revenue lost being financed by broadening the measure of corporate income and the new value-added tax.

VIII

Keep the Wage Tax to Help Fund Social Insurance

I guess you're right on the economics, but those taxes were never
a problem of economics. They are politics all the way through.
We put those payroll taxes there so as to give the contributors a
legal, moral, and political right to collect their pensions and
their unemployment benefits. With those taxes in there, no
damn politician can ever scrap my social security program.
—*Franklin Delano Roosevelt*

Anyone who is serious about coming up with a responsible and realistic way to fund our government must
take into account the growing portion of our federal
budget taken up by the three core social-insurance
programs in this country: Social Security, Medicare, and Medicaid. Though the severity of the crisis facing each of these programs is a matter of debate, as is the time when addressing it

will become necessary, no one denies that each faces an eventual funding crunch given the imminent retirement of the baby boom generation, the aging of our population, and the rise in health care and long-term care costs.

In some more bipartisan future moment there may emerge the possibility of a grand bargain that simultaneously introduces fundamental tax reform and the necessary changes and reforms of these programs. But big changes to the tax system need not await solutions to these most difficult political and economic dilemmas.

It is more realistic to assume that these social-insurance programs will probably have to be tackled on their own. That said, the benefit of the Competitive Tax Plan in the context of social-insurance and wage taxes is that, by maintaining wage taxes in the overall system and replacing most of the income tax with a value-added tax, my plan would provide some needed flexibility in revenue collection down the road to address at least some of the predictable shortfalls in these programs that may have to be paid for out of general revenues. Major competing plans, such as the FairTax and the flat tax, with their starve-the-beast ideology, do not allow for this and thus fail another basic test of providing responsible and reasonable solutions to our nation's challenges.

Ideas from the other side of the political spectrum to replace all or most of our wage taxes that now fund these social-insurance programs—such as with a VAT for this purpose—are also misdirected. Proponents of such a change emphasize that a VAT is more progressive than a wage tax. And they sometimes also note that retirees, as well as workers, will pay VAT, thereby decreasing our reliance on the shrinking ratio of workers to retirees. To be sure, these are advantages of enacting a VAT—advantages the Competitive Tax Plan captures—

but despite these advantages, it would be unwise to reduce payroll taxes substantially before reaching agreement on the future structure, coverage, and financing needs of Social Security, Medicare, and Medicaid. For more than seven decades, payroll taxes have served this nation well as a way of financing our nation's programs of social insurance. It would be unwise to abandon or eviscerate these taxes now—unmooring Social Security and Medicare from their revenue stream, while knowing that we are on the precipice of a large shortfall in the funds necessary to keep these programs viable.

Rising Costs and the Impact on Savings

Clearly the most significant tax legislation of the years between the First and Second World Wars was the Social Security Act of 1935 and its amendments in 1939. This legislation created the federal retirement, survivors, and unemployment insurance system. In 1950 disability insurance was added to Social Security. All of these are financed through a flat-rate payroll tax on a limited amount of wages. The maximum amount of wages subject to the tax that funds Social Security (including retirement, disability, and survivors' benefits) was about $95,000 in 2007. The system of benefits to be paid for by this tax is quite progressive.

The epigraph that opens this chapter was President Roosevelt's answer in 1935 to key New Deal advisers, such as Labor Secretary Frances Perkins, who opposed using a payroll tax to fund benefits and argued that the tax on labor income was inherently regressive. And for more than seventy years Roosevelt has been right about the politics.[1] Notwithstanding great efforts to sell the country on the idea, George W. Bush's proposal in 2005 to replace some Social Security taxes and benefits with individual savings accounts was an abysmal failure in Congress. Bush burned up a lot of his political goodwill in the process.

Lyndon Johnson had recognized Roosevelt's political astuteness when he decided in 1965 also to fund Medicare's hospital insurance with a payroll tax. Concern about those who pay the payroll tax, however, led Congress to fund the federal payments for Medicare's physicians' services from the government's more progressive revenue sources, notably income taxes. And the federal government's share of Medicaid costs is also financed from its general revenues rather than by any particular tax dedicated to this purpose. George W. Bush did not raise any taxes to pay for the Medicare drug benefit added in 2003—the first time a major new entitlement has been added without a funding source. Instead, President Bush and Congress simply increased federal borrowing, thereby pushing down the road the taxes necessary to pay for the new drug benefit.[2]

The politics of using payroll taxes to finance Social Security, unemployment insurance, and Medicare have changed little since Roosevelt's day. Some Democrats still want to replace the payroll tax with a more progressive levy; others do not. And the structure Roosevelt built has been remarkably stable. It is the economics of payroll taxes that are different now.

The most important development in the federal tax structure in the past fifty years has been the growth of the payroll tax to finance these social-insurance programs. These taxes on wages have risen from 10 percent of total budget receipts in 1953 to about 40 percent today. Originally, the Social Security tax rate was set at 1 percent of wages to grow to 5 percent, split evenly between employees and their employers.

Today the combined tax rate on employers and employees is
15.3 percent, including the tax of 2.9 percent of wages imposed
to pay for hospital insurance under Medicare.[3] While the
Medicare tax originally had the same wage ceiling as Social
Security, the ceiling was raised and then eliminated in the
1990s so that this tax is now imposed on all wages without any
dollar ceiling. For most families, payroll taxes are greater than
income taxes; indeed, payroll taxes to fund social insurance
are the most burdensome tax 80 percent of Americans pay
(see Figure 8.1). However, many families underestimate their
payroll tax burden because the employers' share is hidden to
employees.[4]

The increase in payroll taxes has had a major effect on the
take-home pay of low- and middle-income workers. And the
promise of future benefits upon retirement does not completely serve to offset the growing perceptions of both the public and some politicians that the wages of the middle class may
be overtaxed.

Despite the burden, however, people rarely protest payroll taxes because they both know and like what these taxes
pay for. The flat-rate taxes on wages used to finance Social Security and Medicare were designed, and have been embraced
by the American people, as "contributory" social insurance
programs. The Social Security benefits structure is designed so
that low-income workers, who especially need money during
retirement, receive benefits equal to a higher proportion of
their preretirement wages than do higher-income workers.
Moreover, the earned-income tax credit, which was structured
as a refundable credit against income tax in order that it not
reduce the Social Security Trust Fund or the determination of
Social Security benefits, was enacted originally to offset some
of the regressivity of the payroll tax for low-income workers.

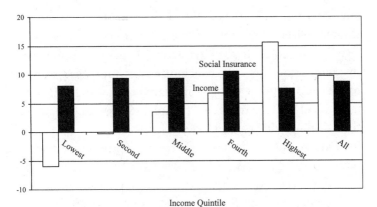

Figure 8.1. Effective federal individual and social insurance tax rates, 2002. *Source:* Congressional Budget Office, "Historical Effective Federal Tax Rates: 1979 to 2002" (2005).

Although the flat-rate Social Security payroll tax is regressive when viewed in isolation, the Social Security system is progressive when its benefits are taken into account. Thus it is misleading to assess the fairness of these flat-rate wage taxes without considering the benefits they finance.[5]

The payroll tax has generally proven surprisingly easy to collect. Employers usually withhold the tax from their employees' wages, and, with the exception of employers of domestic help, nonbusiness taxpayers are not typically required to file returns. However, the application of the tax to self-employed individuals has produced some compliance challenges. Many cash transactions go unreported, especially those involving domestic services, and a few higher-income individuals, including former senator and presidential candidate John Edwards, have formed corporations in an effort to avoid paying the tax. (These corporations are organized as Subchapter S or small limited-liability corporations to avoid any corporate income tax and, at the same time, to convert taxable self-employment income into corporate receipts allegedly not subject to the payroll tax.) Issues have also arisen involving fringe benefits, which often are not subject to payroll taxes. But on the whole—in sharp contrast to the income tax—most Americans face no compliance costs and spend no time dealing with payroll taxes. This is practical because of the flat-rate, no deductions, no credits, no personal exemptions nature of the tax.

Some economists have expressed concern about the economic effects of the Social Security and Medicare systems. While they find taxes on wages to be less distortive than taxes on capital, there is nevertheless some evidence that the Social Security and Medicare systems may have had an adverse impact on the nation's level of savings.[6] Since both Medicare's hospital insurance and Social Security are financed by taxes on wages—taxes that themselves impose no direct burden on savings—the adverse impact of these programs on national savings is generally not a tax problem. These taxes, like any taxes, however, do decrease the amount of after-tax income available to those who pay it and who might otherwise save at least some of it. And the programs' benefits go to retired older citizens, who are likely to—or in the case of Medicare, required to— spend it. The economic security these programs provide our elderly citizens is extremely valuable, but by providing a safety net against unexpected medical expenses and a guaranteed inflation-adjusted monthly income for as long as one lives, Social Security and Medicare may have decreased somewhat people's willingness to save for retirement. As a result, the great benefits of these programs may have come at some cost in reduced national savings.

Giving up the benefits that Social Security and Medicare provide makes no sense, but we must begin looking seriously for ways to reduce their costs. The decline in the rate of U.S. savings has coincided with a substantial increase in total consumption by the elderly, due in substantial part to the intergenerational distribution of income from young to elderly people through Social Security and Medicare. The best way to address the nation's low rate of savings, however, is not by replacing the wage tax but rather by strengthening the ability of all Americans to save. And the Competitive Tax Plan will help us toward this goal by eliminating the income tax for the vast majority of Americans—freeing their savings from any taxation—and by lowering the tax rate on savings for everyone. It also puts in place a tax system that can fund our government's spending, thereby reducing the need for the federal government to soak up private savings through its borrowing.

"Politics All the Way Through"

There are two main reasons why politicians are reluctant to advance changes in Social Security. First, Social Security has long been regarded as the dangerous third rail of American politics, and George Bush's 2005 failed venture into Social Security policy only strengthened that perception. Because of the perceived political risks, politicians want to postpone addressing its problems. Second, Social Security currently is producing cash surpluses, and this has made it easy to avoid tackling the forthcoming problems. The United States government for many years has collected more in Social Security payroll taxes than it pays in benefits. However, in another decade or so, at the latest, the current tax rate will not be adequate to fund cur-

rent benefits. Without any changes, actuaries currently estimate that the Social Security and Medicare trust funds will run
an annual cash deficit of nearly $250 billion by the year 2020, a
deficit of $1 trillion a year by 2030.

The Social Security and Medicare programs for retirees
are immensely popular, but they are also budgetary behe-
moths. The growth in these benefits and in the flat-rate payroll taxes that fund them should disabuse anyone of the no-
tion that a flat-rate tax on everyone will necessarily constrain
growth in government spending. Health and retirement benefits together account for more than half the total annual outlays of the federal government. These costs have grown rapidly over the past six decades, and the aging and increased
longevity of the population guarantee even greater growth in
the years ahead. Not only is the population aging, but increasing life expectancies have made persons aged eighty-five
and older the fastest-growing age group in America.[7] Anticipated demographic changes now imply an average annual
deficit in Social Security funding of more than 2 percent of
taxable wages over the next seventy-five-year period—the
lifetime perspective over which Social Security finances have
typically been measured.[8]

The aging of the population portends new pressures to
raise payroll taxes, pressures that should generally be resisted.
The estimated gap between Social Security benefits and taxes
increases each year, as years of trust fund surpluses are replaced with years of deficit. Accordingly, if no changes are
made, it will take about a 5.5 percent tax rate hike to cover the
gap fifty years from now. Probably the easiest way to compre-
hend the magnitude of the forthcoming demographic changes
is this: In 1950 there were 16.5 workers for each retiree. Today
there are about 3.3. By 2040 there are expected to be only

2.1 workers per recipient. Thus if current benefits were financed only from current taxes and if 3 workers today pay thirty-three cents each for every dollar of benefits, fifty cents each would be required from 2 workers to fund a dollar of benefits. Or if taxes are not increased, benefits would have to be cut by one-third.[9]

Unfortunately, because of rising health care costs, which are outpacing both inflation and wage growth, projections of Medicare finances are even more dire. Health costs have been accelerating since 1999, after a brief slowdown in the 1990s. State finances are also threatened by both the aging of the population and rising health care costs, since most spending on long-term care for the elderly now comes from Medicaid.[10]

If these projections are even close, combined Social Security and Medicare payroll tax rates would have to exceed 25 percent to fund current benefits—10 percentage points more than their current level. Without structural changes, the payroll tax rate will have to be raised to an unacceptably high level, benefits will have to be cut, or federal borrowing will explode. But most politicians regard this as a crisis for the future, even though relatively small steps taken now might produce large positive long-term benefits.

The last time we confronted a significant financial problem with Social Security was 1983. What happened then could provide a template for moving forward. That year projections of Social Security tax revenues and outlays made clear that within a few years taxes would not be adequate to pay benefits, but no one wanted to take the political heat for either cutting Social Security benefits or increasing taxes. Enter a "bipartisan commission," headed by Alan Greenspan, who would later be rewarded with the chairmanship of the Federal Reserve. The Greenspan Commission offered crucial political cover to both

Congress and the administration, and the commission's proposals ultimately were accepted by the Reagan administration
and both political parties in the Congress.

The 1983 Social Security Amendments accelerated into
the 1980s a series of payroll tax increases adopted in 1977 that
had been scheduled to go into effect in 1990, brought federal
civilian employees and most state and local government employees into the Social Security system, gradually increased the
Social Security retirement age from sixty-five to sixty-seven,
and subjected one-half of Social Security benefits to income
taxation for recipients with income above a certain level. The
1983 changes increased Social Security tax revenues by more
than $20 billion annually by the late 1980s, and the 1983
changes, combined with earlier changes in 1977, produced additional tax revenues of about $85 billion a year by 1990, mostly
from middle-income workers. These Social Security tax hikes
contributed substantially to the ability of Bill Clinton to characterize the tax policies of Presidents Reagan and Bush as favoring the rich. They also, I think, presaged a long-term contest between the elderly, who collect the benefits, and younger
workers, who pay the taxes. One important advantage of introducing a VAT into our nation's tax system is that it will impose taxes on everyone's purchases of goods and services regardless of age.

That people are living longer and doing so in better
health is unambiguously a good thing. But an increasing elderly population demands a substantial restructuring of the
social-insurance protections now available to retirees. Whatever increases in life expectancy occur, retirees must have
enough income to live on—income unthreatened by the
prospect of catastrophically expensive health care costs or un-

affordable expenditures for long-term care. The challenge is to provide this retirement security without imposing a payroll tax burden on working people that they cannot afford or shifting needed resources away from workers or children.

This challenge can be met if we adopt a realistic view of when retirement protections should begin, how inflation protections should be calculated, and how social insurance should address medical care costs. We need not abandon the elderly, beggar the future, or drastically increase wage taxes to maintain our successful record of social insurance protections for retirees. No program of retiree income security should allow income protections to drop below current levels. Social Security should continue to replace the 40 percent of wages it now replaces on average under the current system. More than half of the elderly would have incomes below the poverty level without their Social Security benefits, suggesting that at least the current level of benefits for low- and middle-income workers must be maintained to ensure retirees' income security. That level of adequacy must be secured by governmental action that protects workers from general inflation risks and the individual risks inherent in both labor and capital market returns.

In order to accomplish this, politicians will have to make some hard choices. They should, for example, consider accelerating the currently scheduled increase in the retirement age to age sixty-seven and phasing in an additional increase to age seventy to reflect longer longevity. The early retirement age for receiving reduced benefits should be raised from sixty-two to sixty-five. Evidence from around the world suggests that ages for retirement benefit eligibility have a major impact on when people leave the workforce, so higher retirement ages will increase the contribution of earnings to the income of the elderly. A gradual increase in the payroll tax ceiling should also be on the table.

Other smaller changes are also essential. For example, widespread agreement exists that the consumer price index probably overstates inflation and a more accurate measure could enhance the financial outlook for Social Security. Congress should also eliminate the current exemption of certain state and local employees from Social Security. It could also expand the potential financial investments of the Social Security Trust Fund, even if only to commercial paper of financially sound institutions. This could offer a way to increase returns with debt instruments rather than expanding trust fund investments to corporate equities. These are just a handful of suggestions that would help restore Social Security to a sound financial footing. Many others are circulating among policy analysts; they simply require a president and Congress who can muster the political will to act.

Securing Retirement

To date, most of the political debate about the forthcoming gap between payroll taxes and anticipated benefits has focused on whether to institute individual retirement accounts as a substitute for or supplement to Social Security benefits.[11] This remains an important debate, although as President Bush admitted in 2005, it may not have much to do with closing the Social Security financing gap. Despite the great skepticism, which I share, about the wisdom of using individual accounts to replace Social Security benefits, tax-favored asset accumulation devices for a variety of purposes enjoy wide and growing bipartisan support. A movement to universal individual accounts as a supplement to Social Security could create an infrastructure for widespread holding and building of financial wealth. Facilitating savings accumulation for poorer and middle-class families should be a national priority. This could prove to be one of the most significant tax and economic policy developments in decades. Since the current Social Security guarantee is far from generous and private employer–based retirement programs cover only about half of all workers, the government should take a larger role in promoting individual retirement savings and ensuring broad participation in capital markets. Prefunding of retirement is not a silver bullet, but a universal savings program that entails some prefunding may reduce the need for future tax increases or government borrowing. To be effective, however, such savings accounts must be mandatory, not voluntary, and these savings would have to be untouchable until disability or retirement.

Such individual accounts would allow individuals who otherwise would have little or no financial holdings to participate in the higher long-term returns of investments in corporate securities. Our experiences with 401(k)s and IRAs indicate that universality can be accomplished only by requiring that each individual have an account. A mandatory plan would fill the gaps in current employer-based pension coverage—coverage that now benefits only half the workforce and strongly favors higher-paid, better-educated, and older workers, as well as those employed by large firms. Insistence on mandatory accounts, however, departs dramatically from recent proposals for voluntary individual savings accounts.

To see the potential for the expanded retirement security that such a program might provide, consider that in the past seventy years the rate of return on the Standard and Poors portfolio of common stocks has averaged more than 10 percent annually, compared with a 5 percent return on government bonds. Wage compensation, which constitutes the Social Security tax base, has grown even more slowly, at a real rate of less than 3 percent, on average, during the period 1960–2004. At an 8 percent compound return, someone who put $15 a week into a savings account would accumulate more than $250,000 after thirty-five years of working, more than $500,000 after forty-five years. Private retirement savings accounts under such a system ultimately could become an important source of retirement income protection for all workers.

For low-income workers, the difficulty, of course, is finding the funds to save. Obviously, the government would have to contribute. The income tax currently provides a "savers' credit" that promotes savings on a voluntary basis. There are many proposals for expanding the scope and size of this credit to increase savings of low- and moderate-income Americans. Converting the credit into an income-based contribution by the government into individuals' accounts is one possibility. Another is to create mandatory savings accounts for all children, which would allow a smaller government financing of savings: accounts beginning at birth, rather than entry into the labor force, would have many more years for the compounding of investment returns. The payoffs from such a system would be large even though they would not be visible for many years.[12]

The problem of providing an adequate baseline of retirement income for our aging population can readily be solved without major tax increases or cuts in benefits. It is child's play in comparison to the problem of providing the elderly adequate access to health care and long-term care. Solving these problems may also require solutions for our national problems of inadequate health insurance coverage and escalating health care costs. A discussion of those issues would fill another book, so I shall offer just a few observations here. Even optimistic expectations about the health of the elderly and a slowing of health care inflation will not counteract the extreme growth in medical care costs for the population over age sixty-five. We have to rethink our Medicare and Medicaid systems from bottom up.

One option is for higher-income elderly to bear the costs of health insurance themselves. Another would be to refocus health insurance protection to protect the elderly only against the high costs of extensive medical treatment that can cause a substantial decline in their standard of living. This is the direction implied by those who are promoting health savings accounts coupled with high-deductible insurance, for example. It would require that the elderly purchase a high-deductible health insurance policy—or have the government provide such a policy as it now does under Medicare—to ensure the maintenance of adequate income levels and to protect against large shocks to income. The government would have to provide subsidies to help retirees for whom the health insurance policy costs themselves would threaten income adequacy. This would redirect current funding for Medicare and Medicaid toward funding for health insurance when medical spending is large in a given year, either in absolute terms or relative to the retiree's income. As under Medicare today, some financial contribution would be required from all retirees.

Changes of this sort are extensive, and given the political sway of the elderly, may seem unlikely. Much more modest changes in Medicare's coverage and benefits may be a more plausible scenario. This necessarily would mean that the government would face requirements for more funding of these costs in the years ahead. It will be a good trick if our political leadership can keep those funding demands relatively small.

Problems Tax Reform Alone Cannot Solve

The foregoing discussion suggests that the benefits now promised by Social Security, Medicare, and Medicaid will have to be reexamined and likely trimmed. It also raises the question of where more money should come from should we need it, raising the question: What does the future hold for payroll taxes? The answer to the latter may well depend on the political context in which these questions arise.

There are various potential scenarios for tackling these issues. The first is in the normal legislative process, where the House Ways and Means and Senate Finance Committees shape legislation that then proceeds through Congress, taking up each one of these programs at a time. If this occurs, many members of Congress have said that Social Security and Medicare should come up before tax reform. Alternatively, given their political sensitivity, some special bipartisan process may be used, perhaps resembling either the 1983 Social Security commission or the 1990 budget negotiations that took place between the executive and legislative branches. It is impossible to know now what the agenda of such an extraordinary process might be. It could include Social Security, Medicare, or both. It probably would not include tax reform although there has been some talk of a "grand bargain," including all of these issues. Ways and Means Chairman Bill Thomas (R-CA), an extraordinarily effective legislator who retired from Congress in 2006, has long said that the only way to get anything substantial done on any one of these issues is to tackle them all simultaneously.

Given the necessity of reexamining the programs funded by payroll taxes, my Competitive Tax Plan does not set out to restructure payroll taxes as just another aspect of tax reform. This, however, is precisely what some tax reform advocates from both the right and left of the political spectrum have suggested.

From the left, probably the most important idea has come from the Center for American Progress, a relatively new think tank headed by John Podesta, who served as President Clinton's chief of staff. In a tax reform plan released in January 2005, the center proposed repealing the half of the Social Security tax on employees—now 6.2 percent on up to $90,000 of wages—and eliminating the wage ceiling, so that the employers' 6.2 percent tax would apply to all wages without limit. Since, as I have noted, the payroll tax creates few economic problems and is quite simple to comply with, the reason for this proposal is to give low- and middle-income workers a tax cut and shift their tax burden up the income scale. Since most of these workers currently pay little or no income tax, cutting their payroll tax is the only way to offer them substantial tax relief. Given our long-term financial situation, however, this is not the time to be calling for massive tax cuts for the middle class, no matter how politically popular they may be.

Moreover, by eliminating the entire contribution of most employees, the center, ignoring the political wisdom of Franklin Roosevelt's insistence on everyone making "contributions" to Social Security, would divorce the right to receive benefits from workers' payroll tax contributions. Much of the pressure to replace Social Security with individual accounts has already come from higher-income workers who feel that they don't get their "money's worth" from Social Security because of the progressive structure of its benefits. Even now, high-wage workers would be better off if they could put their payroll taxes into individual savings accounts rather than Social Security. The center's strategy runs the risk of converting Social Security into just another spending program and, by doing so, undermining its political support, surely not the center's intention. Moreover, under this proposal, aggregate payroll tax revenues would decrease, further widening the gap between payroll taxes and expected benefits and requiring other taxes to make up the difference. As a policy prescription, therefore, the proposal seems unwise. It may have been designed principally as a political document intended to demonstrate Democrats' concern for the well-being of the middle class and to draw a contrast with the tax policies of George Bush's administration, which the center complains unduly favor the rich.

From the right, the FairTax crowd would replace the payroll tax, along with the individual and corporate income taxes and the estate tax, with a 30 percent national sales tax. The plan would also delink Social Security benefits from any "contributory" financing structure, though the prospect of undermining Social Security does not frighten FairTax advocates. As the president's tax reform panel pointed out, using Treasury estimates and assuming favorable rates of noncompliance, it would take at least a 34 percent sales tax rate simply to replace the income tax.[13] This makes it hard to view the FairTax plan as anything other than a political ploy, designed to appeal to the Republican base and perhaps to expand it. It certainly is not a realistic proposal. But even as a political ploy, it became essential for the plan to include elimination of the payroll tax. If there was to be any hope of generating broad-based grassroots support from the middle class for such a large national sales tax, the payroll tax had to go; so the proposal does away with it. Even with the payroll tax gone, however, the FairTax would shift the tax burden away from those at the top down to others with less income. If payroll taxes were not eliminated, this shift would be even more dramatic, since the income tax and the estate tax primarily burden higher-income groups. Eliminating all of these taxes was also essential for the FairTax proponents to claim that they would eliminate the IRS. Abandoning the idea of repealing payroll taxes would probably be the first move if the FairTax is ever taken seriously as a tax reform alternative.

There are several less drastic proposals for changing the payroll tax that would not completely reject the basic contributory financing structure that Roosevelt insisted on. A number of analysts concerned with Social Security's financing gap have proposed raising the top level of wages subject to the tax above the current level of about $95,000. In 1983 the Social Security Commission and Congress reaffirmed the historical practice of collecting Social Security tax on 90 percent of earnings of workers subject to the tax. Even though the wage ceiling increases automatically each year to reflect the year's increase in average earnings, only about 83 percent of earnings is currently being taxed because earnings for those at the top have risen much more than average wages since 1983. This 7 percent difference reduces payroll taxes by many billions of dollars each year. Some analysts, including former Social Security Commissioner Robert Ball, have proposed moving the wage ceiling up to 90 percent gradually over several decades. Others would impose the full 12.4 percent Social Security tax above the current ceiling; and some would eliminate the ceiling and apply a substantially lower rate. Extending Social Security coverage and the payroll tax to the state and local employees who remain outside the reach of the tax is a common suggestion. In addition, there are various proposals for expanding the amount of taxed wages by including some currently untaxed fringe benefits within the payroll tax base. These ideas merit serious consideration as potential ways to help close the financing gap in Social Security and Medicare. It also would be possible to raise the 2.9 percent Medicare tax rate a bit if necessary. But if a substantial amount of revenue becomes necessary to fund Social Security and health care spending for the elderly, looking to general federal revenues rather than payroll tax increases seems wise.

Returns to capital have outstripped returns to labor over a long period of time.[14] To be fair, if new taxes become necessary to pay for the aging of the nation's population, they should not be imposed, as payroll taxes are, solely on workers. This implies using general revenues, which currently include income taxes (and, for now at least, estate and gift taxes)—and which under the Competitive Tax Plan would also include the value-added tax—for funding the additional government expenditures required by demographic changes and rising health care costs. Down the road, some use of general revenues to fund income and health care for retirees seems inevitable.[15] And if the alternative becomes an increase in payroll taxes paid by low- and moderate-income families, turning to general revenues also seems right.

If the rapid growth in health care spending for the elderly cannot be slowed, a new revenue source will surely be required to fund Medicare and Medicaid. And going forward we may need even more social insurance—for example, for long-term care or to protect workers from economic shocks from unemployment due to technology changes and globalization of the economy. Some are even calling for insurance to protect wage earners against substantial wage reductions due to these forces.

In the near term, relatively modest changes in our tax system and government spending can balance the budget. But down the road—even assuming that changes in Medicare, Medicaid, and Social Security reduce their costs—only by restructuring our nation's tax system can we effectively fund the social contract. We have an archaic tax system, designed in an era when the United States dominated the world economy. Today the U.S. economy must compete worldwide for the investment capital necessary to produce a rising standard of living for the American people.

If large amounts of revenue become necessary, increasing the current income tax by an amount sufficient to provide the necessary funding does not seem a wise option; doing so could threaten our economic prosperity. Financing such spending through additional borrowing would also be wrong and potentially dangerous to our economic health. And economic growth is the engine of both our tax revenues and our prosperity.

This is why people from all parts of the political spectrum have concluded that the United States should implement a relatively low-rate tax on consumption in the form of either a VAT or a retail sales tax to fund future outlays for health insurance and Social Security. Doing this without also using the VAT for income tax reform as my plan proposes to do would be foolish, however. It would retain our existing income tax mess, while putting in place a new revenue source that could soon become a ready vehicle for ever-increasing spending until the tax reaches levels common throughout the world. Instead, the Competitive Tax Plan would use the VAT to fund a $100,000 family exemption from the income tax

($50,000 for singles, with both indexed for inflation)—a threshold no member of Congress will ever suggest lowering in the absence of a genuine national catastrophe—and also permit us to lower substantially the individual and corporate income tax rates.

Tax reform alone cannot solve the major difficulties facing our social insurance programs. But unless those difficulties are at least taken into consideration in crafting a tax system for the twenty-first century, any such reform will eventually be swamped by these enormous budgetary items. The Competitive Tax Plan bites off a lot, but not more than it can chew. It provides a way forward toward fair, efficient, and streamlined tax collection while providing a degree of flexibility in revenue collection that any honest proposal must admit may be necessary.

> *Competitive Tax Plan, Point 4:* Don't delay income tax reform by waiting to solve the social insurance dilemma first. Save payroll tax changes for Social Security and Medicare reform.

IX

Tax Great Wealth but Protect
Farmers and Small Businesses

*The man of great wealth owes a particular obligation
to the state, because he derives special advantages from the
mere existence of government.*
—*Theodore Roosevelt*

Eliminating the income tax for most Americans and introducing a consumption tax in its place will, as I've outlined in previous chapters, have tremendous benefits for businesses large and small and for millions of citizens who will no longer have to file annual returns with the IRS. And my Competitive Tax Plan helps to address our nation's serious fiscal problems. Unfortunately, some of the other fundamental tax reform proposals being discussed in our nation's capital today are tax cuts—especially for the rich—in disguise. As we saw in Chapter 2, with the use of

Rosie Scenarios, many current reform suggestions are more ideological fantasy than responsible policy.

This is certainly the case when it comes to the taxation of very large estates. As Ian Shapiro and I detailed in our book *Death by a Thousand Cuts,* there is perhaps no tax over the past twenty years that has been the subject of a more sustained campaign of misrepresentation and demagoguery that the levy imposed on these accumulations of substantial wealth. Because the estate tax accounts for such a large measure of the progressivity in our current tax system at the very top of the income scale, while affecting so few people, my proposal would retain a reformed version of the tax. Unlike what other proposals might have us think, enacting a consumption tax by no means demands the elimination of all taxes on gifts and inheritances.

Small Tax, Big Benefit

States and local governments typically impose taxes on real estate and some other property such as cars and boats. But the only federal wealth taxes are taxes on gifts and bequests. First adopted in the nineteenth century to fund various wartime government revenue shortfalls, the estate tax has been on the books continuously since 1916. While the rate of tax on large estates has gone up and down over the years, this tax was, until recently, generally considered an uncontroversial means of raising federal revenue from those most able to pay. These estate and gift taxes, which are imposed on transfers of wealth to younger generations, are complex, even though they produce much less revenue than the income tax. The estate tax accounted for about 11 percent of federal revenues at its zenith in 1946, but it has generally not produced more than 2.5 percent of federal revenue since then. Today it accounts for only about 1 percent of federal revenues. Even so, the amount of money raised by this tax is not trivial: $50–70 billion annually is expected for the period 2011–20. And despite their relatively low revenue yield, the estate and gift taxes have contributed significantly to the progressivity of the nation's tax system.[1]

The way the estate tax works is quite straightforward: When a person who is among the very wealthiest in this country dies, his estate has to pay a portion of the value of his assets to the United States government before the rest of the estate can be passed on to his children or other heirs. If the estate is passed to a spouse, there is no tax. Furthermore, if the person leaves the money to charity or sets up a charitable foundation, as so many of America's wealthiest individuals have over the years, none of the money donated is taxed. Depending on where the person lives, the estate may also have to pay state estate taxes.

Until the passage of the 2001 tax law, only individuals with assets of more than $1 million or married couples with assets of more than $2 million were affected by the tax. That is to say, the first $1 million of any individual's estate was exempt from the tax. Any amount above that would be taxed. In the year 2001, just the wealthiest 2.1 percent of all estates were taxed by the federal government. The other 97.9 percent of adults who died that year had estates smaller than the exemption and were unaffected by the law. The average size of the estates taxed that year was about $4 million. Combined, the taxes collected from these estates totaled $24.4 billion, a sum roughly half the size of the 2004 budget for the Departments of Homeland Security or Education.

The 2001 tax law increased the estate tax exemption to $3.5 million ($7 million a couple) for 2009 and reduced the top rate to 45 percent. It repealed the tax altogether in 2010. Like all of the 2001 legislation, unless Congress takes action, in 2011 the tax will reemerge—and with a 55 percent top rate and $1 million exemption. This is highly unlikely, however. By 2006 even liberal Democrats were supporting an exemption of at least $3.5 million and a top rate of 45 percent. The forces favoring repeal of this tax have come a long way from the $700,000 or $800,000 exemption proposed by Newt Gingrich and his fellow Republicans in their 1994 Contract with America. Meanwhile, the uncertainty created by the 2001 act has taken a toll. Estate planning remains a crapshoot; you still don't know what law to plan for. Life insurance premiums still have to be paid, just in case.

In a report issued in July 2005 to assess the impact of the estate tax on family farms and small businesses, the Congressional Budget Office (CBO) observed that more than 60 percent of the wealth subject to the tax was in the form of liquid assets (bonds, corporate stocks, bank accounts, and life insurance) and that the richest 10 percent of estates filing returns— the richest 0.5 percent of Americans—held 45 percent of the wealth and paid two-thirds of the tax. CBO also concluded that with a $3.5 million exemption, only 9,000 Americans would have been required to file estate tax returns in the year 2000, and only 3,676 of those would have owed any tax. Fewer than two hundred estates would have had insufficient liquid assets to pay the tax. Only sixty-five estates of farmers would have been subject to the tax, and only thirteen of these would not have had enough liquid assets to pay the tax.[2]

In short, despite what its determined opponents continue to maintain, the reformed estate tax with higher exemption levels represents a small burden for the few that can substantially benefit the many.

Why We Should Retain a Modified Estate Tax

As recently as the early 1990s the idea of eliminating the estate tax entirely was an idea lingering on the fringes of the right-wing, antitax movement. How it managed to become, by the time of George W. Bush's first run for the White House, a populist cry is a fascinating political saga, which I've elaborated elsewhere.[3] The estate tax clearly has had problems requiring repair, including the need to increase its exemption and to take more family circumstances into account in determining tax liability. There also has long been a political necessity to expand existing relief for intrafamily transfers of closely held businesses and farms, perhaps even to exempt them from estate taxation altogether. Estate tax repeal was enacted in 2001, however, because of the powerful political forces aligned against the tax, not because of its substantive shortcomings.

The National Federation of Independent Business (NFIB), representing owners of small businesses, made estate tax repeal its top legislative priority in 2001, and President Bush concurred.[4] In addition, the aging baby boom generation is now thinking about its mortality. The marketplace—including the market for legislation—has long been responsive to the desires and concerns of this large generation. Moreover, although the estate tax is imposed only on the wealthiest 1 percent or 2 percent of people who die in any year, one Zogby poll found that 71 percent of the public favored its repeal.[5] Some observers dismiss such polls, insisting that two out of every three Americans would be in favor of repealing any tax. Instead, I applaud the unflappable optimism of the American people—polls show that more than 40 percent of Americans believe they are now or will be in the richest 1 percent when they die. But repeal of the estate tax was a mistake.

There are good reasons for retaining a death-time tax on wealth. The first is revenue. Those who want to repeal the estate tax always point out that it has long been a minor source of federal revenues, now less than 1.5 percent of the total. But there are still sizable dollars at stake. In 2004 just over thirty thousand taxable estates contributed $21.5 billion to finance the federal government.[6] Without the 2001 act changes, estate tax receipts had been projected to grow to about $70 billion by 2012.[7] This revenue could pay for a reduction in the top individual income tax rate of about 2 percentage points or a reduction in the corporate income tax rate from 35 percent to 30 percent.[8] Or it could save the nation from borrowing more than an additional $500 billion in the decade ahead. It is not chump change.

Second, estate tax repeal favors the very wealthy, those families who least need tax relief. About half of all estate tax revenue is collected from the largest 10 percent of taxable estates—those valued at more than $5 million, the richest 0.1 percent of our population—and in recent years more than one-fifth of total estate taxes have come from fortunes exceeding $20 million each.[9] Moreover, as the CBO study shows, most of these large estates are composed of liquid assets, not family businesses or farms.[10] Why is repeal of such an important element of progressivity without any replacement appropriate now, given the need for revenues and the fact that the distribution of wealth in the United States has become more unequal in recent years?

Wealth inequality has always been greater than income inequality, and several recent studies suggest that distributions of recent wealth increases have greatly favored the wealthy. Since 1981 the net worth of wealthy individuals in many instances has doubled or tripled, even when adjusted for infla-

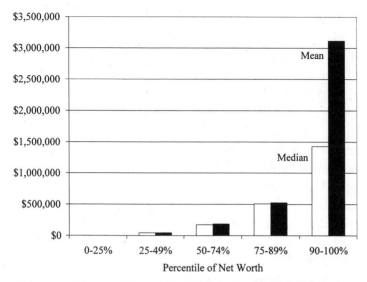

Figure 9.1. Net worth by percentile, 2004. *Source:* Federal Reserve
Board Survey of Consumer Finances, 2004.

tion. In 1986 *Forbes* magazine published its first list of billionaires, numbering 140; by 2006 its list of billionaires included 793
people with a combined wealth of $2.6 trillion. About half of
these were from the United States. The gap between the wealthy
and the poor in the United States has increased to the greatest
level since the 1890s. One study, for example, claims that the top
1 percent of wealth holders enjoyed two-thirds of the increases
in financial wealth during the 1980s and 1990s.[11]

Contrary to the political rhetoric driving the repeal effort, the estate tax targets only the wealthiest segment of the
U.S. population.[12] And as Figure 9.1 shows, our wealthiest families own much of the nation's wealth.[13]

Without a tax on large transfers of wealth, the income tax
will be the only source of progressivity at the top of the income

and wealth scale. Indeed, if repeal of the estate tax were to succeed in increasing capital accumulations, as some of its proponents believe, it will also substantially increase the inequality
of wealth.[14]

When he endorsed the idea of a tax on inheritance back
in 1906, Theodore Roosevelt said that its "primary objective
should be to put a constantly increasing burden on the inheritance of those swollen fortunes, which it is certainly of
no benefit to this country to perpetuate." Andrew Carnegie
agreed, believing that unfettered inheritance of huge fortunes
leads to idleness and profligacy. In the early part of the twentieth century, when the nation's images of wealth came from
Rockefellers and railroad barons, the general public tended to
agree also. They didn't like the idea of an economic aristocracy
perpetuating itself generation after generation in a country
founded on the idea of equal opportunity for all.

In practice, this argument, while applicable to any and all
inheritance, has focused on the legitimacy of taxing large fortunes. That's because no one, not even the most ardent advocate for the estate tax, believes that poor, working, or middle-
class people should have to pay any portion of whatever
savings or assets they've managed to accumulate to the government at the time of their death. The question is and always
has been how to treat the wealthy and the superwealthy.

Third, estate tax repeal is likely to have an important adverse effect upon many charities, particularly universities and
colleges, hospitals, and museums. The estate tax permits unlimited deduction of charitable bequests.[15] If the tax is repealed, it will be no more costly to give a bequest to a family
member than to a charity. Typically, more than one-third of
estates larger than $5 million make charitable bequests; nearly
half of such estates leave assets to charity if the decedent is not

married.[16] In 2000 charitable bequests from otherwise taxable estates totaled $16 billion.[17] And more than $60 billion of assets were held by charitable remainder trusts.[18] Economists have estimated that repeal of the estate tax would reduce charitable bequests by anywhere from 12 percent to 80 percent. And the economist who offered the lowest estimate also predicted that lifetime gifts to charity would drop by as much as 12 percent if the estate tax were repealed.[19]

The major economic argument for eliminating the estate and gift taxes, of course, is that they are taxes on savings, and their elimination might stimulate economic growth. Unsurprisingly, the evidence about the effect of these taxes on the national savings level is uncertain, and the size of the effects is controversial. But, as usual, true believers and truthiness abound. One law professor even argued for repeal of the estate tax on the ground that repealing this tax, which applies only to the wealthiest 1 percent of the population, would increase the wages of the least-advantaged members of our society.[20] He failed, however, to offer one shred of evidence that this kind of wage increase for low-income workers would actually occur. In any event, economic arguments played a surprisingly small role in the 2001 debates over repealing the tax.

What Lies Ahead for Taxes on Wealth

Even in the unlikely event that the 2001 act's repeal of the estate tax actually takes effect, there will be pressures for its reinstatement. Large tax-free bequests will be a fat target for a Congress looking for money. After the retirement of the baby boom generation, financial pressures on Medicare, Medicaid, and Social Security will all escalate. Proposals linking taxation of large bequests to popular spending plans—to help fund

Social Security, Medicare, or long-term care for the elderly—will be hard to defeat.

Moreover, alternative ways of taxing large gifts or bequests of wealth, which might produce about as much revenue as reinstating the estate tax, are available to Congress. And these alternatives would tax the recipients of wealth rather than the person who earned it. This would shift the focus of the tax away from the hardworking business owners and farmers to those who benefit most from inheriting wealth: their rich children. Most have little or no interest in carrying on their father or mother's business. And it is far more difficult to maintain that Paris Hilton deserves her inherited wealth tax free than to argue that her grandfather Conrad Hilton, the hotelier who earned the fortune, should have the ability to do with it whatever he likes.

One possibility would be to tax recipients of large bequests with a so-called accessions tax, a tax studied by the American Law Institute in the 1960s but largely forgotten since.[21] An accessions tax would tax recipients of large gifts and bequests based on the total amount of such gifts and bequests received during their lifetimes rather than according to the total value of each legacy. Like the estate tax, an accessions tax would have a substantial lifetime exemption level, imposing no tax, for example, on a person who receives less than $1 million in gifts or bequests; it would also ignore annual gifts of less than a specified amount, say $10,000.[22] Imposing an accessions tax on recipients rather than an estate tax on transferors would better align the tax rate with the individual's ability to pay taxes. And even with an exemption of the first million dollars received, such a tax might well produce more revenue than a reformed estate tax.

A federal inheritance tax, structured like the taxes now imposed by nearly half the states, offers another way to tax recipients rather than transferors of wealth.[23] Rather than basing the exempt amount or the tax rate on the cumulative amount of wealth transfers received in a lifetime, an inheritance tax would treat each bequest separately. It is feasible under either an accessions tax or an inheritance tax to vary the rate of tax depending upon the recipient's relationship to the transferor and to adjust the tax for other family circumstances. Neither tax, for example, need be imposed upon gifts or bequests of interests in a small business or farm until the asset is sold outside the family.

An inheritance tax or an accessions tax could be imposed at either a progressive or flat rate. A flat rate would simplify both estate planning and tax administration. A flat rate, for example, would facilitate equivalent taxation of outright gifts and those in trust. A flat rate would also substantially alleviate distinctions in tax burdens based on the timing of transfers of wealth. But even with a large exemption that will free all but the wealthiest Americans from the tax and make the tax itself progressive, some people will want to impose higher rates as the size of the inheritance or estate increases. In either event, by taxing recipients rather than transferors of wealth, both an accessions tax and an inheritance tax could also avoid the charge of "double" taxation often leveled at the estate tax. Any of these taxes on "windfalls" might prove politically more popular and more stable than the estate tax. As a third possibility, Congress might decide simply to include large bequests in the recipients' income. Given these alternatives, even if Congress allows the 2001 act's repeal of the estate tax to take effect, I would wager that some tax on large wealth transfers will reappear.

Most current tax reform proposals that would substitute consumption taxes for all or part of the income tax would also eliminate the estate tax, but this is not necessary. Repealing the estate tax would favor the wealthiest families in our country and would require higher rates in some other tax to make up the lost revenue. There is a solid case for reforming and even restructuring our current taxes on transfers of wealth, but not for eliminating a tax on large wealth transfers altogether.

At a time when the gap between the rich and the poor in our country has grown larger than it has been since the 1920s, it is vital that responsible tax reform gain real popular support not simply by being called a "fair" tax but by enacting fairness. In this regard, we must address the question of how to prevent a tax reform from becoming, in effect, a substantial tax cut for the wealthy paid for by an increase on those with less income or wealth.

> *Competitive Tax Plan, Point 5:* Retain a tax on gifts and inheritances with raised exemption levels and relief for small-business owners and farmers.

X

Protect American Workers from a Tax Increase

*[Taxes] upon articles of consumption, may be compared to a
fluid, which will, in time, find its level with the means of paying
them. . . . The rich may be extravagant, the poor can be frugal.*
—*Alexander Hamilton*

Generally speaking, people save more as their income
rises. Conversely, low- and moderate-income people consume a greater proportion of their income
than high earners do. This means that changing
from an income tax to a consumption tax tends to shift taxes
down the income scale.[1] Thus any move toward consumption
taxation requires attention to how the tax burden will be distributed. Without careful design, a shift to a consumption tax
may entail tax cuts for the wealthy and tax increases for low-
and moderate-income people.

To avoid a significant shift in the tax burden away from those at the top down the income scale, I have retained tax on inherited wealth and an income tax on income over $100,000 ($50,000 for singles, with both indexed for inflation). I have urged that the income tax be imposed at a low rate, in the range of 20 percent to 25 percent, but, as I discussed in Chapter 6, the precise contours of both its rate schedule and the definition of income subject to the tax—what exclusions or deductions will be allowed—will have to be worked out in the political process. Moving down the income scale, however, new challenges emerge. The question how to protect low- and middle-income taxpayers from a large tax increase has troubled all tax reform proposals that rely on a consumption tax base, including value-added taxes, the retail sales tax, and the flat tax, all of which have roughly equivalent tax bases and are less progressive than income taxes of the same rate.

There are several ways to address the potentially regressive impact of any consumption tax system. Each involves making trade-offs, along three axes: (1) the targeting of tax relief (making sure that it goes to the people who need it without wasting resources on people who do not); (2) the expense of the relief, which could require higher tax rates overall; and (3) the simplicity of relief (avoiding burdensome and wasteful costs of compliance and administration).[2]

Targeting alone can introduce its own difficulties, as our experience with the earned-income tax credit amply demonstrates. That highly targeted and complex provision has, for example, introduced substantial tax penalties for low- and moderate-income taxpayers who marry as well as work disincentives caused by decline of the credit as wages rise. Targeting also encourages noncompliance as people disguise or mistake facts to claim benefits. Noncompliance, in turn, requires administrative resources and intrusive audits to ferret out wrong-doers. In addition, the more targeted the relief, the more information required; the EITC, for example, demands extensive and detailed information, which is why more then two-thirds of EITC claimants pay someone to help them file their tax returns. On the other hand, as we shall see, overinclusiveness—giving relief to those who don't need it—can be very expensive. In eliminating the filing of tax returns for the vast majority of Americans, I have clearly placed great weight on simplifying our nation's tax system.

In the Competitive Tax Plan two separate but related issues arise. The first is a universal question for all forms of taxes on goods and services, regardless of their form: how to eliminate the regressivity of the tax.[3] Our states and most countries throughout the world have addressed this problem by exempting certain necessities, such as food or clothing. And while I shall argue here that there are better-targeted, simpler, and less economically distortive ways to deal with the problem, no one should be surprised if such exemptions become necessary to make a VAT politically acceptable.

The second issue that occurs under the Competitive Tax is how to replace the benefits of the EITC and child credits that are now paid by the IRS to people who owe no income taxes, benefits that are currently claimed by filing a tax return. As I describe in Chapter 6, these credits are important to low-income workers and their families; together, the EITC and child credit refunds now provide them nearly $60 billion a year in the aggregate. Some new delivery mechanism will be needed. The key is to maintain these benefits without reintroducing the burden of filing annual income tax returns. As I explain below, the Competitive Tax Plan suggests that we avoid this pitfall by providing a "payroll adjustment" or a "smart card" that would replace the EITC and child credit refunds and also redress the burdens of a value-added tax. Before turning to these ideas, however, let's look at how other tax reform proposals have addressed these issues.

Sharing the Burden: How to Handle the Consequences of a Consumption Tax

In one sense, the most straightforward way to introduce a consumption tax might appear to be to personalize it. This technique was employed, for example, in the expenditure tax proposal advanced in the 1990s by Senators Domenici and Nunn.[4] In addition to an 11 percent VAT collected by businesses, the senators proposed taxing individuals at progressive rates on their total annual consumption. Under this personalized consumption tax, a family's annual expenditures on consumption would be computed by adding up all the sources of funds available for consumption and subtracting any amounts saved. Subtracting amounts saved from amounts received in any year will equal that year's consumption, to which progressive rates may then be applied.

The only reason to collect a consumption tax from individuals rather than from businesses is to allow exemptions or to impose progressive tax rates. Senators Nunn and Domenici designed their proposal to include personal exemptions and progressive rates that would increase as annual consumption increased. The progressive rates were included in an effort to avoid the substantial tax reduction for high-income families that would occur under flat-rate consumption tax alternatives. As I noted in Chapter 5, when the details of the Domenici-Nunn proposal were revealed, they demonstrated Congress's inability to impose a personalized tax generally applicable to all Americans without retaining a large number of tax breaks for various types of spending or investments. The proposal also foundered on its unwillingness to tax consumption financed by borrowing or using existing assets. Despite having bipartisan cosponsors, the proposal gained no traction in the Congress. Senator Nunn has since left the Senate, and Senator Domenici has abandoned the effort.

Subsequently, the flat tax and its variations took center stage. As I describe in Chapter 5, the flat tax splits the collection of a (subtraction-method) VAT between businesses and individuals and, unlike standard VATs, collects taxes on wages directly from individuals. The principal advantage of this division of a value-added tax is that it enables Congress to exempt a certain amount of wages from tax and thereby to eliminate some of the regressivity of a standard flat-rate tax on consumption. The amount of the exemption would, of course, vary depending on what distribution of taxes Congress wants, taking into account the rate and any other exclusions, deductions, or tax credits that are allowed. In his version of the flat tax, for example, Congressman Dick Armey would have allowed a personal deduction of about $20,000 for a joint return and an additional deduction of $5,000 for each dependent. (At his proposal's 17 percent flat rate, these deductions would have reduced taxes by $3,400 and $850, respectively.) Armey's flat tax would have allowed no other deductions or tax credits. Thus the individual-level tax would apply to total wages in excess of $30,000 for a married couple with two children. These numbers could, of course, be changed, but the goal of taxing wages directly to individuals, instead of collecting those taxes from businesses as standard VATs do, is to exempt some amount of wages from the tax base. Although the exemption would eliminate the regressivity of a sales tax on the con-

sumption of low-income wage earners, this plan would require workers to give up substantial EITC and child credits in
exchange. A different choice might have been made in this regard. Retaining earned-income tax credits or other tax benefits would complicate the proposal and require a higher tax
rate in order not to lose revenue. That higher rate would apply
to all wages above the exemption level.

Following the lead of the Princeton economist David
Bradford, the president's tax reform panel modified the flat tax
to make its distribution conform more closely to that of current law. It called this tax the Growth and Investment Tax
(GIT). The panel's variation on a subtraction-method VAT
would impose progressive rates of 15, 25, and 30 percent on
wages and would add a flat 15 percent tax rate on dividends, interest, and capital gains.[5] This plan also would retain a modified version of the EITC and child credits as well as various
other tax breaks, including, for example, tax credits for home
mortgage interest and health insurance. The panel pointed to
its priority for economic growth as the reason for taxing only
wages (and not investment income) at progressive rates. Like
the Nunn-Domenici proposal, both the flat tax and the GIT
would require Americans to file tax returns.

As I have indicated, the task of protecting low- and
moderate-income families from a tax increase must take a different tack in consumption tax proposals, such as a common
credit-method VAT or a retail sales tax, that would eliminate
the requirement for individuals to file any tax returns. In virtually all the foreign countries that impose VATs and states
with sales taxes, the typical response to this problem has been
to provide exemptions for purchases of various necessities.
These exemptions often include food (if not consumed in a
restaurant), medicine and medical care, education, rent, and

sometimes a limited amount of clothing. (All VATs contain some of these exemptions, and so would the Competitive Tax. Medical care and education would be exempt, for example.) Some foreign countries also impose higher tax rates on certain "luxury" goods.

Allowing exemptions such as these may make a VAT or sales tax roughly proportional to income, and they are popular politically, even though they require higher VAT rates than a tax without such exclusions. But by providing benefits for various categories of consumption, no matter who is the consumer, such exemptions are not terribly well targeted to their distributional purpose. High-income families enjoy the same exemptions as those with less income. These kinds of exemptions also introduce distortions into people's consumption decisions and thus create new economic inefficiencies. They also often create issues of potential noncompliance depending on how broadly or narrowly the exemptions are drawn. It would be better, therefore, to apply a retail sales tax or VAT to a broad tax base that exempts relatively few goods or services and find another way to provide relief to low- and moderate-income taxpayers. Unfortunately, however, personalizing tax relief means that individuals must provide some government agency with information sufficient to show that they qualify. People must file some form somewhere.

The Fair Tax "Prebate"

Advocates of the so-called FairTax—the national retail sales tax proposal that is supposed to replace corporate and individual income taxes, payroll taxes, and the estate tax with a sales tax—have not tried to maintain anything like the current distribution of taxes. For lower-wage workers, sales tax propo-

nents have not offered any replacement for the EITC, claiming
that the earned-income tax credit should be treated just as any
other government spending program.[6] Thus their plan fails to
match the protections accorded low-income workers under
current law. The middle class would also get squeezed under
the FairTax. These sales tax proponents have, however, proposed what they call a "prebate" to help offset sales taxes on
poverty-level expenditures.

Under this scheme, the government would send every
legal U.S. resident a monthly check equivalent to the amount
of sales tax on a specified amount of goods and services based
on the Department of Health and Human Services' estimated
poverty levels. So even Bill Gates would get a government
check each month. Households with consumption amounts
greater than the tax-free amount covered by the cash grant
would pay a flat rate of tax on any consumption over that
amount. The size of the prebate would depend on the poverty
level, which varies by family size, and the sales tax rate. For example, for a married couple with two children, the 2006 poverty level is $26,400, so with a 30 percent sales tax rate, the fam-
ily would receive $6,072 annually, $506 each month.[7]

Since the prebate depends on government poverty levels,
which vary by family size, some government agency will have
to decide who actually is in each family and make sure that
people are not claiming to be members of more than one family. This could happen either deliberately or inadvertently, for
example, when both divorced parents have joint custody of a
child. The IRS would not investigate these questions, because
the FairTax folks insist that they will get rid of the IRS, but
some agency of the government will have to collect this information before writing the checks.

The aggregate amount of these payments is very large. According to the Treasury Department, it would be $600 billion in 2006; the FairTax folks say "only" $429 billion, but either way it would become one of the biggest entitlement programs in the federal government—along with Social Security, Medicare, and Medicaid. People will quickly become dependent on their monthly checks. "Where's my check from the government?" they'll ask. And there will be pressures to increase the checks a bit for this or that. For example, Congress may well decide to include an additional amount for low-income workers to replace the earned-income tax credit. It may also have difficulty resisting pleas to add amounts for such things as education or child care, once it gets into the business of sending checks to everyone. Any such expansion would, of course, require either a higher sales tax rate to keep revenues constant or offsetting spending cuts elsewhere.

Given the progressivity of the current income tax, fully substituting a revenue-neutral national sales tax necessarily would mean a reduction in the tax share paid by upper-income households relative to the tax share of middle-income households. According to the president's tax reform panel, taking the prebate into account, this national sales tax proposal would, on average, reduce the share of taxes paid by households in the very highest category ($200,000 or more) and in the very lowest income category (cash income of $15,000 or less), but households in other income categories would pay on average a greater share of taxes under the FairTax than under the current tax system. The panel estimated, for example, that a married couple with $39,300 of income, which will pay $5,825 in federal taxes in 2006, would pay 42 percent more, or $7,997 under the retail sales tax with the prebate. According to the panel, a married couple with $66,200 of income would pay an additional $4,791, a tax increase of 36 percent; and a married couple making $99,600 a year would pay an additional $5,789, a 29 percent increase.[8]

The president's panel decided that it would make sense to modify the prebate idea so that the amount families would receive would vary with their incomes. So it developed a related cash grant program which would vary the size of the grant based on the household's income level. It estimated that this grant would cost $780 billion in 2006 and would require a sales tax rate of at least 37 percent (compared with the 34 percent rate it estimated to be necessary to replace only the income tax with the FairTax prebate). This alternative makes the targeting-simplification trade-off clear: a program based on income is more difficult to comply with and to administer than one providing cash grants that vary only with family size.

It is ironic that the self-described advocates of a smaller government, who have invented the FairTax proposal, have put forth a program involving a massive new check-writing scheme from the federal treasury to all Americans. One can readily imagine the possibilities for fraud and abuse, much as conservatives have long complained about such problems in our now shrunken welfare system. We can avoid much of this by relying instead on one part of our tax system that already functions well and with minimal costs of compliance: the payroll tax.

A Consumption Tax, Fair and Practical

The Competitive Tax Plan addresses the potential loss in progressivity from the introduction of a value-added tax in two ways: (1) it retains an income tax for high-income taxpayers, maintaining progressivity at the high end; and (2) it employs a payroll adjustment on the lower end to reduce the tax burden on low- and moderate-income families. This offset would be refundable and would replace entirely the existing EITC and refundable child credits. Nevertheless, protecting low- and moderate-income workers from a tax increase or loss of the EITC without requiring them to file tax returns is probably the most challenging task for the new tax system I am urging here. Allow me to explain.

The current earned-income tax credit supplies important wage subsidies to low-income workers and their children, but it is not working well. The IRS estimated in 2002 that almost one-half of these credits were being claimed by people not entitled to them, at a cost of $10 to $11 billion a year.[9] Even after the IRS audited many low-income workers' tax returns, it recovered just $1.2 billion of this amount, so that somewhere between $8.5 and $10 billion—around 30 percent of the total that year—was paid erroneously. Moreover, the vast majority of workers entitled to the EITC receive their credits as a lump-sum refund after they file their tax returns. Thus workers typically cannot use the EITC to fund their monthly expenditures.

Current law does contain a little-used option for workers to obtain advance payments of the EITC from their employers in their paychecks.[10] Employers fund the costs of the advance payments by reducing the aggregate amount of withheld income and payroll taxes that they pay to the Treasury. The form that the employee must file to claim the advance EITC, the W-5, is quite simple. It asks the employee to supply information only about family status, including marital status and children. The instructions to this form also ask whether the worker expects his or her earned income to exceed the eligibility limits ($33,241 for unmarried parents, $35,241 for married couples with children in 2007) and whether the worker expects her family's investment income to exceed a specified amount ($2,900 in 2007). (Form W-5 and its instructions are reproduced in Appendix 2.) The IRS provides employers with information indicating how much should be added to each worker's paycheck based on how often the worker is paid (weekly, biweekly, or monthly, for example), the worker's annual expected wages, and the worker's number of children.

No one knows why so few workers take advantage of this option today, but one probable reason is that when workers file their income tax returns, they must reconcile the amount of advance payments they have received with the amount they are actually entitled to; if they have received too much, they must repay any overpayment. Many workers no doubt fear finding out that they may owe the IRS a sizable sum when they file their tax returns. Like so many of us, they would rather receive a refund when they file their tax returns. As long as workers can get these funds by filing tax returns, they may remain reluctant to ask their employers for advance EITC payments.

The British also provide benefits for low- and moderate-income workers through their income tax system. Their "working tax credit" is paid in advance through additions to employees' weekly or monthly pay, funded (as are U.S. advance payments) by reductions in aggregate withheld taxes required to be paid by employers.[11] In the United Kingdom, the credit amounts are based on the worker's prior year's income and a reconciliation is done by the U.K. government based annually on information received from employers and payers of investment income. No repayment is required unless the difference exceeds £2,500 (about $5,000). No annual income tax returns are required in the British system, except from the approximately one-third of taxpayers who have substantial amounts of investment income or capital gains, who are self-employed, or who are subject to the highest income tax rate. People who want to claim the British credits must file an initial application with Her Majesty's Revenue and Customs (the British equivalent of our IRS), but after the first year the worker does not need to complete another application. Her Majesty's Revenue and Customs does send each recipient family an annual statement, which asks them to confirm their income and family circumstances.

The Competitive Tax Plan would build on these kinds of advance payment systems—what I call here a "payroll adjustment"—to get EITCs and refundable child credits to low- and moderate-income workers. As I've stated, under my proposed system, income tax withholding from wages would be eliminated for all low- and middle-income workers due to the new $100,000 per family income tax exemption. But Social Security and Medicare payroll taxes would still be withheld from all employees' wages. As a consequence, employers would still report annual wages and withholding to the Social Security Administration (SSA) as they do now on Form W-2. This is necessary for SSA to know what payroll taxes to credit to the workers' accounts for determining their Social Security benefits. This wage information would also be supplied to the IRS, as would information from payers of investment income above certain thresholds, so the IRS can know who has income above the $100,000 threshold and is therefore required to file an annual income tax return. Likewise, self-employed individuals would have to report at least the gross amount they re-

ceive to the IRS and SSA as they do now in determining their
Social Security tax obligations and benefits.

Under the Competitive Tax Plan, a worker would no
longer have to file the income tax withholding Form W-4 that
is now required, but workers who want to claim the EITC and
refundable child credit amounts would have to file a form similar to the current Form W-5 with their employers. Employers
would then increase their workers' take-home pay to provide
the benefits.

Using the payroll tax withholding system to provide
these wage adjustments would allow the elimination of the requirement to file a tax return for these workers without increasing their taxes or eliminating the benefits they currently
receive through the EITC and refunds of child credits. Moreover, payroll adjustments would put money in low-income
workers' pockets when their paychecks are earned rather than
waiting for them to file a year-end tax return.

For several reasons, it is not appropriate that this tax relief and low-wage subsidy correspond precisely to that provided by the current earned-income tax credit. For example,
the EITC now contains serious penalties on marriage, which
should not be replicated in any new system. The president's
panel also recommended eliminating the current restriction
on investment income on the ground that it creates too great a
disincentive for savings by low-wage workers. In addition, depending on how the VAT is structured, relief greater than that
provided by existing earned-income tax credits might be
needed through the payroll adjustment to offset any new tax
burdens created by a consumption tax.

This payroll adjustment should be much simpler than
the current EITC. The EITC would need to be simplified sub-

stantially because the Competitive Tax Plan would no longer use annual tax returns to reconcile payments made during the year with some different "actual" amount. But this is an advantage of my plan, not a disadvantage. Many analysts, including the president's tax reform panel and the national taxpayer advocate, have urged radical simplification of the EITC. The panel's "work credit," which was designed to replace both the current EITC and refundable child credits, could serve as a blueprint for change.[12] (The form the panel suggested to claim this credit is contained in Appendix 2.) Sacrificing some targeting in the interest of simplicity is long overdue.

The British have demonstrated that refundable credits can be delivered through increased paychecks without the need for workers to file annual tax returns. A one-time application may or may not be necessary to demonstrate eligibility, depending on the information requirements of the credit. And workers may be asked to verify their family circumstances from time to time.

Under the Competitive Tax Plan, the government will, as it does now, routinely collect from third parties sufficient financial information to enforce whatever wage or investment income limitations are enacted. And all workers and children will continue to have unique Social Security numbers that can be matched against claims for benefits. Except in the rare instances of massive fraud, enforcement could rely on document matching rather than auditing tax returns and chasing after uncollectible amounts of overpayments, often futilely; future benefits would be adjusted when excessive amounts have been claimed. Resources that the IRS now uses to administer credits—several hundreds of millions of dollars—might be transferred to SSA for these purposes.

Under current law, workers are eligible for some payroll benefit if they earn annual wages of about $35,000 or less.[13] In the aggregate, these adjustments would total about $50 billion to $70 billion a year. If VAT relief were also to be delivered through payroll adjustment, both the aggregate cost and eligible wages would be higher. To avoid an abrupt termination of relief with attendant high marginal tax rates on wages, families with children might be eligible for some tax offset with wages up to about $50,000.[14] But in any event, the payroll adjustment I am suggesting here would be both better-targeted and less expensive than the prebate alternative being urged by sales tax advocates, or the extensive exemptions found in VATs and sales taxes elsewhere.

The exact amounts and parameters of an appropriate payroll adjustment along the lines described here would necessarily depend, of course, on the scope and tax rate of the VAT ultimately enacted. The higher the tax rate, the larger the necessary payroll tax adjustment for low-income workers. The numbers I have used here are intended merely to be illustrative.

Calculating this payroll adjustment should not impose excessive burdens on employers. The IRS would provide tables showing the amounts of the payroll adjustments for employees with different wage levels and numbers of children for different pay periods. If the payroll tax obligations of an employee who claims the benefit are not sufficient to cover the adjustment, the employer would simply reduce the payroll taxes required to be paid over on behalf of other employees to fund the required increases in eligible workers' take-home pay.[15] If these taxes are insufficient to fund the required adjustments—for example, where an employer employs only low-wage workers—the federal government should provide the employer with the necessary funds in a timely fashion. This benefit would be funded from general revenues.[16] (About 2 percentage points of a 14 percent VAT might be dedicated to this purpose: see Appendix 1.)

Although this take-home pay increase for low-income workers is funded from a reduction of the employers' payroll tax deposits, it would not affect individual employees' Social Security eligibility or benefits or the total amounts credited to the Social Security Trust Fund. The current EITC reduces general revenues and affects neither the amounts credited to the Social Security Trust Fund nor the level of individual employees' Social Security benefits. These payroll adjustments would serve merely as a mechanical device for transmitting wage subsidies and perhaps VAT offsets to low-wage workers. Each employee's wages would be reported to the Social Security Administration in full, thereby providing all necessary information to maintain every employee's full eligibility and credits for Social Security benefits.[17]

For retirees, any impact from the new VAT on their cost of living would be largely offset by automatic cost-of-living increases in their monthly Social Security benefits. In addition, retirees with less than $100,000 of income would receive Social Security benefits, private pensions, and IRA distributions free from the income taxes they now pay.

Many other federal programs are also indexed to reflect cost-of-living increases. For cash grant programs directed to low- and moderate-income individuals, which are not indexed for changes in prices, some increases in benefits would probably have to be legislated. Thus, for example, block grants to states, which now fund temporary assistance for needy families, could be increased to offset any additional tax burdens on these families resulting from the enactment of a consumption tax.

A "Smart Card" Alternative

A payroll adjustment is not the only mechanism available for replacing the EITC and refunds of child credits or for mitigating the potential regressive impact of a consumption tax. The digital revolution offers new techniques and technologies for tax administration. I have not lingered in this book over how a VAT should be administered, but there is great potential today to use technologically intensive automated compliance and administration.[18] Indeed, the European Union is currently using digital methods for documenting and reporting VAT transactions. This technology, which will only get better and more pervasive over time, also makes possible new ways to provide tax relief to low- and moderate-income taxpayers. Rather than receiving exemptions for certain categories of necessities, taxpayers could, for example, be issued "smart" cards that would be scanned by retailers to eliminate VAT on either a specified amount of purchases or on purchases of specific goods and services.

Smart cards would provide great flexibility in fashioning VAT relief. VAT relief might, for example, be provided per capita this way based on unique Social Security numbers, or it could be targeted to people based on information the government will automatically receive, such as the person's amount of wages and (substantial) investment income. Each year's smart card VAT tax exemptions might need to be based on the prior year's income to facilitate administration, but this does not seem a major drawback. And smart cards, along with the limited income tax under the Competitive Tax Plan, might be used to eliminate VAT tax cuts for higher-income people. These cards would work like debit cards used throughout the world, or like preferred shopper cards issued by many retailers, including most supermarkets.

Indeed, smart cards might also be used to reduce the potential burdens on employers in providing relief comparable to the current EITC and child credits through payroll tax adjustments. Instead of filing Form W-5 with employers, as described above, employees could file these simple forms with a government agency, probably the Social Security Administration (SSA). SSA could then calculate the employee's payroll adjustment and transfer the amount to the smart card (which would now contain two amounts: one for VAT relief to be used in stores, another for the payroll adjustment to be used by employers). This would eliminate any need for the employer to determine eligibility or amounts of benefits and would also enable employees to get relief without providing any personal information to their employers. As before, the employer would fund payroll adjustments by reducing his aggregate payroll and income tax payments to the government.

If the smart cards look like bank debit cards and are used widely, there will be no stigma from using them. These cards would rely on existing technology that is already in wide commercial use.

Smart cards would allow relief to be granted to unemployed persons as well as to workers. Smart cards could enhance the possibilities for targeting tax relief and eliminate the need for exempting specific categories of spending from the VAT. New data could be added to these cards monthly to offset VAT on current purchases.

Taking advantage of such technological advances does not obviate the need to keep qualifying criteria simple and straightforward. As I have suggested, low-wage workers might be eligible for tax relief based on the amount of their wages, the number of their children, and the absence of a substantial amount of investment income. Efforts to take a host of other criteria into account, as is currently done in determining eligibility for the EITC, would reintroduce the need for more detailed filing of information by low- and moderate-income families and undermine a major reason for freeing them from income tax filing requirements. It would not serve us well to divert the tax return preparation industry from filing tax returns to filing VAT-reduction smart card applications. Simplicity must remain the watchword.

Along the way, liberal populists, who have both pressed for middle-class tax relief and resisted any additional taxes except for the "rich," need to be reminded that the long-term fiscal imbalance due to our aging population and rising health care costs will not simply disappear. Ultimately, the gap will somehow have to be addressed through a combination of spending cuts and tax increases. And although the spending cuts will not show up in the tables distributing the burden of taxes that Congress will inevitably pore over when it considers tax reform, it is spending for Social Security, Medicare, and Medicaid—spending essential to low- and moderate-income Americans—that is at stake. As Franklin Roosevelt proved so well with his Social Security program, combining progressive benefits with a nonprogressive tax can be wise policy indeed.

In sum, there are three techniques that can be used to alleviate concerns about the potential regressivity of a VAT: (1) exempting certain necessities from the tax, (2) instituting a payroll tax adjustment of the sort I have described; or (3) using smart cards to provide tax relief. The last two, either independently or in combination, could also serve to replace

the refundable EITC and child credits that might otherwise
disappear with the repeal of the income tax for most Americans. If we were to take up either the payroll adjustment or the
smart card approach, we could achieve the elasticity of revenue collection, the competitiveness advantages, and the simplification of my Competitive Tax Plan without giving low-
and moderate-income working Americans a substantial tax
hike. That is one priority on which both Democrats and Republicans might agree.

> *Competitive Tax Plan, Point 6:* Prevent a tax in-
> crease on low- and moderate-income Americans
> that could result from a consumption-based tax
> system by introducing payroll adjustments or a
> "smart card."

XI

Bring the States Along

The burden of federal taxation necessarily sets an economic limit to the practical operation of the taxing power of the States, and vice versa.

—Harlan F. Stone, twelfth chief justice of the United States

It is all well and fine to set forth master plans for the reform of our federal tax system in the hopes that a future Congress and president will treat the issue in a serious and responsible fashion and give us a system of revenue collection that addresses today's and tomorrow's problems rather than yesterday's. But in our federalist system, in which many traditional government functions are carried out not by the government in Washington but by states and localities, any durable reform of the federal system should take into account its effects on the tax collections and budgets of states.

While the Competitive Tax Plan I'm proposing for our federal system has certain drawbacks for the states, in that it will pressure them also to eliminate their income taxes for families making less than $100,000, it also has a number of possible benefits for states, especially if they were to adopt similar consumption taxes themselves. Not only do the competing plans not contain such benefits, but some entail real hardships on states. In our system of government, this is no trivial difference.

The States' Diminished Influence

In the fall of 1970, when Richard Nixon was thinking about recommending a value-added tax for the United States, Treasury Secretary David Kennedy hosted a lunch for prominent governors from both political parties. Kennedy planned to ask how the governors might react to the idea of a federal VAT. Just as dessert was being served, Governor Dale Bumpers, an Arkansas Democrat who would later serve as a senator, rose, thanked the secretary for lunch, and preempted the conversation. Bumpers said that the governors were inalterably opposed to a federal VAT, adding that sales taxes in any form were the "exclusive" province of the states and local governments. He urged the federal government to stay out of the consumption tax business altogether and remarked that this was one issue about which all the governors agreed. While it cannot be said for sure that the governors' opposition is the reason that President Nixon never proposed a VAT, it must certainly have given him considerable pause.

Since then, however, governors have lost much of their sway over federal tax policy. Probably the most compelling evidence of that loss came during the machinations leading to the 2001 tax legislation. A number of provisions of that law disadvantaged the states. For example, since many states piggyback their income taxes on federal calculations, without explicit state legislation to deny federal benefits, the states automatically suffered revenue losses due to the tax bill's enactment and enhancement of many federal income tax deductions and credits. But nothing hurt the states like the law's estate-tax provisions. Under prior law, an individual subject to a state-imposed estate tax could subtract up to a certain amount of the state tax from the federal tax liability. Thus when the home state levied an estate tax no larger than the federal credit, as most did, state estate taxes didn't cost taxpayers anything. The 2001 bill, however, immediately lowered the state credit, and repealed it altogether as of 2005— five years before it would repeal the federal estate tax. So in practice, either people would end up having to pay higher estate taxes in the early years of the tax bill's odd phase-in schedule because they could no longer subtract state payments, or the states would have to cut or eliminate their own estate taxes. In essence, federal lawmakers, looking for ways to make their own budget numbers work, had grabbed money from state coffers.

It is not at all clear that the states could have headed off this debacle had they been prepared, but they certainly shot themselves in the foot by not protesting until too late. In 2001 the National Governors Association and the National Council of State Legislatures had decided not to oppose either the repeal of the federal estate tax or the proportional elimination of the state credit, despite the revenue loss it implied for their budgets. Why the silence? For one thing, taking a position on federal tax policy has become hard for state governments and the organizations that represent them in Washington to do. Governors from different political parties can almost never forge a unified position concerning federal tax legislation today. In 2001 Republican governors and legislators wanted to support the tax cuts and the new Republican president. And when George W. Bush came into office, the states, like the federal government, were still enjoying budget surpluses from the economic boom of the 1990s. Many were in the process of enacting their own tax cuts and did not regard the loss of estate tax revenue as significant. Finally, as a political reality, the states knew that there was no point in urging retention of the federal estate tax simply to preserve their own revenues. That argument would not fly. Throughout most of the debate over the 2001 tax cuts, therefore, state governors and legislators remained silent.

The House version of the 2001 tax act would have repealed the state credit in sync with the phase-out of the federal estate tax. Thus a federal tax reduction of 10 percent in a given year would be matched by a 10 percent reduction in the state credit. However, when Senators Chuck Grassley (R-IA) and Max Baucus (D-MT), then the chairman and ranking member of the Senate Finance Committee, respectively, announced their own tax cut plan in May, they proposed repealing the state credit much more rapidly than the federal estate tax. In effect, they planned to deprive the states of nearly $150 billion in revenues over the coming ten-year period in order to help finance more federal tax cuts, while fitting within the Senate's dollar limit for the size of the overall tax cut.[1]

State governors and their representatives in Washington hit the roof. From May 15, the day of the Grassley-Baucus announcement, until the legislation was finalized on May 26, they attempted to scale back repeal of the state credit and restore the House approach. Governors made calls to numerous members of Congress. Florida Governor Jeb Bush, the president's brother, called the White House. The governor was direct with his brother. "While I support the eventual repeal of the estate tax," he said, "shifting the burden merely allows Washington to spend more, while requiring us to spend less." A total of thirty-seven governors, including twenty-one Republicans, signed a letter requesting equal treatment between the states and the federal government for estate-tax changes. In the Senate, Democrat Bob Graham of Florida, whose state stood to lose more than 2.5 percent of its total revenue, took up the states' cause. All to no avail. The final law reduced the state tax credit by 25 percent in 2002, 50 percent in 2003, and 75 percent in 2004 before eliminating it entirely in 2005, even though the federal estate tax was not scheduled for repeal until 2010. The Joint Committee on Taxation's chief of staff Lindy Paull, who had been in the room during the four-man negotiations that produced the final legislation, observed that the state "credit was originally phased out gradually, but when the conference needed money, it was easy money."

Two years later, Governors Paul Patton of Kentucky and Dirk Kempthorne of Idaho, chairmen of the National Governors Association, again wrote to the leaders of the House and Senate tax-writing committees urging them to "ensure equal treatment between states and the federal government with regard to the estate tax changes" of the 2001 act. "Not only have the federal changes imposed difficult conformity choices on states," they added, "but they have also infringed on the authority and flexibility of the states to respond to the needs and priorities of our citizens." They could have saved their paper; nothing changed.

By the time Patton and Kempthorne wrote their letter, most states, like the federal government itself, were confronting serious deficits. A few, including Florida, are prohibited by their constitutions from increasing their own estate or inheritance taxes to make up the lost revenues. Others were reluctant to raise taxes but had little choice. The states had expected to lose some revenue from the 2001 act, but they lost a good bit more than they had anticipated, and much sooner.

The Consequences for the States of Fundamental Reform

Major reform of the federal tax system may pose threats to the states similar to those they faced in the 2001 bill. But none of the plans for tax reform advanced so far—including those that would repeal the income tax completely—take any steps to ease the impact on the states. In fact, most plans, including those that would simply try to reform the federal income tax, are harmful to the states financially. Both the income tax and consumption tax reforms advanced by the president's tax reform panel would, for example, repeal the federal deduction for state and local taxes. So would the flat tax. While repeal or a reduction in that deduction might also happen with the Competitive Tax Plan, it is not an essential element of this reform.

Some plans go even further in disadvantaging the states. By replacing most federal taxes with a national sales tax, the FairTax would not only completely eliminate the federal individual and corporate income taxes that now serve as the starting points for computations of state income taxes, it would also impose a federal sales tax on every purchase state or local governments make. So if a state or locality buys cement to build roads or bricks to build a school, it would have to pay sales tax. And that's not all. While it claims to repeal all other payroll taxes, this so-called FairTax also would impose a 23 percent payroll tax on the wages states and localities (and the federal government) pay to their employees. William Fox and Matthew Murray have estimated that the FairTax would require state and local governments to pay about $346 billion in sales taxes to the federal government, an amount about 50 percent greater than state and local sales tax revenues.[2] The inventors of the so-called FairTax tax claim that they need to impose such taxes in order not to create any advantage for government purchases of goods or services, but, in fact, they are creating a significant incentive for governments to contract out their functions to private enterprises. Making government purchases and government workers subject to tax is how the FairTax folks are able to claim that they can accomplish their goals with "only" a 30% tax rate. If the states and localities were not taxed, a higher rate would be necessary. But where is the money that the states and localities would be required to pay the federal government in sales taxes going to come from?

It would have to come from higher state and local taxes or reduced state and local spending. Somebody is going to have to pay. Ironically, the money might come from state income taxes, which would undermine completely the goal of the FairTax to free individuals and corporations from having to deal with income taxes at all. When the president's tax reform panel looked at the FairTax suggestion, it concluded that in our federal system it would be inappropriate for the federal government to tax state and local governments, and it insisted that the national sales tax rate would have to be higher than the FairTax advocates claim. A federal sales tax on state and local purchases of goods and services is not just inappropriate, it is constitutionally questionable.

Advantages of the Competitive Tax Plan

Although my tax reform plan would pose some challenges for state and local governments, it also would create an important opportunity. Richard Ainsworth has detailed how a federal VAT that relies on current digital technologies, such as those used in connection with European VATs, would create a unique opportunity for the states to modernize and simplify their taxes on consumption.[3] State sales taxes and a federal value added tax could readily coexist. But conformity, or at least coordination, of these taxes would greatly ease the burdens of compliance for businesses and reduce administrative costs for tax collectors. Currently there are 7,579 state and local sales tax jurisdictions in the United States with different tax bases and different legal rules for the activities in the jurisdiction that are subject to tax. Businesses face large and wasteful compliance costs—and sometimes multiple taxes on the same transactions—due to the interstate and intrastate variations. Economists frequently describe our state sales tax regime as a "nutty" system that often imposes invisible and undesirable taxes on businesses. To date, however, the efforts of businesses and economists to get the states to rationalize, standardize, and harmonize these taxes have had only limited success. A federal VAT that applies modern computer technology would create an electronic national database of transactions and would, in Ainsworth's words, "allow state and local governments to seamlessly 'piggyback' the federal tax" without limiting state or local governments' options about their own tax bases or rates, or even about whether their taxes are in the form of retail sales or value-added taxes.[4] If the federal government were to use a digital smart card for providing tax relief to low- and moderate-income taxpayers, states might also piggyback on that technology and methodology to provide similar tax relief if they wished.

Compliance costs might be reduced even further if the states and localities were to follow the federal government's lead and adopt VATs along the lines of the federal tax. This is what happened in Canada, where some of the provinces replaced their retail sales taxes with value-added taxes after adoption of a federal VAT (called a goods and services tax, or GST). Germany and Austria go even further by collecting the VAT at the federal level and sharing its revenue with their states.

Substituting value-added taxes for state sales taxes has additional advantages. State sales taxes are becoming more difficult to collect as Internet retail sales increase. In addition, states now often impose multiple sales taxes on the same goods or services through a cascading of sales taxes that credit-method value-added taxes avoid. Any duplication of state and federal tax-collection processes should be avoided to the extent possible. Indeed, the expertise of state sales tax administrators suggests that there may be a substantial role at the state level for VAT administration, which could ease demands on the IRS.

Given the economic and compliance benefits of federal-state conformity of VAT tax bases, the federal government might supply financial incentives for state conformity when it institutes a federal consumption tax. Because the consumption tax base under the federal VAT I am proposing here would amount to 50 percent to 60 percent of GDP, compared with the median state sales tax, which taxes consumption equal to only 36 percent of GDP, the broader federal consumption tax base could produce greater revenues for most states without increasing their tax rates. This would enable the states to compensate for the inevitable loss of income tax revenues for families with incomes below the $100,000 threshold under my plan (see Table 11.1).

Nearly all states impose an income tax, and although many state income taxes use federal income tax computations as a starting point, filing state income tax returns is a major source of compliance costs and complexity for many Americans. The 150 million Americans who would be freed from filing federal income tax returns under the plan I am advancing here would be substantially less blessed if they still had to file state income tax returns. Bringing the states into conformity with the new federal income tax should be a major tax reform goal and would be a genuine challenge, given the states' taste for fiscal autonomy.

Eliminating the federal income tax for most Americans under the Competitive Tax Plan would create substantial political pressures for the states to do the same. As Table 11.1 shows, states could largely finance their own $100,000 income tax exemption by adopting the substantially larger federal consumption tax base or by increasing excise tax rates on products such as gasoline, alcohol, or tobacco, or through other sources. The federal government should give the states incentives to make changes that conform to the new federal system. For example, the federal government might speed the process of state conformity to the federal system by agreeing to collect and remit the states' remaining income taxes if they conform to the federal income tax. This would permit states to get out of the business of collecting income taxes altogether. This carrot might be accompanied by the stick of allowing federal deductions for state income taxes only for those state income taxes that conform to the federal tax.

Thus with the potential reduction of compliance and administrative costs, the possible simplification of the states' own tax systems, and the potential broadening of states' consumption tax bases, the switch to the Competitive Tax could have substantial benefits, rather than federally imposed hardships, for the states. But the states would have to go along.

Table 11.1
State Tax Bases and Projected Bases Under VAT

	2003 Sales Tax Base (billions of dollars)	VAT Base[a] (billions of dollars)	Ratio (VAT base/sales tax base)	2003 Sales Tax Rate (%)	Change in Revenues Due to VAT (billions of dollars)	2003 Income Tax Revenues (billions of dollars)	Change in Revenues as % of Income Tax Revenues
United States	3501.236	6172.379	1.8	5.94[b]	158.666	186.195	85.21
Alabama	47.365	75.096	1.6	7.95	2.205	2.076	106.21
Alaska	negligible	17.810	—	1.05	0.187	0.000	—
Arizona	76.570	103.151	1.3	7.65	2.033	2.202	92.34
Arkansas	38.081	42.968	1.1	7.95	0.389	1.549	25.08
California	414.984	820.051	2.0	7.95	32.203	34.358	93.73
Colorado	63.214	106.805	1.7	6.15	2.681	3.251	82.47
Connecticut	51.093	98.527	1.9	6.00	2.846	3.778	75.34
Delaware	0.000	28.061	—	—	—	0.724	—
Florida	251.305	311.941	1.2	6.70	4.063	0.000	66.53
Georgia	118.474	182.366	1.5	6.80	4.345	6.530	66.53
Hawaii	42.692	26.536	0.6	4.00	(0.646)	1.068	(60.51)
Idaho	16.840	23.009	1.4	6.10	0.376	0.873	43.11
Illinois	105.817	287.202	2.7	7.50	13.604	7.230	188.15
Indiana	70.171	122.102	1.7	6.00	3.116	3.694	84.36
Iowa	34.538	58.653	1.7	6.60	1.592	1.827	87.13
Kansas	35.633	53.285	1.5	6.75	1.191	1.815	65.63
Kentucky	47.002	73.217	1.6	6.00	1.573	2.792	56.34
Louisiana	69.417	79.187	1.1	8.55	0.835	1.903	43.89
Maine	17.150	23.311	1.4	5.00	0.308	1.101	27.98
Maryland	69.200	120.732	1.7	5.00	2.577	4.964	51.91
Massachusetts	74.161	170.592	2.3	5.00	4.822	8.259	58.38
Michigan	127.796	208.804	1.6	6.00	4.860	5.809	83.67

Minnesota	75.448	119.718	1.6	6.70	2.966	5.525	53.69
Mississippi	35.143	41.212	1.2	7.00	0.425	1.035	41.07
Missouri	66.741	111.358	1.7	6.80	3.034	3.580	84.75
Montana	0.000	14.361	—	—	—	0.552	—
Nebraska	25.828	36.936	1.4	6.30	0.700	1.147	61.02
Nevada	33.728	49.219	1.5	7.35	1.139	0.000	—
New Hampshire	0.000	27.827	—	—	—	0.052	—
New Jersey	98.934	226.601	2.3	5.95	7.596	6.748	112.57
New Mexico	29.822	32.065	1.1	6.50	0.146	0.962	15.15
New York	212.698	470.233	2.2	8.45	21.762	23.312	93.35
North Carolina	88.715	179.090	2.0	7.05	6.371	7.233	88.09
North Dakota	8.599	11.990	1.4	5.50	0.186	0.203	91.68
Ohio	135.230	230.564	1.7	7.15	6.816	8.367	81.46
Oklahoma	33.411	56.971	1.7	8.10	1.908	2.234	85.43
Oregon	0.000	68.603	—	—	—	4.103	—
Pennsylvania	126.019	256.107	2.0	6.25	8.130	6.765	120.19
Rhode Island	10.955	22.309	2.0	7.00	0.795	0.838	94.82
South Carolina	51.526	72.734	1.4	5.60	1.188	2.379	49.93
South Dakota	12.081	15.031	1.2	5.25	0.155	0.000	—
Tennessee	77.352	113.618	1.5	9.40	3.409	0.119	2869.00
Texas	278.547	462.319	1.7	7.90	14.518	0.000	—
Utah	31.307	43.347	1.4	6.45	0.777	1.606	48.35
Vermont	6.338	11.736	1.9	6.00	0.324	0.422	76.78
Virginia	94.456	172.512	1.8	5.00	3.903	7.056	55.31
Washington	92.403	139.245	1.5	8.35	3.911	0.000	—
West Virginia	18.988	27.034	1.4	6.00	0.483	1.047	46.10
Wisconsin	74.829	113.838	1.5	5.40	2.106	5.109	41.23
Wyoming	10.631	12.399	1.2	5.15	0.091	0.000	—

[a] VAT Base is assumed to be 60% of GDP with a compliance rate of 90%.

[b] Average.

Sources: William F. Fox and Matthew N. Murray, "A National Retail Sales Tax: Consequences for the States," State Tax Notes 37 (July 25, 2005): 287; Bureau of Economic Analysis data.

The Road Ahead

As I have discussed, demographic pressures, along with rising health care costs, portend great challenges for the budgets of both federal and state budgets in the years ahead. Today, along with providing health insurance coverage for the poor, Medicaid pays for most of the governmental assistance for the costs of long-term care for the people who need it. Medicaid, for example, provides the safety net of last resort for more than 70 percent of nursing home residents, but for only those elderly who have almost exhausted their assets. The current system condemns many elderly Americans with long-term care needs to finish their lives in or near poverty. And unlike Medicare, which is purely a federal program, Medicaid is financed jointly by the states and the federal government.

The general aging of the population and longer life expectancies will increase the need and expenditures for long-term care, including residence in skilled nursing facilities, community-based adult day care, and medical and personal assistance provided to the elderly in their homes. Over the next fifty years long-term care will nearly double as a share of GDP. Average nursing home costs of more than $50,000 a year already devastate middle-class incomes and plague many retirees with the fear that their long-term care needs will cost them everything that they accumulated during their working lives. There is a variety of proposals for reforming our system—if it can be called that—for financing long-term care, ranging from incentives or mandates for greater private insurance coverage to a new contributory federal system of long-term care insurance. My purpose here is not to argue for any one of these ideas or to evaluate their strengths and weaknesses, but only to suggest that a federal solution to the long-term care problem could provide enormous relief to state budgets in the years ahead. And this is a national problem, not a local one, so a federal solution seems appropriate. If tax reform is considered in the so-called "grand bargain" context, where Social Security, Medicare, and Medicaid taxes and benefits are also up for grabs, federalizing government assistance for the costs of long-term care will surely be one of the options under consideration. And even if these programs and tax reform are taken up by Congress separately, shifting the costs of assistance for long-term care to the federal government will be on the table. Nothing would alleviate more effectively the forthcoming pressures on state budgets—and on their tax systems.

Any federal tax reform will necessarily have to consider its potential impact on state and local finances. Some plans, like the FairTax, would be disastrous for the states. All will require some adjustments at the state level. The size and scope of those adjustments will depend on the details of the tax reform and the differing financial needs of the states. By repealing the federal income tax for most Americans, the plan I am offering here will undoubtedly pressure the states to follow, reducing one of their revenue sources. But the federal VAT I am also recommending will create a great opportunity for offsetting much, if not all, of that revenue loss and for improving the states'—and the nation's—tax systems. Bringing the states along will require care and creativity by Congress and an open mind by the nation's governors and mayors. But we should not reprise the 1970s and allow the recalcitrance or presumed prerogatives of the states to become a roadblock to reform.

Competitive Tax Plan, Point 7: Encourage states to adopt a similar replacement of the income tax with a consumption tax and then conform or at least co-ordinate their methods of collection with the federal government, including harmonizing their tax base with the federal base, simplifying state tax collection, and increasing compliance.

XII
The Plan in Brief

If enacted, Graetz's proposals would make the U.S. one of the
most competitive countries in the world for human capital,
investment and foreign direct investment. . . . The overall tax
burden of the U.S. would not change, staying, as it is this year,
the third lowest in the OECD.

—*"The Tax World Gets Flat and Happy,"* Forbes Global

I n the preceding chapters I have described the situation in which we find ourselves when we take a close look at how our government funds itself. We have seen the failings of the current system and the broken politics that have led to them. And I have offered a reasonable, fiscally responsible, equitable, and internationally competitive plan for fundamentally reforming the tax code. Unlike some other ideas that have become prominent in our political debate, the Competitive Tax Plan does not undermine our nation's long-standing and fundamental commitment to justice—to using progressive taxes as a fair way to alleviate our great inequalities of income and wealth. Nor does it, on the other hand, simply tinker once again within the interstices of our broken income tax as a way of responding to wasteful complexities and economic shortcomings.

The plan centers on eliminating the income tax for most Americans. As discussed in Chapter 6, our current federal income tax is far too complex, containing more than seven hundred provisions affecting individuals and more than fifteen hundred affecting businesses. The code itself and its accompanying regulations total more than 9.4 million words. People spend $150 billion worth of time and money each year complying with it. The IRS, having to administer many policies and programs, has about as much trouble doing its job as taxpayers have doing the job the tax law imposes upon them. Second, there is what I have called the "chicken soup" problem: for any social problem—including education, child care affordability, health insurance coverage, retirement security, or the financing of long-term care— an income tax deduction or credit is supposed to be the answer. That tack has failed us. We have the tax breaks, but the problems remain unsolved. Third, we confront increasing cynicism; the income tax's failings discourage individuals from paying taxes they legally owe. Young people, especially, say that they feel little compunction about dishonestly completing tax forms. Fourth, the growth of the alternative minimum tax (AMT) is an enormous problem: if left unchanged, the AMT will soon be imposed on more than thirty million Americans who will have to calculate their income taxes twice. And finally, there is the challenge of globalization: the internationalization of the economy makes it virtually impossible for the income tax alone to raise the revenue we need—and will need in the future—fairly and without stymieing economic growth.

Given all this, the most reasonable solution is to eliminate for most Americans this broken method of revenue collection and replace the lost revenue with a broad-based tax on consumption. In doing so, we would return the income tax to its pre–World War II status—a low-rate tax on a relatively thin slice of higher-income Americans. A value-added tax imposed at a rate of 10 to 14 percent could finance a $100,000 family exemption from income tax, eliminating 150 million Americans from the income tax rolls and allowing a simpler income tax at a 20 to 25 percent rate to be applied to incomes over $100,000. In combination, these two taxes would produce revenues roughly equivalent to the current income tax (see Appendix 1). This proposal, unlike the flat tax, the FairTax, and other such proposals, would not dramatically shift the tax burden away from high-income families to middle- and lower-income families. Also, rather than relying on tax structures like the flat tax and progressive consumption taxes, which were invented in ivory towers and are untested in today's economy, this plan combines two of the world's most common tax mechanisms, while exploiting our nation's substantial advantages as a low-tax country.

As I've argued, such a proposal, while both feasible and meritorious standing alone, is best considered and understood in the context of a broader reevaluation of other elements of our tax system. A consumption tax replacing most of the income tax is the heart of the Competitive Tax Plan, but it is not its only element.

Here, then, in brief, is what I propose:

1. Enact a Value-Added Tax

The VAT would work like a national sales tax, but instead of depending only on retailers to collect the tax, a VAT is collected piecemeal at all stages of production, so it is much more difficult to evade. This is a common tax used by 141 countries on six continents. Its rate would be between 10 and 14 percent.

Businesses with gross receipts of less than $100,000 annually (which account for nearly 65 percent of the country's twenty-five million businesses) would be exempt from collecting VAT or filing returns.[1] Such an exemption would reduce the number of VAT returns to about nine million.[2] An exemption for small businesses would also relieve them from the costs of compliance and the tax collector from chasing after small amounts of tax. European VATs tend to impose compliance costs about one-fifth to one-third as large as our income tax.[3]

In order to keep the tax rate as low as possible, the VAT base should be broad, covering nearly all goods and services. A broad VAT base with a single tax rate would minimize its economic distortions, and limiting exemptions would simplify compliance and administration. Nevertheless, expenditures on education, religion, most health care, rents, and purchase of existing housing, for example, would be exempt from the consumption tax, as would most expenditures for noncommercial government services.

Many countries that have enacted value-added taxes do not require retailers to state separately the amount of tax imposed on the goods they sell; the tax is buried in the price of products. But this weakness is easily cured if Congress simply requires that the total amount of tax be separately stated whenever goods or services are sold. That way people will know how much tax they are paying.

The key point is this: the consumption tax would be collected only from businesses, and the tax would be imposed on a broad base of goods and services at a level sufficient to free the vast majority of Americans both from any income tax liability and from any requirement to file tax returns (see Chapter 5).

2. Eliminate the Income Tax for Most Americans

All income under $100,000 (for married couples, $50,000 for singles) would be exempt from the income tax, and this cutoff would indexed for inflation. This would eliminate more than 100 million tax returns and free more than 150 million Americans from having to file them. A low rate of tax, say, 20 to 25 percent, would be imposed on the taxable income of high-income individuals. The income tax that would remain for high-income taxpayers could be simplified substantially. The marriage penalties of the existing income tax should be eliminated. Most of the special income tax credits and allowances that now crowd the tax code and complicate tax forms would be repealed. But the deductions for charitable contributions and large medical expenses would be retained. The deduction for home mortgage interest could either be retained in its current form or modified. Congress would have to decide whether to keep, eliminate, or cut back on deductions for state and local taxes. Until better alternative policies are forged, employers would continue to have payroll and income tax incentives to provide their employees retirement savings plans and health insurance. Congress could tax capital gains at the standard rate of 20 to 25 percent or maintain a lower rate, such as the current 15 percent (see chapter 6). Likewise, Congress could retain the current 15 percent rate on dividends, tax dividends at the regular rate, or eliminate dividend taxes completely on income for which corporate taxes have been paid (see Chapter 7).

In order to eliminate the income tax from people's lives quickly upon enactment, an income tax amnesty might allow people to settle their past income tax obligations without the penalties that would normally apply. This could facilitate the transition to the new system.

3. Lower the Corporate Income Tax Rate

The corporate income tax rate would be lowered to 15 or 20 percent, making the United States a far more attractive country in which to do business and making our economy more globally competitive. In addition, the new law should require that book and tax accounting be more closely aligned in order to solve, at last, the tax shelter problem that has plagued the corporate income tax for years. If Congress wants to maintain certain book-tax differences—such as for depreciation, research and development expenses, and foreign income and taxes, for example—these differences should be made explicit. The corporate alternative minimum tax would be repealed. If the corporate and individual rate were closely enough aligned, or if all small businesses were simply taxed at the new lower corporate rate, the income of small corporations could be taxed on a flow-through basis, thereby taxing their income directly to their owners. This would allow small-business income to qualify for the $100,000 income tax exemption, simplifying the taxation of small businesses. The corporate income tax would then apply only to large publicly held companies (see Chapter 7).

4. Retain the Estate and Gift Taxes

Under this plan, in order not to forgo needed revenues and to retain the most steeply progressive element of our tax system, estate and gift taxes would be retained, though exemptions would be raised and farmers and small businesses would be protected. As an alternative, tax could be imposed on recipients of large inheritances (see Chapter 9).

5. Introduce a Payroll Adjustment or "Smart Cards" to Protect Low- and Moderate-Income Workers

To avoid what would otherwise be the regressive impact of imposing a broad-based consumption tax, the Competitive Tax Plan would replace the EITC and refundable child credits with a payroll adjustment or a "smart card" (as described in Chapter 10). Providing low- and middle-income workers benefits this way would allow tax returns to be eliminated for these workers without generally increasing their taxes or eliminating the EITC wage subsidy.[4] Moreover, payroll adjustments or smart cards would put money in low-income workers' pockets when their paychecks are earned rather than through a lump-sum tax refund after year's end, as the EITC now does.

6. Create Incentives for States to Adopt a Similar Model

By offering to assist in the process of state tax collection, and perhaps through other incentives, the federal government could encourage states to adopt a similar replacement of the income tax with a consumption tax and then conform or at

least coordinate their methods of collection with the federal
government, including harmonizing their tax base with the
federal base, simplifying state tax collection, and increasing
compliance (see Chapter 11.)

Why the Major Alternatives
for Fundamental Reform Fail

I have used six straightforward criteria in fashioning the tax reform plan I am advocating here. First, our tax system must be
able to produce the revenue necessary to fund our government
fairly and without limiting our nation's economic potential.
Second, given the disparities of income and wealth in our
country, tax reform should not shift the tax burden away from
our wealthiest citizens down the income scale. Third, a reformed tax system should be much simpler and less costly to
comply with than the one we now have; it should free as many
Americans as is practical from having to file income tax returns, given the other criteria. Fourth, a new tax system should
be designed to halt the madness of relying on tax breaks as the
solution to the nation's social and economic problems. Fifth,
our new tax system should be more favorable to savings, investments, and economic growth than the one we now have.
Finally, a new tax system should improve the international
competitiveness of the American economy and U.S. companies and workers, and it also should fit well with the international economy and our international commitments. Other
prominent tax reform proposals fail to meet these criteria.

Flat tax advocates trumpet their claim that they would
shrink the individual tax return to fit on a postcard. But given
Congress's propensity for enacting tax breaks to encourage
particular expenditures or activities, it is foolish to believe that

a flat tax—which would require all wage earners to file tax returns—would stay flat or simple for very long. The political allure of giving Americans tax breaks for specific expenditures or investments is catnip to both Congress and the White House. Form 1040 itself could once have fit on a postcard.

Nor does the idea of taxing only people's wages seem likely to sit well with the American public over time. The belief that it is unfair to tax only wages and not income from wealth is what led this country to add the Sixteenth Amendment to our Constitution. And this is what prompted the president's panel in 2006 to graft a tax on investment income onto its consumption tax variation (the Growth and Investment Tax). And, as the president's panel as well as the children in the classroom recognize, Americans still believe in progressive tax rates; a flat rate applicable to all is not likely to be enacted, much less remain stable.

In today's global economy, perhaps the greatest political weakness of the flat tax is its treatment of exports and imports—taxing exports, while exempting imports. This makes it anathema to American businesses. Notwithstanding economists' widespread agreement that exchange-rate adjustments will operate to offset this disadvantage, American producers will not stand for a consumption-based tax reform that taxes U.S. production, no matter where the goods are consumed, but fails to tax foreign production of goods consumed in the United States. This treatment of international commerce—which is required for the flat tax proposal under the General Agreement on Trade and Tariffs (GATT)—is enough alone to doom the flat tax politically.

The president's tax reform panel understood this weakness and its problems for tax compliance, so it proposed the opposite treatment, taxing imports and exempting exports.

But it also recognized that achieving that result under its consumption tax proposal would require renegotiation of all of
this nation's income tax treaties and its major trade treaties—
an impossible hurdle.

Proponents of replacing the income tax (including the
corporate income tax, along with the payroll and estate taxes)
with a national sales tax have labeled their proposal the Fair-
Tax and are spending millions of dollars to build grassroots
support. Quite a few congressional Republicans have cospon-
sored legislation endorsing this idea. But there is no reason to
believe that any government can collect a retail sales tax at the
high rates necessary to replace the income tax completely.
Only six countries have ever adopted retail sales taxes at rates
of 10 percent or more; all have abandoned the retail sales tax in
favor of a VAT.[5] The FairTax plan suggests a 30 percent rate—
exceptionally high for a sales tax, and yet according to every
government estimate, too low to replace even the corporate
and individual income taxes. The temptations for retailers to
pocket the money would be just too great. This is why 141 nations have instead adopted value-added taxes, which are similar to sales taxes economically but are collected at all stages of
production.

Like the flat tax, the national sales tax plan would undermine both private employer–based pensions and health insurance. By eliminating any incentives for either, it would threaten
employers' provision of both, which is how most families get
their retirement savings (other than Social Security) and their
health insurance coverage. Both of these plans would also eliminate any incentives for charitable contributions.

But despite the serious shortcomings of the FairTax, we
should not underestimate the political forces that are pushing
it. They resemble the forces that started the effort to repeal the

estate tax in the early 1990s. We now know that the failure to take such a political movement seriously can be costly to its opponents.[6]

Since all reporting of sales taxes would be done by retail businesses and no individual returns would be required, a national sales tax would offer genuine simplification for American families. The rub, however, is that complete replacement of the income tax with a national sales tax would provide a large tax reduction for the country's wealthiest people. Like the flat tax, a national sales tax that completely replaces the income tax would unacceptably shift the tax burden away from those with the greatest ability to pay to families with less income. This plan is simply not fair. But there is no truth-in-labeling requirement in politics.

Given the shortcomings of these (mostly Republican) alternatives to the income tax, we should not be surprised that many Democrats have urged that we simply reform the existing income tax. As we have seen, this was also one of the alternatives recommended by President Bush's tax reform panel in its report. While the details of the proposals vary, the basic idea is straightforward: reprise the 1986 tax reform by eliminating or trimming a long list of income exclusions, deductions, or credits and reduce income tax rates for everyone. The difficulty, as the president's panel learned, is that eliminating the AMT without losing substantial amounts of revenue requires goring many sacred cows, such as employer-provided health insurance, home mortgage interest, and other popular itemized deductions. More important, we have seen how easily an income tax reform can unravel. In the twenty years since the 1986 tax reform, Congress has enacted countless income tax breaks and raised tax rates.[7] Simply trying to fix the income tax is like reaching for a box of Band-aids to cure a cancer.

The Key Advantages of the Competitive Tax Plan

The plan I have offered is fair. It is simple for the average American to understand and comply with. It is fiscally sound. It is designed to replicate existing federal government revenues in the short term and to put in place a tax system flexible enough to permit future tax increases without crippling the economy, should we need more resources down the road.

The plan takes advantage of our status as a low-tax country, something our current income tax fails to do. It would make the United States similar to the average of OECD countries in taxing consumption relative to GDP and in terms of tax rates on consumption (see Figure 12.1).

Our income tax, however, would be very much smaller—and could be very much simpler—than what people generally face abroad (see Figure 12.2).

This new tax system would have a number of important advantages:

- It would be far more favorable for savings and economic growth. Most Americans would owe no tax on their savings, and taxes on savings and investment would be lower for everyone. We would also maintain incentives for employers to provide both health insurance and retirement savings plans for their employees until we can agree on a better system. The United States would be an extremely attractive place for business investments by both U.S. citizens and foreigners. This plan would stimulate economic growth and create additional jobs for American workers, producing substantial long-term benefits for the American economy.

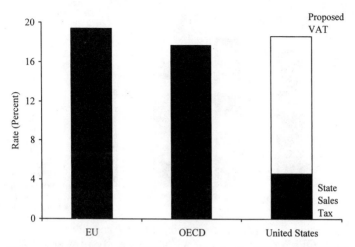

Figure 12.1. Consumption (VAT) tax rates in the EU, among OECD members, and in the United States, 2000 (unweighted rate averages). *Source:* OECD, Consumption Tax Trends, 2001, Table 3.5; U.S. computations based on data from http://salestaxinstitute.com.

- Unlike the current income tax, the plan would eliminate all marriage penalties, something that Congress has so far been unable to do under the current income tax.
- The United States would enjoy a substantial economic leg up in the world economy, while using a combination of taxes common throughout the world. Thus this system would facilitate international coordination and fit well within existing international tax and trade agreements.
- Because it retains the corporate income tax (at a much lower rate) and a dramatically shrunken individual income tax, the plan avoids the difficult issues of transi-

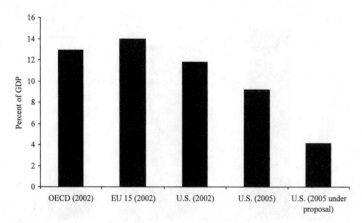

Figure 12.2. Income tax revenue as a percentage of GDP.
Note: OECD reports U.S. revenue for 2003 as 10.9 percent of GDP.
Source: OECD, Revenue Statistics, 2004, release 1; U.S. figures for
2005 are author's estimates.

tion (involving the treatment of unrecovered tax basis)
to an entirely new system that have haunted other proposals to move away from reliance on the income tax.

- By eliminating 100 million tax returns a year, the plan
would drastically reduce compliance costs and head-
aches for the American people. It would also ease the
IRS workload and thus allow it to perform its job far
better (see Figure 6.4). No politician would ever urge
bringing all these people back into the income tax, absent some genuine catastrophe. After all, it took World
War II to persuade Congress originally to extend the
income tax to the masses.

- By diminishing dramatically the political advantages of
income tax incentives, the plan would challenge our

political leaders to produce policies that work and provide increased stability over the long haul, creating more
predictability for both individuals and businesses.

On this final point it is worth adding that the greatest
threat to the stability under my plan, and one of the main criticisms that tax-cut fundamentalists and liberal populists are
likely to lodge against it, is that value-added tax rates might rise
over time. And this might happen to some extent, even though
the VAT has not been the "money machine" throughout the
world that some have claimed.[8] Never-ending VAT rate increases, however, are far less likely with this proposal—where
large amounts of VAT revenue are being used to free most
Americans from the income tax—than with proposals simply
to enact a low-rate VAT to fund Medicare or Medicaid for our
aging population. Starting, as I have proposed here, with a 10 to
14 percent VAT to fund income tax relief greatly reduces the
opportunities for the federal government to use the VAT as a
pocketbook for additional spending. I have urged that we enact
a VAT rate high enough (given existing state sales taxes) to leave
only a relatively limited scope for future increases.

By using the money that a 10 to 14 percent VAT produces
to eliminate income taxation for the vast majority of Americans, while protecting low- and moderate-income families
from a tax increase, the structure of the Competitive Tax Plan
will ensure that we remain a relatively low-tax country. The
VAT rate may go up a bit if needed—as could income tax rates
today—but it would take a political and economic tsunami to
lower substantially the new income tax threshold.

Some have also expressed concern that with an income
tax limited to higher-income taxpayers the risk of future in-

come tax rate increases grows. But this risk is fully present under the income tax today: more than half of its revenue comes from the 5 percent of returns with the highest income, nearly two-thirds from the top 10 percent.[9] And capital mobility in today's global economy offers genuine protection against substantial individual and corporate income tax rate increases. The trend around the world is toward lower, not higher, income tax rates. When corporate and individual income tax rates on capital income are high, that income tends to move to a jurisdiction with lower rates. Often, the capital—and its accompanying jobs—move. Sometimes only the revenue is lost through tax planning. In today's highly competitive global economy, high income tax rates are counterproductive.[10]

In 2005 *Forbes* magazine evaluated a version of my Competitive Tax Plan, assuming a 25 percent rate for both the individual and corporate income taxes. It concluded that the plan would make the United States the most attractive location for savings and investment in the world and would make the U.S. "tax misery index" lower than forty-four of the top fifty industrialized countries in the world.[11] With this Competitive Tax Plan, the American people may look forward confidently to a simple, fair, pro-growth tax system for the twenty-first century.

In an interview with *Tax Analysts* in 2006, former Senator John Breaux, cochairman of the president's tax reform panel, was asked what about this plan appealed to him. Breaux responded: "I thought that it simplified the system; it would have lowered the rates dramatically, but still allow the rates . . . to include some type of progressivity, whereas strictly a VAT tax, like the 'flat tax,' would have been difficult to make reasonably progressive. So if you combine a value-added tax with a much lower income tax, you can have some progressivity and yet have a tax that functions and operates in a more simplified fashion."

The Competitive Tax Plan returns the U.S. income tax to its original and proper place as a tax on higher-income individuals, and it employs a time-tested form of tax collection, the value-added tax, to put in place a stable system of funding our government. In the process, it can help our economy and dramatically reduce the cost of compliance and enforcement. While there is no one silver bullet when it comes to a thing as complex as federal tax policy, the plan I've put forward here comes far closer to the mark than the alternatives. The time for tinkering at the edges of the problem has passed. We owe it to ourselves and to future generations to put our house in order. To fix it, and to get the fix right.

Appendix 1: Revenues

In a 2002 essay in the *Yale Law Journal* describing a tax reform idea that has here become the Competitive Tax Plan, I included a series of ten-year revenue tables demonstrating the fiscal soundness of this plan: enact a 10 to 14 percent VAT to eliminate the income tax for families with $100,000 or less of income, substantially lower tax rates of both the remaining individual income and the corporate (or business) income taxes, replace the EITC and refundable child credits, and provide relief to offset the potential regressivity of the VAT.[1] These estimates were prepared for a seminar delivered to the U.S. Treasury Office of Tax Policy in August 2002, and that office assisted in the development of those estimates, which I shall not reproduce here.

Analyses by the Treasury Department and the Joint Committee on Taxation have criticized other plans like the FairTax and Congressman Armey's flat tax as being unrealistic in their revenue projections. No such criticism has been leveled at my plan. It is a practical and realistic alternative to our existing system.

I have argued in this book for a new *structure* for taxation in the United States. I have not drafted a tax code ready for enactment; Congress and a president must do that. So many important details of the Competitive Tax Plan, including the precise tax bases of both the VAT and the corporate and individual income taxes and their rates, will need to be worked out in the political process. Nevertheless, I shall share here my best estimates about some of the general revenue parameters. All of the estimates that follow have been calculated at 2008 levels (and in 2008 dollars):

1. The VAT

A 10 percent VAT should raise somewhere between $735 billion and $850 billion annually, depending on what goods and services are subject to tax.[2] Each additional percentage point would produce an additional $70–85 billion per year. This assumes a reasonably broad-based VAT with relatively few exceptions. If exceptions for more "necessities" were enacted, the VAT revenue would be lower, but so would the cost of the VAT regressivity offsets discussed below.

2. The Individual Income Tax

Individual income tax relief would cost about $575 billion to $650 billion annually. This assumes that the income tax will apply only to married couples with more than $100,000 of income ($50,000 for singles), indexed for inflation. If the current AMT tax base were used, for example, with these exemptions and a 25 percent rate while maintaining the existing 15 percent rates for dividends and capital gains, the revenue lost would be about $600 billion per year.[3] Adding a deduction for state and local taxes, with neither ceiling nor floor, would cost about an additional $70 billion; limiting the deduction would reduce its cost. Each additional percentage point to the 25 percent rate would add about $20–25 billion in annual revenues. An additional 30 percent rate bracket on taxable income of more than $1 million (without increasing the rates on dividends or capital gains) would raise about $15 billion annually. Alternatively, a uniform tax rate of 20 percent on ordinary income, dividends, and capital gains in excess of the exemption would lose about $650 billion of revenue. At these exemption levels, only about 30 million income tax returns would need to be filed, compared with about 140 million under current law.

It would take a VAT of about 8 or 9 percent to fund this major shrinking of the income tax without any further broadening of the definition of income subject to tax. In February 2007 the Congressional Budget Office presented many options for revenue-raising income tax changes.[4] These included limiting charitable deductions to the amount in excess of 2 percent of one's income, restructuring the home mortgage deduction, changing the income taxation of insurance, revising the treatment of tax-exempt state and local bonds, limiting or eliminating the deduction for costs of child care, and others. Congress may or may not want to take on such issues in the context of making the kinds of structural changes I am urging here. If they do, obviously, any such income tax base broadening would increase revenues and could permit lower VAT or income tax rates.

3. The Corporate Income Tax

Reducing the corporate tax rate to 15 percent would cost approximately $180 billion to $190 billion annually; a 20 percent rate would cost about $50 billion less. This, however, is almost certainly greater, relative to GDP, than the long-term cost of such a change. Corporate tax revenues have been especially robust in recent years, and CBO has predicted that they will return closer to their lesser long-term relationship to the overall size of the economy. And as corporate tax rates continue to move downward around the world, our nation will find that corporate income subject to our tax will move offshore. In any event, these numbers fail to account for any broadening of the corporate tax base. With a rate reduction of this magnitude the elimination of some corporate tax breaks is surely appropriate. In February 2007 CBO identified nearly a dozen potential base-broadening ideas, including such things as lessening or eliminating benefits for the extraction of minerals, taxing large credit unions the same way as similar financial institutions, taxing public power utilities, and others.[5] A rate cut of the magnitude I am urging here might also trigger, for example, a modification of depreciation allowances and, I would hope, greater conformity between book and tax accounting. With income tax base broadening it would be feasible to fund both the individual corporate income tax changes with a VAT of about 10 or 11 percent.

4. Payroll Adjustments and VAT Regressivity Offsets

In Chapter 10 I describe a payroll adjustment or "smart card" to replace EITCs and refundable child credits (amounts now paid to low-income workers through the current income tax) and to redress the potential regressivity of the VAT. The latter might also be addressed, in whole or in part, by removing certain necessities from the VAT base. Replacing the EITC and refundable child credits would cost nearly $60 billion in 2008—less than 1 percentage point of VAT or 3 percentage points of the income tax that remains. Relieving VAT regressivity might cost $150 billion to $225 billion more, depending on the details of the VAT base, its rate, and the ultimate trade-offs among targeting, expense, and complexity (discussed in Chapter 10). As a result, the VAT rate might go as high as 14 percent.

5. Retaining the Estate Tax with a Higher Exemption

Unlike for other numbers in this appendix, the year 2008 is not apt in the case of the estate tax because the repeal of the estate tax is not scheduled until 2010. I suggest in Chapter 9, however, that an estate tax should be retained with a higher exemption than currently and with additional relief for farmers and small businesses. Or, as an alternative, large inheritances would be taxed to recipients. CBO has evaluated a number of options, including one that would set the estate tax exemption level at $3.5 million and the tax rate at 45 percent. CBO estimated that, in 2012, this option would produce revenues of about $30 billion to $40 billion, compared with none if the repeal is made permanent.[6]

6. Other Potential Revenue Sources

I have not discussed here (except in Chapter 8 in connection with the payroll taxes) other revenue options that might be used to finance long-term spending demands. All I will say now is that there are others. Carbon taxes or auctioning off rights under a cap-and-trade emissions program offer two possibilities, and large sums of revenue may be possible in such cases. Equalizing federal alcohol taxes on beer, wine, and spirits by alcohol content would be another source of revenue, though much smaller.

My point is this: Congress and future presidents should strive to keep tax rates as low as possible, but revenues must be adequate to finance government spending. I have proposed a major shift in the financing of our government here, but I have not attempted to exhaust the possibilities. The fat lady never sings in tax policy. Changes are inevitable. But the Competitive Tax Plan I have proposed here offers a fiscally responsible, fair, simple, and economically sensible structure for funding our government in the years ahead.

Appendix 2: Earned-Income Credit Forms and Worksheet

Figure A.2.1. 2007 Form W-5

20**07** Form W-5

 Department of the Treasury
Internal Revenue Service

Instructions

Purpose of Form

Use Form W-5 if you are eligible to get part of the earned income credit (EIC) in advance with your pay and choose to do so. See *Who Is Eligible To Get Advance EIC Payments?* below. The amount you can get in advance generally depends on your wages. If you are married, the amount of your advance EIC payments also depends on whether your spouse has filed a Form W-5 with his or her employer. However, your employer cannot give you more than $1,712 throughout 2007 with your pay. You will get the rest of any EIC you are entitled to when you file your tax return and claim the EIC.

If you do not choose to get advance payments, you can still claim the EIC on your 2007 tax return.

What Is the EIC?

The EIC is a credit for certain workers. It reduces the tax you owe. It may give you a refund even if you do not owe any tax.

Who Is Eligible To Get Advance EIC Payments?

You are eligible to get advance EIC payments if **all four** of the following apply.

1. You (and your spouse, if filing a joint return) have a valid social security number (SSN) issued by the Social Security Administration. For more information on valid SSNs, see Pub. 596, Earned Income Credit (EIC).

2. You expect to have at least one qualifying child and to be able to claim the credit using that child. If you do not expect to have a qualifying child, you may still be eligible for the EIC, but you **cannot** receive advance EIC payments. See *Who Is a Qualifying Child?* below.

3. You expect that your 2007 earned income and adjusted gross income (AGI) will each be less than $33,241 ($35,241 if you expect to file a joint return for 2007). Include your spouse's income if you plan to file a joint return. As used on this form, earned income does not include amounts inmates in

penal institutions are paid for their work, amounts received as a pension or annuity from a nonqualified deferred compensation plan or a nongovernmental section 457 plan, or nontaxable earned income.

4. You expect to be able to claim the EIC for 2007. To find out if you may be able to claim the EIC, answer the questions on page 2.

How To Get Advance EIC Payments

If you are eligible to get advance EIC payments, fill in the 2007 Form W-5 at the bottom of this page. Then, detach it and give it to your employer. If you get advance payments, you must file a 2007 Form 1040 or 1040A income tax return.

You may have only one Form W-5 in effect at one time. If you and your spouse are both employed, you should file separate Forms W-5.

This Form W-5 expires on December 31, 2007. If you are eligible to get advance EIC payments for 2008, you must file a new Form W-5 next year.

> **TIP** You may be able to get a larger credit when you file your 2007 return. For details, see Additional Credit on page 3.

Who Is a Qualifying Child?

A qualifying child is any child who meets all three of the following conditions.

1. The child is your:

Son, daughter, stepchild, eligible foster child, brother, sister, half brother, half sister, stepbrother, stepsister, or a descendant of any of them (for example, your grandchild, niece, or nephew).

Note. An adopted child is always treated as your own child. An adopted child includes a child lawfully placed with you for legal adoption. An eligible foster child is any child placed with you by an authorized placement agency or by judgment, decree, or other order of any court of competent jurisdiction.

(continued on page 3)

Give the bottom part to your employer; keep the top part for your records.

.... Detach here ....

Form **W-5** Department of the Treasury Internal Revenue Service	**Earned Income Credit Advance Payment Certificate** Use the current year's certificate only. Give this certificate to your employer. This certificate expires on December 31, 2007.	OMB No. 1545-0074 20**07**

Print or type your full name	Your social security number

Note. If you get advance payments of the earned income credit for 2007, you **must** file a 2007 federal income tax return. To get advance payments, you **must** have a qualifying child and your filing status must be any status **except** married filing a separate return.

1 I expect to have a qualifying child and be able to claim the earned income credit for 2007 using that child. I do not have another Form W-5 in effect with any other current employer, and I choose to get advance EIC payments . . . . ☐ Yes ☐ No

2 Check the box that shows your expected filing status for 2007:
☐ Single, head of household, or qualifying widow(er)   ☐ Married filing jointly

3 If you are married, does your spouse have a Form W-5 in effect for 2007 with any employer? . . . . ☐ Yes ☐ No

Under penalties of perjury, I declare that the information I have furnished above is, to the best of my knowledge, true, correct, and complete.

Signature _____   Date _____

Cat. No. 10227P

Form W-5 (2007)   Page **2**

Questions To See if You May Be Able To Claim the EIC for 2007

⚠ You **cannot** claim the EIC if you file either Form 2555 or Form 2555-EZ (relating to foreign earned income) for 2007. You also **cannot** claim the EIC if you are a nonresident alien for any part of 2007 unless you are married to a U.S. citizen or resident, file a joint return, and elect to be taxed as a resident alien for all of 2007.

1 Do you expect to have a qualifying child? Read *Who Is a Qualifying Child?* that starts on page 1 before you answer this question. If the child is married, be sure you also read *Married child* on page 3.

  ☐☐ **No.** (STOP) You may be able to claim the EIC but you **cannot** get advance EIC payments.
  ☐☐ **Yes.** *Continue.*

⚠ If the child meets the conditions to be a qualifying child for both you and another person, see *Qualifying child of more than one person* on page 3.

2 Do you expect your 2007 filing status to be married filing a separate return?

  ☐☐ **Yes.** (STOP) You **cannot** claim the EIC.
  ☐☐ **No.** *Continue.*

  (TIP) If you expect to file a joint return for 2007, include your spouse's income when answering questions 3 and 4.

3 Do you expect that your 2007 earned income and AGI will each be less than: $33,241 ($35,241 if married filing jointly) if you expect to have 1 qualifying child; $37,783 ($39,783 if married filing jointly) if you expect to have 2 or more qualifying children?

  ☐☐ **No.** (STOP) You **cannot** claim the EIC.
  ☐☐ **Yes.** *Continue.* But remember, you **cannot** get advance EIC payments if you expect your 2007 earned income or AGI will be $33,241 or more ($35,241 or more if married filing jointly).

4 Do you expect that your 2007 investment income will be more than $2,900? For most people, investment income is the total of their taxable interest, ordinary dividends, capital gain distributions, and tax-exempt interest. However, if you plan to file a 2007 Form 1040, see the 2006 Form 1040 instructions to figure your investment income.

  ☐☐ **Yes.** (STOP) You **cannot** claim the EIC.
  ☐☐ **No.** *Continue.*

5 Do you expect that you, or your spouse if filing a joint return, will be a qualifying child of another person for 2007?

  ☐☐ **Yes.** You **cannot** claim the EIC.
  ☐☐ **No.** You may be able to claim the EIC.

Figure A.2.2. Work credit form proposed by the president's advisory panel on tax reform

Line 26—Work Credit

Step 1 How To Figure the Credit

1. Do you want the IRS to figure the credit for you?

   ☐ **Yes.** Just check the   ☐ **No.** Go to Step 2.
   box and enter your
   tax-exempt interest
   and dividends at the
   bottom of Schedule A
   if you meet the
   conditions listed on
   Schedule A.

Step 2 Can You Take the Credit?

1. Can you or your spouse be claimed as a dependent on someone else's 200X return?

   ☐ **Yes.** (STOP)   ☐ **No.** Continue
   You cannot take this
   credit.

2. Do you and your spouse have a social security number that allows you to work or is valid for the work credit (see page xx)?

   ☐ **Yes.** Continue   ☐ **No.** (STOP)
                               You cannot take this credit.

3. Did you and your spouse live in the United States for more than half of 200X? Members of the military, see page xx before you answer.

   ☐ **Yes.** Continue   ☐ **No.** (STOP)
                               You cannot take this credit.

4. Were you married at the end of 200X and are electing **not** to file your 200X return with your spouse? If you are separated from your spouse, see page xx.

   ☐ **Yes.** (STOP)   ☐ **No.** Continue
   You cannot take this
   credit.

5. Were you a nonresident alien for any part of 200X?

   ☐ **Yes.** See *Nonresident* ☐ **No.** Continue
   aliens on page xx.

6. Are you filing Form 2555 or 2555-EZ (relating to foreign earned income)?

   ☐ **Yes.** (STOP)   ☐ **No.** Go to question 7.
   You cannot take this
   credit.

7. Do any of the following apply to you?
   - The amount on your Schedule A, line 4, is more than the amount on your Schedule A, line 5.
   - You lived with 2 or more child dependents in the United States for more than half of 200X and the amount on 1040-SIMPLE, line 16, is less than $37,800 ($41,800 if married).
   - You lived with 1 child dependent in the United States for more than half of 200X and the amount on 1040-SIMPLE, line 16, is less than $28,600 ($32,600 if married).

   ☐ **Yes.** Go to Step 3.   ☐ **No.** (STOP)
                               You cannot take this credit.

Step 3 Work Income

1. Figure work income:

   1040-SIMPLE, line 1

   Add:
   - All of your nontaxable combat pay if you elect to include it in work income. See *Combat pay, Nontaxable* on page xx.
   - Your business income or (loss) from 1040-SIMPLE, line 2. But if line 2 includes an amount from Schedule E or you were a statutory employee, see *Schedule E filers* or *Statutory employees*, whichever applies, on page xx.
   - Any amounts from Schedule SE, lines 15 and 17, if you elected to use either optional method to figure your net earnings from self-employment.

   Work Income =

2. Do any of the following apply to you?
   - The amount on your Schedule A, line 4, is more than the amount on your Schedule A, line 5.
   - You lived with 2 or more child dependents in the United States for more than half of 200X and your work income is less than $37,800 ($41,800 if married).
   - You lived with 1 child dependent in the United States for more than half of 200X and your work income is less than $28,600 ($32,600 if married).

   ☐ **Yes.** Use the work-   ☐ **No.** (STOP)
   sheet on page xx to   You cannot take this credit.
   figure your credit.

Work Credit Worksheet—Line 26

Keep for Your Records

TIP *The IRS can figure your work credit for you. Just check the box and enter your tax-exempt interest and dividends at the bottom of Schedule A if you qualify.*

Otherwise, be sure you answered the questions on page XX to see if you can take this credit before completing this worksheet.

Part 1

All Filers

1 Is the amount on Schedule A, line 4, more than the amount on Schedule A, line 5?

☐ **Yes.** Subtract Schedule A, line 5, from Schedule A, line 4, and enter the result.
☐ **No.** Skip lines 1 through 3 and enter -0- on line 4.

| 1 | |

2 Enter your work income from Step 3 on page XX.

| 2 | |

3 Look up the amount on line 2 in the blue table on page XX to find the credit. Enter the credit here.

| 3 | |

4 Enter the smaller of line 1 or line 3.

| 4 | |

Next. If you have at least one child dependent who lived with you in the United States for more than half of 200X, go to Part 2. Otherwise, enter the amount from line 4 on line 11.

Part 2

Filers With At Least One Child Dependent

5 Look up the amount on line 2 in the orange table on pages XX through XX to find the credit. Enter the credit here.

| 5 | |

6 Enter your taxable income from 1040-SIMPLE, line 16.

| 6 | |

7 Enter your tax-exempt interest and dividends.

| 7 | |

8 Add lines 6 and 7.

| 8 | |

9 Look up the amount on line 8 in the orange table on pages XX through XX to find the credit. Enter the credit here.

| 9 | |

10 Enter the smaller of line 5 or line 9.

| 10 | |

Then, add the amounts on lines 4 and 10 and enter the result on line 11.

Part 3

Work Credit

11 This is your work credit.

| 11 | |

⚠ **CAUTION** *If you take the work credit even though you are not eligible, you may not be allowed to take the credit for up to 10 years. See Form 8862, Who must file, on page XX. You may also have to pay penalties.*

Enter this amount on 1040-SIMPLE, line 26.

1040-SIMPLE

Notes

Prologue

1. Benjamin M. Friedman, *The Moral Consequences of Economic Growth* (New York: Vintage, 2005), 183.

2. Ibid., 413.

3. Congressional Budget Office, "Budget and Economic Outlook, Fixed Years 2008–2017," January 2007.

4. Government Accountability Office, "The Nation's Long-Term Fiscal Outlook," September 2006. GAO's estimates of the long-term gap between federal revenues and spending ranges from 2.7 percent ($378 billion in 2008) to 6 percent of GDP.

5. CBO, "Budget and Economic Outlook," 78.

1. The Case for Fundamental Reform

1. Benjamin M. Friedman, "Deficits and Debt in the Short and Long Run," NBER working paper no. 11630, October 2005, http://www.nber.org/papers/w11630, last visited May 14, 2007. Friedman speculates that the increased private investment that might have occurred in the absence of deficits since the 1980s might have meant a national income some 5 percent greater—roughly $500 billion a year in a $10 trillion annual economy. He also notes that the only way the United States managed to achieve even its much lower average investment rate was by "borrowing heavily from abroad," and wonders whether our nation's large and growing net foreign debt position will

create "turmoil in the dollar exchange market, or even more importantly lead to an erosion of American influence in world affairs." Ibid at 24–25.

2. For analysis of the inadequacy of immigration increases to fund retirement benefits for an aging population, see Martin Feldstein, "The Effects of the Ageing European Population on Economic Growth and Budgets: Implications for Immigration and Other Policies," NBER working paper no. 12736, December 2006, http://www.nber.org/papers/w12736, last visited May 14, 2007.

3. Douglas Holtz-Eakin, Testimony Before the Committee on the Budget, United States House of Representatives, Washington, D.C., Feb. 15, 2006.

4. Estimates of tax expenditures cannot simply be added together as a way of estimating the amount of revenues that could be produced if they were repealed. I have added them together here simply to provide an overall sense of their magnitude and to illustrate how they have changed over time.

5. Pamela J. Jackson, "Higher Education Tax Credits: An Economic Analysis," in Linda W. Cooke, ed., *Higher Education Tax Credits* (New York: Nova, 2006), 25–57.

6. For example, the so-called HOPE education credit provides a 100 percent nonrefundable tax credit for the first $1,000 of postsecondary tuition and a 50 percent credit for the second $1,000 of tuition and related expenses for the first two years of a student's undergraduate education. The Lifetime Learning credit provides a 20 percent credit for the first $10,000 of a family's postsecondary education, including all undergraduate, graduate, and professional education. Both credits are reduced as income exceeds $40,000 ($80,000 for a married couple) and disappear for taxpayers with more than $50,000 of income ($100,000 for a married couple). Only one of these credits is available per year per student. Other overlapping provisions, which include limited deductions for tuition, savings incentives such as tax-advantaged education accounts and qualified state tuition programs, exclusions from income for amounts used to pay for educational expenses (for example, interest on education savings bonds), and deductions for the costs of borrowing to pay for educational expenses, have different income limits.

7. If amounts distributed from an education savings account are excludable from income because they are used to pay the qualified higher-education expenses of the beneficiary, neither the HOPE nor the Lifetime Learning credit may be claimed for the same year for the same individual. The individual may elect to forgo the exclusion, in which case a HOPE or Lifetime Learning credit may be claimed.

2. The Broken Politics of Taxation

1. Bruce Bartlett, "'Starve the Beast': Origins and Development of a Budgetary Metaphor," on file with author.

2. Milton Friedman, "The Kemp-Roth Free Lunch," *Newsweek,* Aug. 7, 1978.

3. William Niskanen, *Autocratic, Democratic, and Optimal Government: Fiscal Choices and Economic Outcomes* (Surrey, U.K.: Edward Elger, 2004).

4. David A. Stockman, *The Triumph of Politics: Why the Reagan Revolution Failed* (New York: HarperCollins, 1986).

5. Department of the Treasury, Office of Tax Analysis, *A Dynamic Analysis of Permanent Extension of the President's Tax Relief* (Washington, D.C.: Department of the Treasury, 2006), 5.

6. Congressional Budget Office, "Budget and Economic Outlook, Fixed Years 2008–2017," January 2007, 78, 100.

7. If no AMT relief is provided, thirty-five million people will be affected by the AMT by 2016 even if the 2001 and 2003 tax cuts are not extended, fifty million if these tax cuts are made permanent. Leonard E. Burman, William G. Gale, Gregory Leiserson, and Jeffrey Rohaly, "Options to Fix the AMT," Tax Policy Center, Washington, D.C., Jan. 19, 2007.

8. Ronald Reagan, "Remarks on Signing H.R. 3838 into Law," Washington, D.C., Oct. 22, 1986.

9. Jeffrey Owens, Testimony before the President's Advisory Panel on Tax Reform, Washington, D.C., Mar. 31, 2005. See also Cedric Sandford, *Successful Tax Reform: Lessons from an Analysis of Tax Reform in Six Countries* (Bedfordshire, U.K.: Fiscal Publications, 1993).

10. Richard A. Musgrave, "Short of Euphoria," *Journal of Economic Perspectives* 1, no. 1 (1987): 59–71.

11. Alan J. Auerbach and Joel Slemrod, "The Economic Effects of the Tax Reform Act of 1986," *Journal of Economic Literature* 35 (1997): 589–632. See also Joel Slemrod, ed., *Do Taxes Matter? The Impact of the Tax Reform Act of 1986* (Cambridge: MIT Press, 1990).

12. Six enactments were particularly important: (1) the Omnibus Budget Reconciliation Act of 1990, a bipartisan deficit-reduction measure that broke George H. W. Bush's famous "no new taxes" pledge, probably costing him reelection; (2) the Omnibus Budget Reconciliation Act of 1993, Bill Clinton's rate-raising deficit-reduction effort, which was enacted with only Democratic votes; (3) the Taxpayer Relief Act of 1997, a bipartisan tax-cutting law, most notable for cutting capital gains rates; (4) the Economic Growth and

Tax Relief Reconciliation Act of 2001, a tax-reduction measure fulfilling George W. Bush's campaign promises to cut income tax rates and eliminate the estate tax; (5) the Jobs and Growth Tax Relief Reconciliation Act of 2003, another George W. Bush tax-cutting measure, most notable for lowering taxes on dividends and capital gains; and (6) the American Jobs Creation Act of 2004, a corporate tax cut, responding in part to a decision of the World Trade Organization, which had declared income tax benefits for exports illegal. These laws unraveled the 1986 reform by narrowing the corporate and individual income tax bases and raising the top individual income tax rate.

13. Adam Clymer, "Doubt Found on Fairness and Cuts," *New York Times,* June 25, 1986.

14. Duanjie Chen and Jack M. Mintz, "U.S. Business Tax Reform Would Be Healthy for the World Economy," C. D. Howe Institute, Sept. 20, 2006, http://www.cdhowe.org/pdf/ebrief_34.pdf, last visited May 14, 2007; Duanjie Chen, Jack M. Mintz, and Finn Poschmann, "Attention G-7 Leaders: Investment Taxes Can Harm Your Nations' Health," C. D. Howe Institute, Set. 20, 2005, http://www.cdhowe.org/pdf/ebrief_18.pdf, last visited May 14, 2007.

15. *Simple, Fair, and Pro-Growth: Proposals to Fix America's Tax System, Report of the President's Advisory Panel on Tax Reform* (Washington, D.C.: Government Printing Office, 2005), available at http://www.taxreformpanel .gov/final-report, last visited May 14, 2007.

16. Dustin Stamper, "CEA Chair Says Significant Tax Reform Already Done," *Tax Notes,* May 8, 2006.

17. The president eased the panel's difficulty a bit by requiring that its recommendations be revenue neutral only vis-à-vis his own budget, which assumed that virtually all of the tax cuts enacted in his first term would be made permanent; even so, the panel could not advance new tax cuts.

18. See Jeffrey L. Yablon, *As Certain as Death: Quotations About Taxes* (Falls Church, Va.: Tax Analysts, 2004), http://www.taxanalysts.com/www/ freefiles.nsf/Files/Yablon.pdf/$file/Yablon.pdf, last visited May 14, 2007.

19. Karlyn Bowman, *Public Opinion on Taxes,* Apr. 6, 2007, American Enterprise Institute <http://www.aei.org/publications/pubID.16838/pub_ detail.asp>, last visited May 14, 2007.

3. Of Pleaders, Zealots, and the Rest of Us

1. Marc Peyser, "The Truthiness Teller," *Newsweek,* Feb. 13, 2006.

2. Here, for example, is how Jane G. Gravelle, a senior specialist in eco-

nomic policy at the Congressional Research Service, described the optimistic predictions of economic growth in the report of President Bush's 2005 tax reform panel: "The growth effects for this plan are uncertain and may be quite modest. . . . The largest results are based on complex econometric models whose assumptions are probably not realistic and whose main results are not based on empirical evidence. In addition, the parameters chosen for the model lead to results that are large relative to the empirical evidence that is available." Jane G. Gravelle, *The Advisory Panel's Tax Reform Proposals* (Washington, D.C.: Congressional Research Service, 2006). How, then, can an ordinary American distinguish truth from truthiness?

3. By far the most comprehensive collection of polling data on the subject of taxes has been compiled by the American Enterprise Institute. Karlyn Bowman, *Public Opinion on Taxes,* Apr. 6, 2007, American Enterprise Institute, Oct. 25, 2006, http://www.aei.org/publications/pubID.16838/pub_detail.asp, last visited May 14, 2007. The data here are taken from this collection.

4. Michael J. Graetz and Ian Shapiro, *Death by a Thousand Cuts: The Fight Over Taxing Inherited Wealth* (Princeton: Princeton University Press, 2005), 118–31.

5. Neal Boortz and John Linder, *The FairTax Book* (New York: Regan, 2005), 84.

6. The 23 percent rate is computed on a tax-inclusive basis, which includes the amount of tax in the base of the tax. This is the way income and payroll tax rates are usually expressed. The 30 percent rate is the same tax expressed on a tax-exclusive basis, which does not include the amount of the tax in the base, the common way of describing sales tax rates. For example, if a gallon of gas costs a total of $3.90, 90 cents of which is tax, the tax is 23 percent on a tax-inclusive basis (.90 divided by 3.90) and 30 percent on a tax-exclusive basis (.90 divided by 3.00). A simple mathematical formula allows both kinds of rates to be computed.

7. Laurence J. Kotlikoff and David Rapson, "Would the FairTax Raise or Lower Marginal Average Tax Rates?" NBER working paper no. 11831, December 2005, http://papers.nber.org/papers/w11831, 29–30, last visited May 14, 2007. See also George K. Yin, "Accommodating the 'Low-Income' in a Cash-Flow or Consumed Income Tax World," *Florida Tax Review* 2 (1995): 445. Using what he describes as a "highly stylized" economic model and "dynamic scoring," Kotlikoff and a colleague also predict that the FairTax would almost double the U.S. capital stock and increase real wages by 19 percent. Sabine Jokisch and Laurence J. Kotlikoff, "Simulating the Dynamic Macroeconomic and Micro-economic Effects of the FairTax," NBER working paper

no. 11858, December 2005, http://papers.nber.org/papers/w11858, last visited May 14, 2007.

8. Evan Halpor, "Second Life for State Tax Program," *Los Angeles Times,* Dec. 5, 2006.

4. Until the Second Child Speaks

1. Dan T. Smith, "High Progressive Tax Rates: Inequity and Immorality?" *University of Florida Law Review* 20 (1968): 451–63, 452.

2. Remarks by Federal Reserve Chairman Ben S. Bernanke before the Greater Omaha Chamber of Commerce, Omaha, Nebraska, February 6, 2007, available at http://www.federalreserve.gov/boarddocs/speeches/2007/20070206/default.htm, last visited May 14, 2007.

3. Congressional Budget Office, "Historical Effective Tax Rates: 1979 to 2004," Washington, D.C., 2006, available at http://www.cbo.gov/ftpdoc.cfm?index=7718.&type=1, last visited May 14, 2007.

4. Austan Goolsbee, "Democratizing Capitalism," *Blueprint,* July 22, 2006.

5. These one-year "snapshots" do not take into account the fact that over time people move up and down the income scale. But as Federal Reserve Chairman Bernanke has explained, economists disagree about whether income mobility has changed much over time, and if it has not, mobility cannot explain away the upward trend in measures of inequality.

6. William Safire, "The 25% Solution," *New York Times,* Apr. 20, 1995.

7. Stephen Weisman, *The Great Tax Wars* (New York: Simon and Schuster, 2002), 6, 18.

8. Thomas Piketty and Emmanuel Saez have concluded that "although the share of the top 0.1 percent of the income distribution has increased substantially over the last 30 years, the average tax rate of the top 0.1 percent has declined substantially over that time." "How Progressive Is the U.S. Federal Tax System? A Historical and International Perspective," *Journal of Economic Perspectives* 21, no. 1 (2007): 3–24.

5. Tax Spending

1. This number includes 47 states, 1,732 counties, 5,571 cities, and 229 districts. Richard T. Ainsworth, "The Digital VAT (D-VAT)," *Virginia Tax Review* 25 (2006): 875–938, n. 16.

2. For an analysis of the main forms of noncompliance under a VAT and how they might be addressed, see Michael Keen and Stephen Smith, "VAT Fraud and Evasion: What Do We Know and What Can Be Done," *National Tax Journal* 59 (2006): 861–87 (also concluding that current VAT enforcement difficulties in the EU largely reflect circumstances that would not apply in the United States).

3. For a detailed analysis of taxing financial services under a VAT, see European Commission, "Value Added Tax: A Study of Methods of Taxing Financial and Insurance Services" (1996), available at http://ec.europa.eu/tax ation_customs/resources/documents/taxation/vat/key_documents/re ports_published/methods_taxing.pdf, last visited May 14, 2007.

4. The extent to which substituting a VAT for corporate income taxes will help imports of U.S. products is controversial. Most business executives believe that the current corporate income tax raises the prices of their products and that, by exempting exports, a VAT would make their products more competitive worldwide. The consensus among economists, however, has been that the corporate income tax does not affect prices but instead reduces returns to those who supply capital, although this may be changing with the internationalization of the economy. Economists have also concluded that adjustments to exchange rates will offset any trade advantages of taxing imports and exempting imports.

5. A broad, but realistic, consumption tax base would include approximately 50 to 60 percent of the nation's gross domestic product, less than the percentage of consumption taxed in some nations but higher than the OECD average, which is about 40 percent of gross domestic product. Liam P. Ebrill, Michael Keen, Jean-Paul Bodin, and Victoria Summers, *The Modern VAT* (Washington, D.C.: International Monetary Fund, 2001), 40–42, 43, 46. The president's panel recommended that a VAT base should include about 60 percent of GDP. *Simple, Fair, and Pro-Growth: Proposals to Fix America's Tax System, Report of the President's Advisory Panel on Tax Reform* (Washington, D.C.: Government Printing Office, 2005), 191–205, 249–55, available at http://www .taxreformpanel.gov/final-report, last visited May 14, 2007.

6. Even though an exemption for small businesses will help reduce the costs of compliance and administration of a VAT, it would have little effect on VAT revenues. When an exempt small wholesaler, for example, sells a product to a non-exempt retailer, the retailer will collect the full VAT on a sale to a consumer and will get no credit for taxes paid to the wholesaler, since the wholesaler was exempt.

7. Joel Slemrod, Testimony before the President's Advisory Panel on Tax Reform, Washington, D.C., Mar. 3, 2005, available at http://www.taxre

formpanel.gov/meetings/docs/slemrod_03032005.ppt, last visited May 14, 2007.

8. Bernard D. Reams, Jr., ed., *United States Revenue Acts: 1909–1950, The Laws, Legislative Histories, and Administrative Documents,* vol. 1 (Buffalo: William S. Hein, 1979). *Internal Revenue Hearings Before the Committee on Finance of the U.S. Senate: The Proposed Revenue Act of 1921,* 67th Cong., 1st sess., May 9–27, 1921. Testimony of Chester A. Jordan, public accountant of Portland, Maine, 487. "Before the law came into effect I had three or four men in my employ. Since being obliged to undertake all of these problems for my clients I am obliged to employ seven or eight men and two and three women. Those men are college graduates and they are employed about six months of the year on tax work. I believe that if the tax law were simplified as it should be I might not be obliged to employ more than half that number."

9. Reams, *United States Revenue Acts.* Internal Revenue Hearings before the Committee on Ways and Means of the U.S. House of Representatives, Washington, D.C., July 26–29, 1921, 144, 153.

10. Department of the Treasury, *Report of the Secretary of the Treasury* (Washington, D.C.: Department of the Treasury, 1942), 92–95, 408–21.

11. Frank V. Fowles, "Administration Leans to Value-Added Tax to Help Solve National Fiscal Crisis," *National Journal* 6 (1972): 210.

12. Robert E. Hall and Alvin Robushka, *The Flat Tax,* 2nd ed. (Stanford: Hoover Institution Press, 1995), 55.

13. David F. Bradford, *The X Tax in the World Economy: Going Global with a Simple, Progressive Tax* (Washington, D.C.: American Enterprise Institute Press, 2004).

14. Martin D. Ginsburg, "Life Under a Personal Consumption Tax: Some Thoughts on Working, Saving, and Consuming in Nunn-Domenici's Tax World," working paper, September 1995, Nov. 8, 2006, http://www.bus.umich.edu/otpr/workingpaper.htm; Alvin C. Warren, Jr., "The Proposal for an 'Unlimited Savings Allowance,'" *Tax Notes,* Aug. 18, 1995.

15. David Bradford, "What Are Consumption Taxes and Who Pays Them?" *Tax Notes,* Apr. 18, 1988; Charles E. McLure and George Zodrow, "A Hybrid Approach to Direct Taxation of Consumption," *Tax Notes,* Dec. 5, 1995.

16. For illustrations of the relationships among these various ways of imposing consumption taxes, see Itai Grinberg, "Implementing a Progressive Consumption Tax: Advantages of Adopting the VAT Credit-Method System," *National Tax Journal* 59 (2006): 929–54. Under both the flat tax and the GIT, businesses, including corporations, partnerships, and self-employed individ-

uals, would be taxed on gross business receipts from the sales of goods or services minus the costs of business purchases of goods or services, cash wages paid, and any contributions to retirement plans for employees. The tax rate applicable to businesses would be identical to that for individuals, but unlike in my Competitive Tax Plan, no exemption would be provided for small businesses or for businesses with only a small amount of taxable net receipts. Neither the flat tax nor the GIT would tax businesses on any financial receipts from interest, dividends, borrowings, or equity issues, nor would they be allowed any deduction for interest, dividends, repayments of loans, or retirements of equity. Since an immediate deduction would be allowed whenever a business purchased goods or services, there would be no depreciation or inventory accounting required. It is far from clear, however, that U.S. businesses would be willing to give up their interest deductions in exchange for the immediate deduction of the costs of investment assets and inventory. Allowing such deductions without disallowing interest deductions, however, would be a disaster. Investments that are nonproductive before tax would become advantageous after tax. Capital would be deployed in uneconomic enterprises, and borrowing would pave the easy street to tax shelters.

Under the flat tax (but not the GIT), no deductions would be allowed for any business costs of providing fringe benefits to employees. Businesses therefore would get no deductions for health insurance, life insurance, or child care they provide their employees, to name only a few. This aspect of the flat tax seems politically unrealistic and certain to be changed if Congress ever gets serious about the proposal; allowing such deductions, however, would necessarily require a higher tax rate to maintain revenues.

17. PricewaterhouseCoopers, "United States in the World Economy, 1960–2005," on file with author.

18. Grinberg, "Implementing a Progressive Consumption Tax."

6. Shrink the Income Tax

1. Cited in Stephen A. Bank, "Origins of a Flat Tax," *Denver University Law Review* 73 (1996): 329–403, 374.

2. This is the view expressed, for example, by Justice Harlan, dissenting in *Pollock v. Farmers' Loan & Trust Co.*, 158 U.S. 601 (1895), 671. (The income tax "is or may become vital to the very existence and preservation of the Union in a national emergency, such as that of war with a great commercial nation, during which the collection of all duties upon imports will cease or be materially diminished.")

3. Carolyn C. Jones, "Class Tax to Mass Tax: The Role of Propaganda in the Expansion of Income Tax During World War II," *Buffalo Law Review* 37 (1994): 685–739.

4. A Disney cartoon featuring Donald Duck paying his "Taxes to Beat the Axis" to engender popular support for the income tax showed him throwing his aspirin bottle away when he prepared his tax return.

5. Department of the Treasury, Internal Revenue Service, *IRS Earned Income Tax Credit (EITC) Initiative* (Washington, D.C.: Internal Revenue Service, 2005), available at http://www.irs.gov/pub/irs-utl/irs_earned_in come_tax_credit_initiative_final_report_to_congress_october_2005.pdf, last visited May 14, 2007; Michael Parisi and Scott Hollenbeck, "Individual Income Tax Returns, 2002," in Department of the Treasury, Internal Revenue Service, *Statistics of Income Bulletin* (Washington, D.C.: Internal Revenue Service, 2004), available at http://www.irs.gov/pub/irs-soi/02indtr.pdf, last visited May 14, 2007.

6. Gregg Esenwein, *Federal Income Tax Thresholds for Selected Years, 1996 Through 2006* (Washington, D.C.: Congressional Research Service, 2005).

7. Parisi and Hollenbeck, "Individual Income Tax Returns, 2002."

8. The earned-income tax credit also imposes a large "marriage penalty" on low-income families. Imagine two low-income workers, with one or both eligible for the EITC. When they marry, their joint income becomes high enough that their EITC benefits after marriage either are much lower or disappear altogether.

9. Joint Committee on Taxation, *Present Law and Background Relating to the Individual Alternative Minimum Tax* (Washington, D.C.: Joint Committee on Taxation, 2005), available at http://www.house.gov/jct/x-37-05 .pdf, last visited May 14, 2007; Leonard E. Burman, William G. Gale, and Jeffrey Rohaly, "The Expanding Reach of the Individual Alternative Minimum Tax," *Journal of Economic Perspectives* 17, no. 2 (2003): 173–86. See also David Cay Johnston, "The Untaxed Rich, Found and Then Lost," *New York Times,* Mar. 4, 2007 (stating that repeal of the AMT would be more costly than repeal of the regular income tax now).

10. Although it also included a "bubble" rate of 33 percent that applied below the top income level, the 1986 law was constructed so that the highest average tax rate never exceeded 28 percent.

11. Michael Strudler et al., "Further Analysis of the Distribution of Income and Taxes," in Department of the Treasury, Internal Revenue Service, *Statistics of Income Bulletin* (Washington, D.C.: Internal Revenue Service,

2004), available at http://www.irs.gov/pub/irs-soi/04asastr.pdf, last visited May 14, 2007.

12. For further detail, see also Michael J. Graetz, "100 Million Unnecessary Returns: A Fresh Start for the U.S. Tax System," *Yale Law Journal* 112 (2002): 261–310.

13. Congress could tax capital gains at the standard 20 or 25 percent rate or retain a lower rate. Likewise, Congress could keep the special 15 percent rate on dividends, adopt the panel's revisions, or, as I would prefer, enact the original 2003 proposal of President Bush, eliminating dividend taxes completely when corporate taxes are paid. As the following chapter describes, I would also simplify and reduce taxes on small businesses and corporations.

14. If the AMT were to serve as the income tax, certain changes would be necessary. For example, expenses of earning income, including miscellaneous business expenses, should be deductible. The $100,000 exemption should make other personal exemptions and credits for children unnecessary. Deductions might or might not be allowed for state and local taxes.

7. Reduce the Corporate Income Tax Rate

1. Alan Auerbach, "The U.S. Tax System in International Perspective: A Review of the 2006 Economic Report of the President's Tax Chapter," University of California Berkeley working paper, Apr. 12, 2006, http://www.econ.berkeley.edu/~auerbach/taxsystem.pdf, last visited May 14, 2007; William C. Randolph, "International Burdens of the Corporate Income Tax," Congressional Budget Office working paper no. 2006-09, August 2006, http://www.cbo.gov/ftpdocs/75xx/doc7503/2006-09.pdf, last visited May 14, 2007.

2. *Pollock v. Farmers' Loan & Trust Co.*, 157 U.S. 429 (1895).

3. Important studies were produced by the U.S. Department of the Treasury and the American Law Institute in the early 1990s. Department of the Treasury, *Integration of the Individual and Corporate Tax Systems: Taxing Business Income Once* (Washington, D.C.: Department of the Treasury, 1992); Alvin C. Warren, Jr., *Integration of Individual and Corporate Income Taxes* (Philadelphia: American Law Institute, 1993); Michael J. Graetz and Alvin C. Warren, Jr., *Integration of the U.S. Corporate and Individual Income Taxes: The Treasury Department and American Law Institute Reports* (Falls Church, Va.: Tax Analysts, 1998).

4. A third option, deduction of dividends, is usually rejected because it would automatically extend the benefits of integration to tax-exempt and foreign shareholders.

5. Michael J. Graetz and Alvin C. Warren, Jr., "Income Tax Discrimination and the Political and Economic Integration of Europe," *Yale Law Journal* 115 (2006): 1186–1255; Richard J. Vann, "Trends in Company/Shareholder Taxation: Single or Double Taxation?" *Cahiers de Droit Fiscal International* 88a (2003): 21–70.

6. This would complete a trend of recent years. There has been much growth, for example, in the number of Subchapter S corporations, which are treated as flow-through entities under current law.

7. See, e.g., Celia Whitaker, "Note: Bridging the Book-Tax Accounting Gap," *Yale Law Journal* 115 (2005): 680.

8. See U.S. Bureau of Economic Analysis, http://www.bea.gov/bea/di/home/iip.htm, last visited May 14, 2007.

9. Congressional Budget Office, *Corporate Income Tax Rates: International Comparisons* (Washington, D.C.: Congressional Budget Office, 2005). available at http://www.cbo.gov/ftpdocs/69xx/doc6902/11-28-CorporateTax.pdf, last visited May 14, 2007; Martin A. Sullivan, "A New Era in Corporate Taxation," Testimony before the Committee on Finance, United States Senate, June 13, 2006.

10. Both the Joint Committee on Taxation and the President's Tax Reform Panel have urged replacing the U.S. foreign tax credit with an exemption for dividends paid out of foreign-source business income. Depending on how royalties and certain business deductions are treated, such a change might increase U.S. corporate revenues, a fact that demonstrates how little tax revenue is being collected from foreign-source income. I have elsewhere urged an exemption for dividends paid from foreign-source active business income. Michael J. Graetz and Paul W. Oosterhuis, "Structuring and Exemption System for Foreign Income of U.S. Corporations," *National Tax Journal* 54 (2001): 771–86.

11. Joint Committee on Taxation, *General Explanation of the Tax Reform Act of 1986* (Washington, D.C.: Joint Committee on Taxation, 1987).

12. This cut in corporate tax rates need not be financed entirely by a new consumption tax. A number of possibilities exist for broadening the corporate tax base. For example, additional revenue would be provided and depreciation allowances for corporations would be simplified by requiring that plant and equipment be depreciated using a 150 percent declining balance method. The Treasury Department has shown that with the elimi-

nation of "special provisions that reduce taxes for particular types of activities, industries and businesses," the 35 percent corporate tax rate could be reduced to 27 percent and produce approximately the same revenue as current law. U.S. Treasury, Background Paper for Treasury Conference on Business Taxation and Global Competitiveness, July 23, 2007, at 7–11. If the additional level of corporate tax were eliminated through integration of the corporate and individual taxes, incentives under current law to use the noncorporate form of business would disappear in the new regime.

8. Keep the Wage Tax to Help Fund Social Insurance

1. He was not right on the law, however. The Supreme Court in *Flemming v. Nestor*, 363 U.S. 603 (1960), held that the promises of Social Security benefits do not create any legal entitlement to receive them.

2. After passage of the prescription drug benefit (in the Medicare Modernization Act of 2003), Medicare now has three parts. First, Hospitalization Insurance (called HI, or Medicare Part A) helps pay the costs associated with hospital stays and the costs of home health, hospice, and skilled nursing facility care. Medicare Part A is financed by a dedicated 2.9 percent payroll tax and some revenues from income taxes on Social Security benefits. Second, Supplementary Medical Insurance now includes both Parts B and D. Part B helps pay the cost of physician visits, outpatient bills, and home health bills and is financed by beneficiaries' premium payments and general revenues. These premiums cover about 25 percent of the program's costs, with the remainder paid by general revenues. Third, the prescription drug benefit (Medicare Part D) is also financed by premium payments and general revenue transfers, along with state transfers that are reimbursed from the Medicaid program for those Medicare beneficiaries who are also eligible for Medicaid. The combination of premiums and state transfers is expected to cover about 25 percent of the total cost of the prescription drug benefit, with general revenues covering the remainder.

3. The tax to fund Social Security's Old Age, Survivors, and Disability program (OASDI) is now 12.4 percent; the tax to fund Part A of Medicare is 2.9 percent.

4. Employers and employees pay one-half of the payroll tax attributable to an employee's wages. Internal Revenue Code §3101 (employees); ibid., §3111 (employers). Economists agree, however, that both halves of the tax

generally burden employees in the form of lower wages. Janet Stotsky, "Payroll Taxes and the Funding of Social Security Systems," in Parthasarathi Shome, ed., *Tax Policy Handbook* (Washington, D.C.: International Monetary Fund, 1995), 177, 178–79.

5. One could make a similar claim for all taxes and all spending, but few taxes, at least at the federal level, are earmarked for specified spending, and efforts to allocate to specific people the costs of spending for such things as homeland security or national defense are inherently controversial. Social Security, with its payroll tax, on the other hand, was designed and is implemented as a unified system of taxes and spending.

6. See, for example, Lawrence Summers and Chris Carroll, "Why Is U.S. National Saving So Low?" Brookings Papers on Economic Activity (1987), http://links.jstor.org/sici?sici=0007-2303%281987%291987%3A2%3C607%3AWIUNSS%3E2.0.CO%3B2-S, last visited May 14, 2007; Alan J. Auerbach and Laurence J. Kotlikoff, "Demographics, Fiscal Policy, and U.S. Savings," in L. Summers ed., *Tax Policy and the Economy*, vol. 4 (Cambridge: MIT Press, 1990), 73–102; Jagadeesh Gokhale, Laurence J. Kotlikoff, and John Sabelhaus, "Understanding Postwar Decline in U.S. Saving: A Cohort Analysis," NBER working paper no. 5571, May 1996, http://papers.nber.org/papers/w5571, last visited May 14, 2007; Laurence J. Kotlikoff, *Generational Accounting* (New York: Free Press, 1992).

7. Michael J. Graetz and Jerry L. Mashaw, *True Security: Rethinking American Social Insurance* (New Haven: Yale University Press, 1999), 104–5.

8. United States Social Security Administration, *2002 Annual Report of the Board of Trustees of the Federal Old-Age and Survivors Insurance and Disability Insurance Trust Funds* (Washington, D.C.: Social Security Administration, 2002).

9. Graetz and Mashaw, *True Security*, 48, tbl. IV.B1; 52. For further discussion, see ibid., 106–7.

10. According to a study by the Kaiser Family Foundation's Kaiser Commission on Medicaid and the Uninsured, Medicaid spending averages 15 percent of state budgets. Henry J. Kaiser Family Foundation, "The Role of Medicaid in State Economies: A Look at the Research," 2004, http://www.kff.org/medicaid/7075a.cfm, last visited May 14, 2007.

11. See, e.g., Laurence J. Kotlikoff and Jeffrey Sachs, "It's High Time to Privatize," *Brookings Review,* summer 1997, 16; Steven Greenhouse, "Union Warning Label on Social Security," *New York Times,* Feb. 19, 1999; Hugh Price and Julian Bond, "Social Security's Stable Benefit," *New York Times,* July 16, 2001; Daniel J. Mitchell, "A Brief Guide to Social Security Reform," Aug. 7, 1997, on file with author; Kilolo Kijakazi and Robert Greenstein, "Market

Risk Versus Political Risk: Why Social Security Faces Greater Risk Under Privatization," Mar. 28, 2002, http://www.cbpp.org/3-28-02socsec.pdf, last visited May 14, 2007.

12. There are many practical issues that arise here, including how to get money into such accounts, how the money is to be invested, and how the money will come out of the accounts. I have investigated these elsewhere and will not discuss them here. Fred T. Goldberg, Jr., and Michael J. Graetz, "Reforming Social Security: A Practical and Workable System of Personal Retirement Accounts," in John B. Shoren, ed., *Administrative Aspects of Investment-Based Social Security Reform* (Chicago: University of Chicago Press, 2000), 9–39.

13. *Simple, Fair, and Pro-Growth: Proposals to Fix America's Tax System, Report of the President's Advisory Panel on Tax Reform* (Washington, D.C.: Government Printing Office, 2005), 216, available at http://www.taxre formpanel.gov/final-report, last visited May 14, 2007. The panel estimates that a *64 percent rate* would be necessary to replace the income tax using a sales tax base like those typically used in the states.

14. See, e.g., Carmen DeNavas-Walt, Robert W. Cleveland, and Marc I. Roemer, *Money Income in the United States: 2000* (Washington, D.C.: United States Department of Commerce, 2001), 11–13 (describing income inequality over time); Graetz and Mashaw, *True Security,* 31–32.

15. Some have suggested dedicating estate and gift tax revenues to the Social Security Trust Fund; e.g., Nancy J. Altman, *The Battle for Social Security: From FDR's Vision to Bush's Gamble* (Hoboken, N.J.: Wiley, 2005).

9. Tax Great Wealth but Protect Farmers and Small Businesses

1. See Michael Graetz, "To Praise the Estate Tax, Not to Bury It," *Yale Law Journal* 93 (1983): 259–86.

2. Congressional Budget Office, *Effects of the Federal Estate Tax on Farms and Small Businesses* (Washington, D.C.: Congressional Budget Office, 2005).

3. Michael J. Graetz and Ian Shapiro, *Death by a Thousand Cuts: The Fight Over Taxing Inherited Wealth* (Princeton: Princeton University Press, 2005).

4. George W. Bush, "Remarks on Transmitting Proposed Tax Cut Plan to the Congress," 36 Weekly Comp. Pres. Doc. 271, Feb. 12, 2001. See also Statement of Senator Feingold, 146 *Congressional Record* S6431, July 11, 2000 (daily

ed.); William H. Miller, "The New Congress," *Industry Week,* Jan. 5, 1999, http://www.industryweek.com/currentarticles/asp/articles.asp?ArticleID=399, last visited May 14, 2007; Cal Dooley, Press Release, "Dooley Urges Conferees to Adopt Senate Estate Tax Version," July 21, 1997 ("This is NFIB's top tax priority").

5. National Public Radio, *Talk of the Nation,* Feb. 21, 2001 (reporting on a Zogby poll conducted December 2000). See also Mayling Birney, Michael J. Graetz, and Ian Shapiro, "Public Opinion and the Push to Repeal the Estate Tax," *National Tax Journal* 49 (2006): 439–62.

6. William G. Gale and Joel Slemrod, "Overview," in William G. Gale, James R. Hines, Jr., and Joel Slemrod, eds., *Rethinking Estate and Gift Taxation* (Washington, D.C.: Brookings, 2000): 1, 24 tables 1–7; David Joulfaian, "Taxing Wealth Transfers and Its Behavioral Consequences," *National Tax Journal* 53 (2001): 933.

7. Joint Committee on Taxation, *Description and Analysis of Present Law and Proposals Relating to Federal Estate and Gift Taxation* (Washington, D.C.: Joint Committee on Taxation, 2001), 26, available at http://www.house.gov/jct/x-14-01.pdf, last visited May 14, 2007.

8. Joulfaian, "Taxing Wealth Transfers," 933; Matthew Scoffic and Patrice Treubert, "Corporation Income Tax Returns, 1996," in Department of the Treasury, Internal Revenue Service, *Statistics of Income Bulletin* (Washington, D.C.: Internal Revenue Service, 1999), 50, 61–63 table 1, available at http://www.irs.gov/pub/irs-soi/99corart.pdf, last visited May 14, 2007; Congressional Budget Office, *Budget Options* (Washington, D.C.: Congressional Budget Office, 2007), available at http://www.cbo.gov/ftpdoc.cfm?index =7821&type=1, last visited May 14, 2007.

9. Joulfaian, "Taxing Wealth Transfers," 938 table 3; see also Barry W. Johnson and Jacob M. Mikow, "Federal Estate Tax Returns, 1998–2000," in Department of the Treasury, Internal Revenue Service, *Statistics of Income Bulletin* (Washington, D.C.: Internal Revenue Service, 2002), 133, 156 table 1a, available at http://www.irs.gov/pub/irs-soi/00esart.pdf, last visited May 14, 2007; Barry W. Johnson and Jacob M. Mikow, "Federal Estate Tax Returns, 1995–1997," in Department of the Treasury, Internal Revenue Service, *Statistics of Income Bulletin* (Washington, D.C.: Internal Revenue Service, 1999): 69, 113 table 2, available at http://www.irs.gov/pub/irs-soi/97esart.pdf, last visited May 14, 2007.

10. CBO, *Effects of the Federal Estate Tax.*

11. Edward N. Wolff, *Top Heavy: A Study of the Increasing Inequality of Wealth in America* (New York: Twentieth Century Fund, 1995).

12. Joulfaian, "Taxing Wealth Transfers," 938.

13. Wolff, *Top Heavy,* 65–67.

14. See John Laitner, "Inequality and Wealth Accumulation: Eliminating the Federal Gift and Estate Tax," in Gale, Hines, and Slemrod, *Rethinking Estate and Gift Taxation,* 258, 278–81 (stating that the replacement of the estate tax with a proportional income tax could cause a 16 percent to 32 percent increase in the wealth held by the top 1 percent).

15. Internal Revenue Code §2055 (2000).

16. David Joulfaian, "Estate Taxes and Charitable Bequests by the Wealthy," *National Tax Journal* 53 (2000): 743, 753 table 5c; Joulfaian, "Taxing Wealth Transfers," 949 table 12A.

17. Johnson and Mikow, "Returns, 1998–2000," 166, table 1c.

18. Melissa J. Belvedere, "Charitable Remainder Trusts, 1998," in Department of the Treasury, Internal Revenue Service, *Statistics of Income Bulletin* (Washington, D.C.: Internal Revenue Service, 2001), 58, 58 fig. A, available at http://www.irs.gov/pub/irs-soi/98chrmtr.pdf, last visited May 14, 2007.

19. See B. Douglas Bernheim, "Does the Estate Tax Raise Revenue?" in Laurence H. Summers, ed., *Tax Policy and the Economy* (Cambridge: MIT Press, 1987), 113, 131 (estimating a 79.3 percent decrease in charitable giving); Charles T. Clotfelter and Richard L. Schmalbeck, "The Impact of Fundamental Tax Reform on Nonprofit Organizations," in Henry J. Aaron and William G. Gale, eds., *Economic Effects of Fundamental Tax Reform* (Washington, D.C.: Brookings, 1996), 211, 233–34 (estimating a 24 percent to 44 percent decrease in charitable giving); David Joulfaian, "Charitable Giving in Life and in Death," in Gale, Hines, and Slemrod, *Rethinking Estate and Gift Taxation,* 350, 364 (estimating a 31 percent decrease in charitable giving); Joulfaian, "Taxing Wealth Transfers," 951 (estimating a 12 percent decrease in charitable giving), 952.

20. Edward J. McCaffery, "The Uneasy Case for Wealth Transfer Taxation," *Yale Law Journal* 104 (1994): 283–367.

21. The accessions tax was first proposed in 1945 by Harry J. Rudick, "A Proposal for an Accessions Tax," *Tax Law Review* 1 (1945): 25. For further discussion of the accessions tax, see Institute for Fiscal Studies, *The Structure and Reform of Direct Taxation* (London: Allen and Unwin, 1978), 321; William D. Andrews, "The Accessions Tax Proposal," *Tax Law Review* 22 (1967): 589–633; William D. Andrews, "Reporter's Study of the Accessions Tax Proposal," in American Law Institute, *Federal Estate and Gift Taxation* (Philadelphia: American Law Institute, 1969), 446; Edward C. Halbach, Jr., "An Accessions Tax," *Real Property Probate and Trust Journal* 23 (1988): 211–74; Richard D. Kirshberg, "The Accessions Tax: Administrative Bramblebush or Instrument

of Social Policy?" *UCLA Law Review* 14 (1966): 135–240; Harry J. Rudick, "What Alternative to the Estate and Gift Taxes?" *California Law Review* 38 (1950): 150–82; and Stanley S. Surrey, "An Introduction to Revision of the Federal Estate and Gift Taxes," *California Law Review* 38 (1950): 1–27.

22. An exclusion for annual gifts of $12,000 or less is a feature of current law. Internal Revenue Code §2503(b) (2000).

23. See John M. Janiga and Louis S. Harrison, "The Case for the Retention of the State Death Tax Credit in the Federal Transfer Tax Scheme: 'Just Say No' to a Deduction," *Pepperdine Law Review* 21 (1994): 695–731, 701–2 (reporting that eighteen states impose both the inheritance and estate taxes while five states use just the estate tax). Since the publication of this article, Montana and North Carolina have repealed their inheritance taxes. Act Repealing State Inheritance Taxes, §36, 2000 Montana Laws 46, 69; Act effective Jan. 1, 1999, 1997 N.C. Sess. Laws 1295.

10. Protect American Workers from a Tax Increase

1. Flat-rate tax systems such as the flat tax and the retail sales tax are also less progressive than revenue-equivalent graduated taxes since lower-income individuals must pay the same tax rate as higher-income individuals. There are difficult conceptual issues as to how to distribute the burdens of a consumption tax to families. Economists have shown that if economically equivalent taxes, such as the VAT and the flat tax, are distributed based on who nominally pays the tax, starkly different pictures and policy implications emerge. See Leonard E. Berman, Jane G. Gravelle, and Jeffery Rohaly, "Toward a More Consistent Distributional Analysis," *National Tax Journal,* Proceedings of the 98th Annual Conference on Taxation (2006): 223–36. I do not deal with these issues in this book.

2. For an excellent discussion of these trade-offs, see Janet Holtzblatt, "Trade-Offs Between Targeting and Simplicity: Lessons from the U.S. and British Experiences with Refundable Tax Credits," in J. Alm, Jorge Martinez-Vazquez, and Mark Rider, eds., *The Challenges of Tax Reform in a Global Economy* (New York: Springer, 2006), 39–74.

3. It is worth noting that the degree of regressivity of such taxes is itself a controversial matter. Looking at the distribution of taxes over a lifetime, rather than annually, suggests more modest regressivity since today's savings often finance consumption in the near future.

4. See "USA Tax Act of 1995," Senate Bill 722, Apr. 25, 1995; Edward J. McCaffrey, *Fair Not Flat: How to Make the Tax System Better and Simpler*

(Chicago: University of Chicago Press, 2002); Laurence S. Seidman, *The USA Tax: A Progressive Consumption Tax* (Cambridge: MIT Press, 1997); Michael J. Graetz, "Implementing a Progressive Consumption Tax," *Harvard Law Review* 92 (1979): 1575; William D. Andrews, "A Consumption-Type or Cash Flow Personal Income Tax," *Harvard Law Review* 87 (1974): 1113.

5. *Simple, Fair, and Pro-Growth: Proposals to Fix America's Tax System, Report of the President's Advisory Panel on Tax Reform* (Washington, D.C.: Government Printing Office, 2005), available at http://www.taxreformpanel .gov/final-report, last visited May 14, 2007; see also, David Bradford, "What Are Consumption Taxes and Who Pays Them?" *Tax Notes,* Apr. 18, 1988; Charles E. McLure and George Zodrow, "A Hybrid Approach to Direct Taxation of Consumption," *Tax Notes,* Dec. 5, 1995.

6. See "The Fair Tax Act of 1999," H.R. 2525, July 14, 1999; Neal Boortz and John Linder, *The FairTax Book* (New York: Regan, 2005).

7. The numbers in the text may be surprising. Thirty percent of $26,400 is $7,920, which suggests a prebate of $660 a month, but spending $26,400 total, including the tax, would require only $506 a month in prebates to reimburse the taxes actually paid. The president's panel calculated somewhat different amounts for the uniform cash grants (prebates) in 2006: $2,494 for singles, $4,988 for married couples, plus $853 for each child. See *Simple, Fair, and Pro-Growth,* 255–56.

8. *Simple, Fair, and Pro-Growth,* 213 figure 9.4, 213–14.

9. Robert S. McIntyre, "Free Money: Take Some," *American Prospect,* Apr. 8, 2002; Holtzblatt, "Trade-Offs Between Targeting and Simplicity."

10. The advance-payment option came into the law in 1978. Tax Counseling for the Elderly, Pub. L. No. 95-600, §105, 92 Stat. 2763, 2773-76 (1978) (codified as amended at I.R.C. §3507). Only about $160 million of the total $26 billion in refunded earned-income credits were refunded in advance in 2000. Department of the Treasury, Internal Revenue Service, *Data Book* (Washington, D.C.: Internal Revenue Service, 2001): 10. There is much room for improving the delivery of this tax relief and wage subsidy to low-income workers. See Edmund S. Phelps, *Rewarding Work: How to Restore Participation and Self-Support to Free Enterprise* (Cambridge: Harvard University Press, 1997) (proposing a system of graduated tax subsidies to employers of low-wage workers).

11. An additional child tax credit is paid directly by the U.K. government into bank accounts or through the post office.

12. *Simple, Fair, and Pro-Growth,* 225–32, 269–72.

13. Under both the child credit and the EITC, there often have been difficulty and controversy over who is eligible to claim credits, because the

claimant might be able to show that he or she has provided more than one-half of the child's financial support. Internal Revenue Code §152(c) (2000). The EITC is now allowed to the parent who lives with the child. Ibid., §32(c). Alternatively, it would be much simpler and, given the increasing efforts of enforcing child support obligations, perhaps equitable to allow payroll off-sets for both parents.

14. For a discussion of the problems with such high-marginal rates from withdrawing benefits, see Michael J. Graetz and Jerry L. Mashaw, *True Security: Rethinking American Social Insurance* (New Haven: Yale University Press, 1999), 296–99. The increase in take-home pay from this offset would grow with the number of children in the family. This tax relief for low-income workers would be quite expensive, requiring not only dedication of the full amount of revenues and outlays currently attributable to the earned-income tax credit but also an additional amount, which might be as much as 2 or 3 percentage points of total consumption tax revenues. See also Appendix 1.

15. This is equivalent to the refundability feature of the EITC. It will not require additional funding by employers, since they will simply reduce their aggregate payroll tax deposits by the total adjustments for all employees. It would therefore be rare for an employer to have an overall negative withholding balance. In the handful of cases in which the employer's total adjustments exceed its total payroll tax deposits, the employer could be provided a refundable credit against its income taxes. The Social Security Administration would reconcile each employer's withholding adjustments with wages reported at year end, as it now does with W-2 forms for Social Security purposes.

16. This follows the current practice for the EITC, which was originally enacted to offset payroll tax burdens for low-income workers.

17. This payroll tax adjustment would be available only to employees. For low-income self-employed independent contractors, relief would have to be obtained through reduced estimated tax payments. This might require a year-end reconciliation through some form of tax return, although the Social Security Administration might already get enough information for self-employment tax purposes without such a return.

18. Richard T. Ainsworth, "Biometrics: Solving the Regressivity of VATs and RSTs with 'Smart Card' Technology," working paper, Aug. 7, 2006, http://www.bu.edu/law/faculty/scholarship/workingpapers/documents/AinsworthR080706.pdf, last visited May 14, 2007; Richard T. Ainsworth, "Carousel Fraud in the EU: A Digital VAT Solution," *Worldwide Tax Daily*, May 4, 2006; Richard T. Ainsworth, "The Digital VAT (D-VAT)," *Virginia Tax*

Review 25 (2006): 875–938; Richard T. Ainsworth, "Digital VAT and Development: D-VAT and D-Velopment," *Worldwide Tax Daily,* Aug. 17, 2005.

11. Bring the States Along

1. The Senate had to make sure that all of its tax cuts did not cost more than $1.35 trillion over the budget period in order to pass the bill under special rules applicable to budget reconciliation legislation that prevent filibusters. Senate proponents did not have the sixty votes necessary to halt a filibuster on the bill. Shortly after they made this announcement, Russ Sullivan, a Senate Finance Committee staffer, told members of the National Conference of State Legislators that the money being taken from the states was necessary to get the cost of the tax bill down to its $1.35 trillion limit. He also observed that the previous silence of state groups had helped make this money grab politically palatable.

2. William F. Fox and Matthew N. Murray, "A National Retail Sales Tax: Consequences for the States," *State Tax Notes,* July 25, 2005, 287.

3. Richard T. Ainsworth, "Biometrics: Solving the Regressivity of VATs and RSTs with 'Smart Card' Technology," working paper, Aug. 7, 2006, http://www.bu.edu/law/faculty/scholarship/workingpapers/documents/AinsworthR080706.pdf, last visited May 14, 2007; Richard T. Ainsworth, "Carousel Fraud in the EU: A Digital VAT Solution," *Worldwide Tax Daily,* May 4, 2006; Richard T. Ainsworth, "The Digital VAT (D-VAT)," *Virginia Tax Review* 25 (2006): 875–938; Richard T. Ainsworth, "Digital VAT and Development: D-VAT and D-Velopment," *Worldwide Tax Daily,* Aug. 17, 2005.

4. Ainsworth, "The Digital VAT (D-VAT)," 884. For a thoughtful discussion of both the advantages of the states harmonizing their consumption taxes with a federal VAT and how a federal VAT can coexist with different state VATs and retail sales taxes, see Richard M. Bird, Jack M. Mintz, and Thomas A. Wilson, "Coordinating Federal and Provincial Sales Taxes: Lessons from the Canadian Experience," *National Tax Journal* 59 (2006): 889–904.

12. The Plan in Brief

1. This kind of exemption does not cost a lot of revenue under a VAT because except in the case of small retailers, the tax will be picked up further down the line. So for businesses that are selling goods and services to other

businesses (like wholesalers and manufacturers), the exemption might be considerably higher.

2. GAO has estimated that an exemption for small businesses with gross receipts of $100,000 or less would reduce the required number of VAT returns from 24 million to 5.4 million. We assume here that such a small business exemption would be included in a VAT and show 8 million VAT returns filed, since some small businesses will opt into the VAT to obtain refunds and to account for growth since the GAO report was published. General Accountability Office, *Tax Policy: Value-Added Tax: Administrative Costs Vary with Complexity and Number of Businesses* (Washington, D.C.: General Accountability Office, 1993), 62.

3. Joel Slemrod, Testimony before the President's Advisory Panel on Tax Reform, Mar. 3, 2005, http://www.taxreformpanel.gov/meetings/docs/slemrod_03032005.ppt, last visited May 14, 2007.

4. Alternately, the payroll adjustment or smart card relief might be combined with some VAT exceptions for necessities.

5. Slemrod, Testimony before the President's Advisory Panel.

6. Michael J. Graetz and Ian Shapiro, *Death by a Thousand Cuts: The Fight Over Taxing Inherited Wealth* (Princeton: Princeton University Press, 2005).

7. Details of how the 1986 Tax Reform subsequently fell apart are contained in Michael J. Graetz, "Tax Reform Unraveling," *Journal of Economic Perspectives* 21, no. 1 (2007): 69–90.

8. See generally Michael Keen and Ben Lockwood, "Is the VAT a Money Machine?" *National Tax Journal* 59 (2006): 905–28. In Canada, whose experience is likely to be closer than that of Europe to ours, the VAT (called a goods and services tax) was introduced at a 7 percent rate. For the fifteen years after its enactment, the tax rate remained unchanged and the tax base was adjusted only in minor ways. As a result, VAT revenues essentially tracked rises in nominal GDP and consumer spending over this period. See Richard M. Bird, Jack M. Mintz, and Thomas A. Wilson, "Coordinating Federal and Provincial Sales Taxes: Lessons from the Canadian Experience," *National Tax Journal* 59 (2006): 889–904.

9. Michael Strudler et al., "Further Analysis of the Distribution of Income and Taxes," in Department of the Treasury, Internal Revenue Service, *Statistics of Income Bulletin* (Washington: Internal Revenue Service, 2004), available at http://www.irs.gov/pub/irs-soi/04asastr.pdf, last visited May 14, 2007.

10. In the past to assuage fears of rising VAT or income taxes, I have suggested that for this plan to be viable politically, it might become necessary

to impose a supermajority voting requirement—a 60 percent vote of both the House and the Senate—to raise either VAT or income tax rates or to lower the income tax exemption. Michael J. Graetz, "100 Million Unnecessary Returns: A Fresh Start for the U.S. Tax System," *Yale Law Journal* 112 (2002): 261–303. While such a requirement remains possible, I am less convinced that it remains necessary.

11. "Tax Misery and Reform Index," *Forbes Global*, May 23, 2005, 24.

Appendix 1

1. See Michael J. Graetz, "100 Million Unnecessary Returns: A Fresh Start for the U.S. Tax System," *Yale Law Journal* 112 (2002): 261–310, Appendix: Estimates for proposal, 304–10.

2. The lower number in this range is calculated based on a VAT base equal to about 50 percent of GDP, which in 2008 is expected to be about 14.7 billion. The president's panel recommended a VAT base of approximately 60 percent of GDP, which accounts for the high end of this range.

3. This assumes that the $100,000 ($50,000 for singles) exemption will phase out at a rate of $20 for every $100 of income above $200,000 for married couples ($100,000 singles).

4. Congressional Budget Office, *Budget Options* (Washington, D.C.: Congressional Budget Office, 2007), available at http://www.cbo.gov/ftpdoc .cfm?index=7821&type=1, last visited May 14, 2007.

5. Ibid., 292–306. In July 2007 the Treasury Department illustrated how broadening the corporate tax base would allow a reduction of the corporate tax rate from 35 to 27 percent without losing revenues. U.S.Treasury, Background Paper for Treasury Conference on Business Taxation and Global Competitiveness, July 23, 2007, at 7–11. Some of the changes described, involving provisions for research and development and the taxation of income earned abroad, would be very controversial, however.

6. CBO, *Budget Options*, 313–15.

Glossary

AFDC (Aid for Families with Dependent Children). Welfare program operated from 1935 until 1997, succeeded by Temporary Assistance for Needy Families (TANF).

AMT (alternative minimum tax). A supplement to the personal income tax structure originally intended to ensure that those with high incomes pay some minimum level of tax. A taxpayer must pay the higher of the AMT or the regular income tax.

CBO (Congressional Budget Office). Staff responsible for providing nonpartisan data and economic analysis for Congress to use in creating the federal budget.

consumption tax. A levy on the basis of consumption (rather than, for example, income or wealth). Retail sales taxes and value-added taxes are examples of consumption taxes.

deduction. A subtraction from a taxpayer's gross income or adjusted gross income sanctioned by the tax code in calculating the amount of taxable income.

double taxation of corporate income. The taxation of corporate income once when earned by the corporation and again when paid out as dividends to shareholders.

EITC (earned income tax credit). Tax credit for low-income working individuals and families. The amount of credit is determined by family size and earnings. Refundable, so that if the amount of credit exceeds the amount of taxes owed, government pays the difference.

estate tax. Tax imposed on the value of large amounts of wealth at the time of a donor's death. Also known as the death tax.

exclusion. An element of income the taxpayer is permitted to exclude from gross income for tax purposes.

exemption. An allowance that offsets income on the number of dependents and on special conditions, such as blindness. Along with the standard deduction, the figure is used to determine the threshold below which no tax will be due.

FairTax. National sales tax advanced by Congressman John Linder and radio personality Neal Boortz.

flat tax. Subtraction-method value-added tax proposed by Robert Hall and Alvin Rabushka in *The Flat Tax,* made popular by Steve Forbes in his 1992 presidential campaign, and urged by former Congressman Dick Armey (R-TX). A uniform-rate subtraction-method value-added tax under which wages are taxed to individuals rather than businesses to allow exemptions.

GAO (Government Accountability Office). Formerly Government Accounting Office. The nonpartisan investigatory arm of Congress that audits and evaluates executive branch departments and activities and existing and proposed legislation.

GATT (General Agreement on Tariffs and Trade). One of the major multilateral trade treaties signed by the United States. Originally created by the Bretton Woods Conference as part of a larger plan for economic recovery after World War II.

GDP (gross domestic product). The market value of all final goods and services produced within a country in a given year.

gift tax. Tax imposed on the value of property that a donor gives voluntarily. Because it applies to gifts of property that are conferred on recipients before the donor's death, the gift tax is linked to the estate tax. This tax does not apply to annual gifts to any one person of less than $12,000 ($24,000 for married couples).

GIT (growth and investment tax). A variation on a subtraction-method value-added tax, plus a 15 percent income tax on dividends, interest, and capital gains. Would tax wages in three brackets (15 percent, 25 percent, 30 percent), provide a family credit in place of the standard deduction and child tax credit, a work credit in place of the EITC, and a home credit in place of a deduction for home mortgage interest. Suggested by President Bush's panel on tax reform in 2005.

GNP (gross national product). The total value of all final goods and services produced by a country's factors of production and sold on the worldwide market in a given year.

GST (goods and services tax). Canada's name for its VAT, also used by some other countries.

JCT (Joint Tax Committee). Congressional committee composed of members from both the U.S. House of Representatives and Senate that provides staff responsible for various aspects of the tax legislative process, including estimating revenue effects of pending legislation. Committee staff members also assist the congressional tax-making committees in preparing and revising drafts of tax bills and oversee the process by which the House and Senate reach agreement on bill provisions.

marriage penalty. Feature of the U.S. tax code that imposes a higher tax on a married couple than the total that they would pay as single persons.

OECD (Organisation for Economic Co-operation and Development). Group of thirty industrialized nations, including the United States, Mexico, Canada, Australia, New Zealand, Japan, South Korea, and nearly all of Europe.

OMB (Office of Management and Budget). White House office in charge of overseeing the White House's role in the federal budget process.

paint-by-numbers lawmaking. Process by which members of the U.S. Congress, in conformity with statutory requirements, tailor tax legislation to meet a fixed revenue target for the requisite federal budget period.

partnership. An association of one or more persons created for the purposes of owning and running a business. Partnerships themselves are not taxed; taxes are imposed only on partnership members.

payroll tax. Tax imposed on employees and employers (including the self-employed) based on the amount of wages. Social Security taxes are an important example.

phase-in. Gradual implementation of a policy, for example with respect to time or income level.

President's Advisory Panel on Federal Tax Reform. Bipartisan panel created by President Bush in January 2005 that released a report in November of 2005 proposing a number of tax reforms.

progressive-rate tax. A tax whose marginal rate increases as the amount to which it is applied increases.

proprietorship. A business in which an individual owns all assets and liabilities in his or her personal capacity.

retail sales tax. Tax collected from consumers on sales by retail businesses, which remit the tax to the government. Widely used by states and local governments.

Rosie Scenario. Relentless optimism in forecasting key economic variables, including overestimation of economic growth and other key economic predictors that determine the size of total government spending and revenues.

Social Security Administration. An independent federal agency, established by congressional statute, that manages the federal social-insurance programs providing retirement, disability, and survivors' benefits.

subtraction-method value-added tax. Tax applied to the difference between the total receipts from a business's sales of goods or services and the total amount of the business's purchases of goods or services from other businesses. Has been used in New Hampshire and Michigan.

sunset. A statutory expiration after a set period of time in the absence of the statute's formal renewal.

TANF (Temporary Assistance for Needy Families). Successor to AFDC, provides cash assistance to indigent families with dependent children.

tax base. Parameters on which taxation is levied as defined by law. In an income tax, for example, taxable income as determined by statutory inclusions and exclusions. In a VAT or retail sales tax, the specified goods and services subject to the tax, to the exclusion of those exempted.

tax gap. The difference between what taxpayers should pay and what they actually pay on a timely basis, estimated by the IRS to be more than $300 billion annually.

VAT (value-added tax). Tax collected at every level of production as value is added. Similar to a retail sales tax in which tax is withheld by manufacturers and wholesalers. Used by 141 countries in 2007, including every member of the OECD except the United States.

Acknowledgments

In writing this book I have had the great advantage of extraordinarily generous friends, colleagues, and students who helped me along the way. I had the benefit of excellent research assistance from Nicholas Caton, a Yale Law School student, who devoted great energy and untold hours to this project. Many colleagues and friends read the entire manuscript and offered valuable suggestions; they include Bruce Ackerman, Anne Alstott, Tom Downey, Fred Goldberg, Itai Grinberg, Daniel Halperin, Brian Jenn, Daniel Markovits, Jerry Mashaw, Pamela Olson, Joel Platt, Ian Shapiro, Alvin Warren, and two anonymous readers. My editor at Yale University Press, Michael O'Malley, was enthusiastic about this project from the outset and offered many helpful suggestions along the way. Seunghee Ham, a Yale undergraduate, assisted with both proofreading and research. And Karen Williams typed the entire manuscript, retyped it, and then typed it again and again with unfailing good humor.

My greatest debt goes to my good friend Adam Haslett, a Yale Law School graduate and a hugely talented writer. Adam took time away from writing a novel to consult with me about this book's structure, to offer many detailed suggestions for improvement, and, in the last round, to save me from using three different metaphors in one paragraph. I never failed to take his advice. When it comes to writing, I am his student, and he is a great teacher to have.

I also want to thank Jeffrey Yablon, whose ever-growing collection of quotations about taxation published annually in *Tax Notes Magazine* saved me many hours in unearthing many of the quotations I have used at the beginning of these chapters and often gave me good laughs when I most needed them.

Harold Koh, dean of the Yale Law School, and Ian Shapiro, director of Yale's MacMillan Center for International and Area Studies, provided encouragement and important financial support.

I first expressed my idea for what has here become the Competitive Tax Plan in a couple of pages of a book, *The Decline (and Fall?) of the Income Tax*, published in 1997 by W. W. Norton. I then elaborated on the idea in the paperback edition of that book (retitled by Norton *The U.S. Income Tax*) and in an essay published in 2002 in the Yale Law Journal: "100 Million Unnecessary Returns: A Fresh Start for the U.S. Income Tax." (112 [2002]: 261–310). I have also testified before Congress and the president's panel on tax reform, advancing the basic plan described here. Chapter 12, summarizing the plan, is largely taken from a chapter I contributed to *Toward Fundamental Tax Reform* (Alan J. Auerback and Kevin Hasset, eds. [Washington D.C.: American Enterprise Institute, 2005]), and was also published as "Taxes That Work: A Simple American Plan" in the *Florida Law Review* (58 [2006]: 1043–62). I thank all of these publishers for giving me permission to reprint or excerpt this work here.

Finally, I thank my family—my wife, Brett Dignam, and my children, Lucas, Dylan, Jake, Sydney, and Casey—for putting up with me through another book ordeal. They are everything to me.

Index